MW01491862

EMPIRE OF
BRUTALITY

LOUISIANA STATE UNIVERSITY PRESS   BATON ROUGE

CHRISTOPHER MICHAEL BLAKLEY

EMPIRE OF BRUTALITY

Enslaved
People and
Animals in the
British Atlantic World

Published by Louisiana State University Press
lsupress.org

DESIGNER: Mandy McDonald Scallan
TYPEFACE: text, Whitman; display, Yanone Kaffeesatz

COVER ILLUSTRATION: Edmund Ollier, *Cassell's History of the United States*, vol. 3 (London:
Cassell, Petter, & Galpin, 1874–77), 91. Courtesy of the Library of Congress.

Chapter 1 first appeared, in somewhat different form, as "'To Get a Cargo of Flesh, Bone, and
Blood': Animals in the Slave Trade in West Africa," *International Review of Environmental
History,* vol. 5, issue 1 (2019): 85–111.

Library of Congress Cataloging-in-Publication Data

Names: Blakley, Christopher Michael, author.
Title: Empire of brutality : enslaved people and animals in the British
    Atlantic world / Christopher Michael Blakley.
Description: Baton Rouge : Louisiana State University Press, [2023] |
    Includes bibliographical references and index.
Identifiers: LCCN 2023007823 (print) | LCCN 2023007824 (ebook) | ISBN
    978-0-8071-7886-7 (cloth) | ISBN 978-0-8071-8101-0 (pdf) | ISBN 978-0-8071-8100-3
    (epub)
Subjects: LCSH: Slavery—Atlantic Ocean Region—History. | Human-animal
    relationships—Atlantic Ocean Region—History
Classification: LCC HT1331 .B59 2023 (print) | LCC HT1331 (ebook) | DDC
    306.3/62—dc23/eng/20230501
LC record available at https://lccn.loc.gov/2023007823
LC ebook record available at https://lccn.loc.gov/2023007824

CONTENTS

ACKNOWLEDGMENTS

Many institutions and communities supported this book, and I am indebted to their generosity and goodwill. Helen E. Deutsch, former director of the Center for 17th- & 18th-Century Studies of the University of California, Los Angeles, welcomed me to West Adams as a postdoctoral fellow and set a high standard for scholarly excellence. Brenda Elaine Stevenson and Sharla M. Fett mentored me as I developed the book, and I am in awe of their brilliance and kindness as scholars. Lauren Robin Derby did much to spur me on through conversations over coffee in Westwood. Andrew Kettler advised me during and after our postdoctoral year on revising and improving the text. Kathryn Renton read drafts and offered advice in Eagle Rock. Thanks are also due to the UCLA Atlantic History Group and Carla Gardina Pestana for supporting the Animals, Agency, and Slaving in the Atlantic World conference, and to the William Andrews Clark Memorial Library for hosting the Contested Foundations conference series. I am thankful for the suggestions for revision offered by the anonymous referee for the press, the encouragement and support of the dedicated professionals of the Louisiana State University Press, including Alisa Plant, Catherine Kadair, Neal Novak, and Ashley Gilly, and most especially to the wise counsel of Editor in Chief Rand Dotson, who guided this project with enthusiasm and keen eyes during a global pandemic.

I am appreciative of the financial resources and scholarly groups I benefited from through Rutgers University, the McNeil Center for Early American Studies at the University of Pennsylvania, John Carter Brown Library, William L. Clements Library, Huntington Library, Social Science Research Council, Andrew W. Mellon Foundation, and Folger Shakespeare Library. Funds from the National Science Foundation made it possible for me to present this research at the annual meetings of the American Society for Environmental History, History of Science Society, and Society for the History of Technology. Archivists at Rutgers University Libraries, American Philosophical Society Library, Barbados Department of Archives, Sidney Martin Library at University of the West Indies, Cave Hill, Shilstone Memorial Library of the Barbados Museum and Historical Society, Swem Library at the College of William and

Mary, John D. Rockefeller Jr. Library of the Colonial Williamsburg Foundation, South Caroliniana Library of the University of South Carolina, South Carolina Department of Archives and History, and Jamaica Archives and Records Department, Spanish Town, helpfully aided my research. Librarians at University of Michigan, University of Pennsylvania, Brown University, Occidental College, Chaffey College, and California State University, Northridge, fulfilled requests with alacrity.

Several readers graciously read and critiqued drafts of this book, most especially James Delbourgo, as well as Daniel K. Richter, Marisa J. Fuentes, Neil Maher, Toby C. Jones, and Marcy Norton, whom I am gratified to acknowledge. Through conferences and workshops I benefited from suggestions from Jennifer Anderson, Karl Appuhn, Rick Bell, Etienne Benson, Katherine Bergevin, John Blanton, Christopher Bonner, Holly Brewer, Charlotte Carrington-Farmer, Joyce E. Chaplin, Paul G. E. Clemens, Deirdre Coleman, Matthew Crawford, Kevin Dawson, Bathesheba Demuth, Rayvon Fouché, Eric Herschthal, Joshua Kercsmar, Julie Chun Kim, Philip D. Morgan, Matthew Mulcahy, Tyler D. Parry, Christopher Parsons, Keith Pluymers, Elizabeth Polcha, Jayne Ptolemy, Seth Rockman, Harriet Ritvo, Neil Safier, Casey Schmitt, Laura Keenan Spero, Mary Terrall, Zeb Tortorici, Lorena Walsh, Molly Warsh, Charlton Yingling, and Anya Zilberstein, as well as audiences at the Washington Early American Seminar of the University of Maryland, Agricultural History Society, Organization of American Historians, Early American Seminar of the CUNY Graduate Center, Columbia University, Yale University, Brown University, and German Historical Institute.

Participants of the American Origins Seminar of the University of Southern California-Huntington Library Early Modern Studies Institute engaged with the book, and I thank Carole Shammas and Peter Mancall for their conviviality, as well as Alejandra Dubcovsky, Lindsay O'Neill, Michael Block, Amy Braden, Will Cowan, Kathleen Murphy, Kate Mulry, and Strother Roberts for their camaraderie.

Kind words from Bryan Givens of Pepperdine University, as well as from Kevin McDonald and Elizabeth Drummond at Loyola Marymount University, kept me in good spirits in the early days of the pandemic. Morale boosts from Susan Fitzpatrick-Behrens, Jeffrey Auerbach, Jeffrey Kaja, Josh Sides, Thomas Devine, and Natale A. Zappia at CSUN have been tremendous while revising the book during a pandemic. Thanks, too, to Donal O'Sullivan for sharing their office with me in Sierra Tower. My colleagues at Occidental College, Devin

Fromm, Jacqueline Elam, and Lauren Brown, kept me sane with friendship. Tim Greene, Omar Dphrepaulezz, and my colleagues at Chaffey College in Rancho Cucamonga helped too, in many ways.

Conversations with students made this book possible, and this work is as much a result of spontaneous classroom discussions about some of the primary sources the book takes up as of research with archives, libraries, and academic institutions. It's a real privilege to learn from extremely resilient students in Los Angeles and San Bernardino Counties, including undergraduates experiencing homelessness, economic precarity, incarceration, slow violence and environmental racism, and a global pandemic. Teaching is a dialogue, and I am wiser for listening to and learning from my students' voices.

Mi Gyung Kim of North Carolina State University sparked my love of history. Many teachers nurtured me as a student and I am glad to know them now as colleagues, namely Ross Bassett, Judy Kertesz, David Sepkoski, Jamie Pietruska, Phyllis Mack, Lynn Mollenauer, Johanna Schoen, Walter Rucker, and Camilla Townsend.

Family and friends in Raleigh and Durham cheered me on every step of the way, including my parents, Mike and Linda Blakley; Amanda and Erin Gunter; my nephew, Graeme, and niece, Eliot; and my second mom, Susan Cook. Thanks also to the Cook and Kohler clans for adopting me at family reunions in Chicago and Iowa City. Belinda Paige Blakley is my intellectual partner, relentless advocate, dearest friend, and honored teacher. I am inspired by their deep spirit of curiosity, care, empathy, and love.

EMPIRE OF BRUTALITY

Prologue

Meeting in secret, beyond the range of sight and hearing of overseers, over several weeks in the late summer of 1723, a community of enslaved women and men in Virginia began to write a letter. When they met to write is unclear, perhaps after nightfall or just before dawn. Addressed to the "Lord Arch Bishop of Lonnd," Edmund Gibson, whom the Church of England had recently appointed, the letter is a remarkable document of intellectual critique produced within the eighteenth-century worlds of the African diaspora and the Black Atlantic.[1] And it is a surprising key to the intellectual, material, and social histories of what it meant to belong and be seen as either human or animal in early America.

Writing from the "Land of verJennia," the group identified themselves as baptized and multiracial enslaved people dedicated to following the edicts of their Christian faith and the tenets of the Anglican Church. Staking their claims to belonging within the Church, the collective made demands on the bishop as one community of his "poore partishinners," who deserved as much assistance as any other within Britain's North American colonies. The group requested that the bishop appeal to King George I to release them "out of this Cruell Bondegg" and reminded the clergyman that they were brothers and sisters bound together by their common identity as Christian believers.

Describing their lives in Virginia, the group put forward the contention to their audience that their enslavers subjected them and their children to an unjust "Sevarity and Sorrowfull Sarvice we are hard used up on Every account." Slaveholders, they put forth, denied women and men of African descent the right to marriage. Overseers forced slaves to labor on the Sabbath, coercing them into transgressing one of the Ten Commandments given to Moses by God in the Book of Exodus. Beyond these fundamental rights of the faithful, the community expressed their hope that the Church would provide schools and teachers to instruct their children in reading the Bible, reciting the Lord's Prayer, and learning the doctrines of Protestant Christianity.

Their letter was not only the plea of a devoted congregation of disciples but also a testament of individuals who asserted their essential humanity. In the letter, the authors—among whom were both literate and nonliterate people—added a statement about what they understood to be one of the foundational cruxes of their enslavement. Their ideas are worth considering in depth: "And to be plain they doo Look no more up on us then if wee ware dogs which I hope when these Strange Lines comes to Lord Ships hands will be Looket in to." In sum, the group tasked Gibson with investigating the denial of their humanity by slaveholders and charged him with looking into their dehumanization under slavery as a threat to the lives of Christians on both sides of the British Atlantic world.

Historians of slavery rightly point out that English slavers and slaveholders in the early modern Atlantic world did not literally believe people of African descent were animals. Rather, enslavers exploited the humanity of the enslaved by treating them as private property akin to animals.[2] Indeed, the writers of the letter sent to Fulham Palace, Gibson's residence in London, articulated that they understood themselves to be first and foremost fully human subjects whose humanity ought to have been recognized by their status as Christians. Nevertheless, their self-understanding of enslavement as an institution that reduced them socially and ethically to an animal-like position, to the status of dogs, is worth looking into.

Some of the letter writers may have remembered being pursued by the working dogs that slavers used to intimidate captives in Atlantic Africa, often Newfoundland dogs. Others might have seen dogs, either lap dogs or hunting companions, as the favorite pets of their slaveholders. Britons associated dogs with cultural values such as obedience and the subordination of inferiors by dominant superiors.[3] Despite a few forerunners in the Caribbean and the mid-Atlantic, abolitionist thought was not a significant intellectual movement in Virginia in 1723, and it is unlikely that the group's description of their lives as being doglike was the result of white rhetorical coaching or white abolitionist ventriloquism. Instead, historians must necessarily approach this text as one originating in Black and diasporic African intellectual milieus of thinking about the environment, the more-than-human world of plants, wind, sunlight, and water that included nonhuman animals, embedded in material, lived experience.[4]

Rather than reflecting an affective, sympathetic bond linking Blackness and animality, the letter is a repudiation of the animalizing project settler-slaveholders strove to instantiate and is indicative of Black claims on humanism and the human itself.[5] In this sense, the letter can be understood as a philosophical assault on the logic of dehumanization in the early modern Anglophone Atlantic. This concept indexes an intellectual agenda upheld by English-speaking slaveholders and, crucially, a vision for enslaver–enslaved relations that never achieved its full realization in the colonial Atlantic.

Dehumanization, as formulated by philosopher David Livingstone Smith, includes three key principles. First, those who seek to dehumanize others must hold the notion of an essential difference between multiple and circumscribed groups of people, which are further divided into natural kinds. Second, these differences must necessitate the creation and maintenance of an ordered social hierarchy wherein superiors ought to rule over inferiors. And third, these essential differences in peoples must be inextricably linked to ancestry.[6] Central to Smith's theory is the dehumanizer's belief that classes of people categorized as inferiors are discursively marked as subhuman, less than human, or animal-like. Dehumanization is not a modern invention. Scholars have shown, for instance, how European medieval theologians within Christendom in the twelfth and thirteenth centuries elaborated such a cultural logic through discussions equating people of Jewish descent with dogs.[7] Animalizing rhetoric is malleable, and in this context the Catholic thinkers' theological comparison of Jews with dogs did not indicate Jews' obedience to Christians but rather their alleged shared irrationality and impurity.

Adopting the interpretive lens of dehumanization does not require historians to argue that slavery obliterated the humanity and intellect of enslaved people via the "crude psychic impact" of human trafficking.[8] The real psychic shocks of the first, middle, and final passages, the scramble and the auction block, and the brutality of the plantation complex did not transform enslaved captives into "infantile" or bestial things or make them so traumatized as to be utterly dependent on their slaveholder.[9] Given that the 1723 letter writers' text invokes the human–animal binary—containing within it the conceptual terrain of the human and animal as ontologically separate categories within European cosmology—and tasks the Church to probe the dehumanizing nature of slavery, the historical record of Black thought in this period is a stark contrast to the now outdated and discredited "Sambo" thesis. Generations of scholars, including Michael A. Gomez, Gwendolyn Midlo Hall, Alexander X. Byrd, Jason R. Young, Yvonne P. Chireau, and Frederick Knight, teach us that diverse people from multiethnic and multilingual backgrounds preserved ideas, beliefs, languages, philosophies, attitudes, technologies, and ways of knowing the natural world through their unfree journeys from Atlantic Africa to the Americas. Atlantic slaving did not annihilate African cultures or the minds of African people and render human beings into animal-like subjects.

So, what questions can scholars ask after reading the letter? If the letter writers demanded the bishop "looket in to" their being treated as "if wee ware dogs," then historians might begin by asking, Why did slaveholders act and think of the enslaved as animal-like chattel? And what real human–animal relations existed throughout slaving and slavery to support English speakers' agenda of dehumanization? What I am interested in is further understanding how slaveholders *aimed* to effect and induce feelings of abjection and debasement while simultaneously exploiting the very human feelings of the enslaved.[10]

And beyond that intellectual question, this book seeks to examine if ambitious settler-slaver worldviews emerged from material human–animal relationships involving trade, curiosity, and labor. What happens if historians consider that dehumanization as a value system came about in both conscious and improvised ways? Here it is useful to flag that Smith is not the only, or most recent, philosopher who has discussed the role of dehumanization in slavery and colonialism. Critiques of European imperialism, of Enlightenment philosophies of race, and of universalist narratives of humanity and its opposite, animality, produced during the so-called Age of Reason and Age of Revolution, can be traced to thinkers of Black existentialism and Négritude, including Aimé Césaire, Léopold Sédar Senghor, Frantz Fanon, and Sylvia Wynter.[11] More recently, their ideas have been elaborated, complicated, and updated by scholars like Achille Mbembe, Zakiyyah Iman Jackson, Lewis R. Gordon, Joshua Bennett, Bénédicte Boisseron, and the Afropessimist framework of Frank B. Wilderson III.[12]

At the start, it may be useful to stake out here what this study is *not* intended to achieve. Given that my analysis here will focus on ideas and material human–animal interactions in a decidedly European cosmological context—the moral cosmos to which the 1723 letter writers appealed—this book takes the form of a European rather than indigenous Atlantic African intellectual and cultural history. While I may occasionally note Fante, Akan-Twi, Igbo, Fulbe, or Yoruba ideas about animals, humanity, or animality, this is decidedly not a work of Africanist scholarship, and such work will necessarily need to be the result of scholars equipped with the requisite linguistic training. Instead, my focus will begin with the ideas and culture of the English speakers who dehumanized Atlantic Africans, alongside Indigenous Americans and others, in the early modern world. And the analysis and evidence presented do not support the thesis that slaveholders literally intended to effect biological forms of neoteny among enslaved people. Instead, *dehumanization,* as it is used here, refers to a socio-intellectual register, an ongoing, incomplete, and unfinished process that saturated the minds of slaveholders and shaped their actions.

Introduction

SLAVERY AND HUMAN–ANIMAL RELATIONSHIPS

S cholars of the Atlantic slave trade have shown how English slavers and slaveholders produced rhetorical comparisons binding Atlantic Africans to animals from the very beginnings of encounters between West Africans and English mariners in the sixteenth century.[1] Metaphors of "brutish," "bestial," or "beastly" sub-Saharan African nations appeared in travel narratives, such as John Lok's account of a merchant voyage to Cape Palmas, the Cestos River, and Cape Three Points in 1554. Lok described all African people living south of the Sahara Desert as "a people of beastly living, without a God, lawe, religion, or common wealth, and so scorched and vexed with the heat of the sunne, that in many places they curse it when it riseth."[2] Despite Africans' allegedly primitive character and lack of social institutions, Lok and other Tudor-era merchants expected to gain great wealth from trading in West Africa by exploiting the region's storied goldfields.[3]

Lok and his companions also sought to purchase animal goods from Atlantic African traders on the coast, including "two hundred and fifty Elephants teeth of all quantities," and their partners made animal gifts to them, including an elephant skull and civet cats. English artisans, as Kim F. Hall has shown, manipulated ivory to make decorative luxury goods like furniture details and window lattices. Sixteenth-century Europeans lavished praise on ivory as a material imbued with racialized beauty. The "whitenesse thereof was so much esteemed, that it was thought to represent the natural fairnesse of mans skinne: insomuch that such as went about to set foorth (or rather corrupt) naturall beautie with colours and painting, were reproved," by a popular proverb instructing craftspeople against darkening the naturally white tusks.[4] Lok contrasted the beauty of white ivory against the Black skin of Atlantic Africans and numerous other "monstrous things that are engendred in Africke." Theorists of race and racial formations point out that Tudor intellectuals gradually associated Blackness with the monstrous, the diabolical, and the nonhuman.[5] In

1584, an English writer, for instance, reported that children learned that demons possessed "fanges like a dog, clawes like a bear, a skin like a Niger, and a voice roaring like a lion."[6] Encounters via travel and trade in West Africa engendered racial ideas shot through with conceptions of a human–animal binary.

Defining *human, humanity, animal, animality, human–animal binary, or human–animal relationship* is a difficult but necessary task at the start. For early moderns, as Erica Fudge notes, the human or humanity itself is an ontological category defined in a binary opposition to the animal or animality.[7] Among the qualities that made humans unique, according to early moderns in the sixteenth and seventeenth centuries, were speech, rationality, free will, belief in and devotion to God, and authority over the living subjects that God created to serve humans: animals. Given these attributes and ideas, it is not surprising, as Fudge shows, that sixteenth-century jurists like Diego de Covarrubias argued that Amerindians, who he claimed lived "without laws or any form of government," were "born to serve others as the beasts and wild animals are."[8] To examine slavery as a more-than-human event within an early modern context, this book aims to take up the categories of human and animal as they were understood between the sixteenth and eighteenth centuries. Moreover, the concept of a human–animal relationship refers to a structured interaction or position between humans and animals to achieve some end, and the relationships or interactions discussed here include trade, curiosity, labor, and resistance.

In addition to the ivory, Lok and his crew returned to England with five human captives from their voyage. Though they did not principally set out on a slaving voyage, many Tudor expeditions, especially piratical ventures to attack rival empire merchant fleets, became impromptu slaving missions.[9] In the early seventeenth century and through the Stuart era, English joint-stock companies organized trading missions around acquiring animal goods and human captives. In September 1651, the Guinea Company instructed its employees to purchase animal "hides, wax, and teeth" and "15 or 20 young lusty Negers" from traders on the Gambia River.[10] That winter, the company ordered Bartholomew Haward to sail for Gambia to purchase as many slaves as his ship could hold.[11] If Haward could not fill the hold with captives, the company directed him to fill the remaining cargo space with cattle and provisions for the "Cargo of negers and Cattel." Haward's ship then traveled from the Gambia to Barbados, where one observer commented that enslaved laborers were "the life of this place" due to their labor on ginger, indigo, and sugar plantations.[12]

In 1657, Richard Ligon, an English visitor to Barbados, affirmed the growing connection between frequent arrivals of captives and livestock on the island. Describing Atlantic Africans for sale at Bridgetown, Ligon wrote that slaves "are as neer beasts as may be."[13]

Reports of the combined sale of enslaved people and chattel livestock led to descriptions of slave markets and barracoons, or temporary holding huts, as comparable to animal pens. Jean Barbot, a French slaver who traveled to West Africa between 1678 and 1682, observed that captives incarcerated north of Ouidah in the Bight of Benin waited "above two hundred leagues up the country, where they are kept like cattle in Europe." Barbot further learned that "those slaves we transport from Guinea to America are prepossessed with the opinion, that they are carried like sheep to the slaughter, and that Europeans are fond of their flesh."[14]

Exchanges of animal goods and livestock nurtured links between Atlantic Africans and animals in the minds of Europeans. Yet these ideas came about through material human–animal relationships via trade. In the fifteenth century, Portuguese mariners bartered horses for human captives when approaching states in the Senegal River valley, such as the Jolof Empire and others along the Niger River.[15] Trade cycles of horses for slaves, in this context, were not unique to African-European relations and resembled similar patterns of commerce, like the gun–slave cycles prevalent in western Central Africa.[16] Rather, Portugal inserted itself within human–animal networks originating with North African Muslim merchants who had sold warhorses to West African states since at least the fourteenth century.[17]

Though English slavers did not engage in any significant exchange of horses for slaves, travelers in West Africa employed animal comparisons to distance themselves from Africans. Thomas Herbert began his discussion of the people he encountered in the Atlantic islands in the early seventeenth century by describing them as being licentious and careless, "so as little difference was 'twixt them and other Animals, and according to the custome of the first Age." While somewhere in western Central Africa—the precise location is ambiguous in the text—Herbert claimed that a "Dog was of that value here, that 20 salvages [sic] have been exchanged for one of them" by English slavers bound for the "Caribae Isles."[18] Though I have found no other documented evidence of exchanges of dogs for captives, it is possible that one of the letter writers from Virginia in 1723 remembered witnessing one of his fellow prisoners being sold for a dog.

Likening slaves to livestock was not limited to the cultures of the Anglophone Atlantic. In seventeenth-century Brazil, Jesuit missionaries, such as António Vieira and his colleagues, justified Black slavery in Portugal's South American colony as rescuing slaves from "savagery" by transforming them into the "hands and feet of the sugar planter."[19] Even while the Jesuits deplored the sight of "masters treating the slaves like beasts," they defended plantation slavery as a fundamentally benevolent institution. A century later, Samuel Martin, an Antigua planter whom we will discuss, would likewise hold that enslaved people and livestock were the "nerves" of a sugar estate, and he employed similar anatomical rhetoric to discuss plantation hierarchies.

Early critics of slavery in the Anglophone Atlantic foregrounded such human–animal distinctions in their writing. Morgan Godwyn, an English critic of slavery in the Caribbean, argued in *The Negro's and Indians Advocate* (1680) that slaveholders believed that Atlantic Africans "carry some resemblances of Manhood, yet are indeed *no Men.*" Godwyn contended that slaveholders in Barbados considered their horses and slaves to be of equivalent worth and that slavery corroded African humanity by reducing slaves to the "state and degree of *Brutes.*"[20] Thomas Tryon, another seventeenth-century writer who attacked slavery, lamented that slavery undermined Christianity and the moral authority of England's empire altogether by denying Africans their rights as Christians.[21]

New England slaveholders, including clergy, held similar attitudes about the social status of enslaved Atlantic Africans, seeing them as animal-like. The Puritan minister and natural philosopher Cotton Mather wrote in 1689 that white enslavers in Massachusetts valued enslaved Africans "as *Horses* or *Oxen,* to do our Drudgeries," despite their innate soul being "as white and good as those" of people of European descent.[22]

Defenders of the harmonious relationship between Christianity and slavery felt shock upon witnessing the behavior of slaveholders in British America. The evangelist and slaveholder George Whitefield complained in an open letter to the enslavers of the southern colonies that "your Slaves, who are frequently stiled Dogs or Beasts, have not an equal Privilege" to actual dogs.[23] Whitefield lamented that slaveholders denied African slaves the possibility of becoming fully Christian through baptism, other sacraments, or further religious education.

Godwyn's claims that slaveholders in the Caribbean treated slaves as if they were "brutes" were also shared among farmers in Britain's North American colonies who did not own slaves and resented slavery as an institution and for the economic and political powers slaveholding granted to elites. In 1756, Hermon Husband wrote a letter from Orange County, North Carolina, to John Carteret, 2nd Earl Granville, reflecting on the changing society of the Piedmont in the mid-eighteenth century. Husband had managed copper mines in Maryland before turning his attention to his landholdings in Orange County, and he opposed the expansion of plantation slavery into rural North Carolina as a "destructive canker" that hurt the economic opportunities of poor whites. Husband complained to Carteret that "the Negroes are imported in greater numbers and do encrease two to one to what the white people do, and unless the white people take to beat out their brains as they do the piggs when over stocked, as the Egyptians did the Hebrews, they must unavoidably (according to the naturall course of things) wholy over run in a serious of time the whole provinces." Husband feared that North Carolina would become like Jamaica or South Carolina, a colony where white settlers were "obligued to come to terms" with being demographically outnumbered by Atlantic Africans. Husband made explicit in his letter to Carteret his comparison of people of African descent and livestock animals. "And even were they like cows and horses in respect to look for freedom and liberty," he wrote, "yet being of human shape and understanding are not to be stoped from breeding or destroyed when overstocked with them."[24]

In addition to textual sources, early modern portraiture presents a critical visual archive that complements the documentary record for understanding and seeing human–animal relationships inflected with ideas about race in early modern Europe. Aristocratic portraits in the seventeenth century featured subjects accompanied by enslaved people and a spectrum of animal companions. Jan Mitjen's *Portrait of Maria of Orange, with Hendrik van Zuijlestein and a Servant* includes an enslaved person holding the reins of their enslaver's horse in the background while the slaveholder occupies the foreground. Abraham Wuchters depicted Sophie Amalie of Brunswick-Calenberg, queen of Denmark and Norway, with an enslaved person and a raptor in a falconer's hood perched next to the royal person. This painting can be understood via Marcy Norton's discussion of early modern falconry, which argues that aristocratic falconers saw both raptors and human servants as extensions of their body and mastery over others.[25]

In other paintings from this period, animals and enslaved people appear as exotic curiosities. Anton Domenico Gabbiani's *Portrait of Three Musicians of the Medici Court,* circa 1687, includes an enslaved person with a parrot resting on their arm behind the musicians. Likewise, Nicolas de Largillière's portrait of a woman, possibly Madame Claude Lambert de Thorigny, features a noblewoman flanked by a parrot and an enslaved servant. Into the eighteenth century, slaveholders chose to be portrayed with pets and exotic animals—including parrots and monkeys—and enslaved people, as is evident in several of William Hogarth's engravings.[26] Phillipe Vignon's portrait of Françoise Marie de Bourbon and Louise Françoise de Bourbon is staged such that the two sisters—the Duchess of Orléans and Duchess of Bourbon—are being served by an enslaved person while Louise Françoise holds a lapdog. In terms of the painting's verticality, the slave is visually located between the noblewomen and the dog. Charles Seymour, 6th Duke of Somerset, chose to be portrayed by John Closterman with a hunting dog and an enslaved boy.

In the portraits by Mitjen, Wuchters, and Closterman, enslaved people are visually paired with loyal, tame animal subjects: the horse, the raptor, and the hunting dog. In these artworks, the enslaved and the animals are emblematic of the slaveholder's ability to command servile beings. By contrast, in Gabbiani's, Largillière's, and Vignon's work, the enslaved are doubled with pets, ranging from exotic parrots to the domestic lapdog. Here, enslaved people stand in for curiosity and control over forms of animal life valued not for their labor but for their novelty.

Visual culture from the early eighteenth century likewise reflects the imagined racial hierarchy that Britons and others strove to build in the early modern Atlantic world. Bartholomew Dandridge's portrait of a young aristocratic English girl from 1725 neatly encapsulates these ideals. In the painting, the girl, dressed in a white gown, stands tall and gazes confidently forward toward the viewer. In her hands, she cradles the head of a dog, whose eyes are turned up toward her face. Between the girl and the dog, an enslaved servant is posed in a crouch, just behind her. Like the dog, the slave's face and eyes, undoubtedly posed by Dandridge, are dutifully fixed on the girl. This painting appeared in an exhibition in 2014 curated by Esther Chadwick, Meredith Gamer, and Cyra Levenson titled *Figures of Empire: Slavery and Portraiture in Eighteenth-Century Atlantic Britain* and staged at the Yale Center for British Art. In the museum label for the portrait, which the curators retitled *A Young Girl with an Enslaved Servant and a Dog,* gallery visitors learned that the matching metal collars looping around the necks of the slave and the dog marked them both as the property of the girl's father.

Dandridge positioned the slave and the dog to look upward toward the girl in a gesture signifying their loyalty and devotion for their mistress. Moreover, the curators remind us, an image from classical antiquity of cherubs taming a wild goat appears on an urn behind the girl. The curators contend that this background image of an untamed animal serves as a contrast to the painting's foreground, which revolves around the girl and her "domesticated" subjects: the tamed slave and the dog.

Dandridge's visual assembly of the girl, the enslaved adolescent, and the canine embodied a social hierarchical ideal in the British Atlantic. In their self-conscious vision of empire, slaveholders ruled atop the enslaved and animals alike. Through their self-presentation in artworks and in the real practice of slaveholding, slaveowners' identities were bound up with their ability to simultaneously tame and govern over a world of racially foreign, alien subjects and nonhuman animals, ranging from domestic pets to livestock and even exotic scientific specimens.

Justus Englehardt Kühn's artworks invite further comparison between enslaved people and loyal animals and tame pets. In a portrait of Eleanor Darnall as a child, circa 1710, the young girl and daughter of a wealthy Maryland slaveholder, Henry Darnall II, is posed with a dog below her. In Kühn's painting of her brother, Henry Darnall III, circa 1712, the artist portrays the scion of the Prince George's County planter in a similar fashion, although in this portrait the dog is replaced with what is an apparently equivalent figure—an enslaved man with a silver collar. The silver collar reappeared in another of Kühn's portraits of the children of slaveholders, this time his depiction of Charles Carroll II of Annapolis. In this portrait, the future inheritor of his father's plantations and enslaved property is posed with another animal, a deer, bedecked with the same sort of silver collar worn by the enslaved man in the previous portrait.

Numerous eighteenth-century portraits reproduce this theme. George Knapton depicted John Spencer and his son engaged in hunting, in another oil portrait from 1744. Like Dandridge's portrait, this one includes an enslaved man, Caesar Shaw.[27] In the foreground, the elder Spencer stands erect, pointing a hunting rifle toward the ground. To his right, his son sits astride a brown horse. Crouched below the horse, Shaw holds on to a small dog, likely used for retrieving the slaveowner's quarry. Again, viewers are invited to appreciate a visual logic to the painting's hierarchy: Spencer and his son are placed at the top, with the horse and Shaw occupying the middle, and below them is the dog on the ground.

Another painting from 1765 exhibited in *Figures of Empire,* titled *An Unknown Man, Perhaps Charles Goring of Wiston (1744–1829), out Shooting with his Servant,* repeats this visual association of enslaved people with loyal animals. In this portrait, the slave and the dog dutifully attend to the unknown man on a hunt, and again they are staged below him. Joshua Reynolds's 1766 portrait of John Manners, Marquess of Granby, similarly includes an enslaved groom, depicted behind a horse while the aristocrat is foregrounded.

Enslaved people and other kinds of animals appear in other eighteenth-century portraits. The portrait of Tekla Róża Radziwiłł held at the Belarusian National Arts Museum and dated to the 1720s includes an enslaved child, and a bird perched on the hand of the Polish and Lithuanian duchess. François Dagobert Jouvenet's portrait of Antoine Barthélemy de Vire Duliron de Montivers, a soldier for the Compagnie des Indes, includes an enslaved person in the background—likely taken from Senegal or Gambia—while the portrait's subject offers a fruit to a small monkey in the foreground. When Lady Grace Carteret posed for her portrait, she, or perhaps the painter John Giles Eccardt, surrounded her with her spaniel, a cockatoo, and an enslaved servant. Jean-Louis Voille's portrait of Evdokiya Nikolayevna Chesmenskaya features an enslaved servant holding a bird in a small cage. And an anonymous painting of Maria Karolina Sobieska, a Polish noblewoman, incorporates an enslaved servant on one side of the subject and a lamb on the other.

One final painting that illustrates the multiplicity of relationships between enslaved people and animals is Agostino Brunias's *Servants Washing a Deer* (1755). The painting depicts a group of enslaved people, two women and two young men, bathing their enslaver's pet deer. Brunias spent much of his career painting in Dominica, an island where deer are not native.[28] The scene is an enigmatic one that deserves a second look. It reminds us that enslaved people's daily, and sometimes intimate, contact with animals beyond livestock included caring for and even thinking about animals. The deer was a pet, not unlike the monkey depicted in the portrait of de Vire Duliron de Montivers, and it is worth imagining the range of emotions or sensibilities the enslaved felt while caring for the animal. Perhaps they resented the deer for its privileged status as the pet of an elite planter. Or maybe they felt affection or curiosity and regarded the animal with real care and kindness.

Despite the possibility of enslaved people's kind feelings for animals like the deer in Brunias's painting, the human–animal binary emerging out of the logic of race and racism in the British Atlantic nevertheless placed sub-

Saharan Africans in the middle of a social hierarchy, between white Europeans and nonhuman animals. Such ideas may not even have been limited to the Atlantic world. In the later decades of the eighteenth century, British colonial administrators residing in cities on the empire's peripheries defended their imperium, and its relationship to slavery as an institution, as fundamentally humane and benevolent. William Jones, a jurist, philologist, and scholar of Indian antiquity, wrote a brief essay, "Slavery in Bengal," from his post in Kolkata, West Bengal, in 1785. Despite his location in South Asia and the Indian Ocean world, Jones's views on slavery are worth considering within the intellectual currents of the wider Anglophone colonial world.

Jones argued that "absolute unconditional slavery, by which one human creature becomes the property of another, like a horse or an ox, is happily unknown to the laws of England, and that no human law could give it a just sanction." Jones, himself a slaveholder, considered "slaves as servants under a contract, express or implied" and made by "such persons as are authorized by nature or by law" to license such contracts. While Jones lamented that many slaveholders cruelly abused their slaves, he praised himself for treating his own slaves, whom he had "rescued" from a life of misery, as servants.[29] For Jones and others, the law guaranteed a certain moral and philosophical justification for chattel slavery despite his insistence here that Britain's form of slavery was *not* chattel slavery.[30]

Rather than being principally concerned with the history of human–canine relations or representations, or with the specific relations between slaves and individual animal species, this book explores the diffuse and varied human and animal relationships generated by slaving and slavery in the British Atlantic world. If historians take seriously the Virginia petitioners' claims in their letter to Edmund Gibson that slaveholders "doo Look no more up on us then if wee ware dogs," that raises several questions: How did the material, lived experiences of enslaved people and different kinds of animals lead slaveholders to perceive the two as interlinked subjects? And why did enslaved people themselves emphasize in their writings and speeches their own understanding of slavery as a phenomenological transformation through which they moved down a hierarchical gradation of existence from fully human subjects to being seen as and treated as if they were objects reduced to an animal-like state? To answer these questions, this book combines approaches from histories of Atlantic slavery in West Africa, plantation slavery in the Caribbean and the Chesapeake, the African diaspora, the history of science, animal studies, and cultural history, and moves chronologically from the late seventeenth century until the legal abolition of the Atlantic slave trade by British Parliament and the United States Congress at the start of the early nineteenth century, in 1807.

What is at stake in following routes of slaving through the archive and answering these questions is how historians of early America, slavery, early African American history, and even histories of science and the environment grapple with the historical and philosophical problem of dehumanization. Rather than tracing a straight line from the moment that slavers seized the bodies of human captives to their sale, transportation, and multiple final passages to plantations and other spaces where Atlantic Africans endured servitude, I seek to understand multiple pathways and trajectories that emerged by which the lives of enslaved people came to be inextricably bound up with disparate forms of animal life.[31] Looking at diverse human–animal relationships tells us something about the ways in which the mingling of enslaved people and animals—including animal remains, scientific specimens, and livestock for agriculture—occurred across a spectrum of activities, and that dehumanization was not always an obviously violent process.

Several historians of slavery and racial capitalism caution against unselfconsciously embracing the thesis that slaveholders dehumanized enslaved people, and their critiques are vital for clarifying the stakes of this book.[32] Arguing that enslavers dehumanized the enslaved, their line of thinking goes, implies that slaveholders did not recognize slaves as human, or ultimately succeeded in obliterating the humanity of people of African descent, and that those enslaved became literally drone-like objects who assimilated their bestial status.

This critique is crucial to bear in mind. Slaveholders consciously preyed upon the humanity of the enslaved by threatening to separate mothers and fathers from their children, wives from their husbands, and sisters from their brothers. Slavers consciously preyed upon universal human fears of being beaten, drowned, raped, or maimed. And enslaved people retained their humanity and rejected slavery frequently, through conscious acts of resistance and through everyday acts of humanity such as fostering friendships and nurturing kinship, singing and prayer, speaking autochthonous languages, and countless other forms of spiritual and personal renewal.

So no serious scholar could claim that slaveholders either literally believed slaves to be animals or that enslaved people ever believed themselves to be animals. As Jennifer L. Morgan puts it, the "ultimate contradiction" in slavery is the slaveholder's simultaneous recognition of humanity and inhumanity among the enslaved. A slaveholder's inventory might include "Bessie" under "Women," and "Bessy" under "Cows," as Morgan shows, but neither enslaver nor enslaved held the illusion that they were literally animals.[33] Thus, the key point to bear in mind at the start is that dehumanization, in this context, refers to an ongoing degradation of humanity that disciplined, controlled, or otherwise diminished enslaved people by *likening* them to animals.

Further, some critics of the dehumanization frame argue that the concept relies on anachronistic categories like human or inhuman that were not widely shared or understood in the early modern period. Here I disagree. The 1723 letter to the bishop of London, discussed earlier, demonstrates that enslaved people argued that their enslavers "Look no more up on us then if wee ware dogs" and excluded them from the realm of who ought to be seen as human. One way to think about how to reconcile the fact that the letter writers articulated their humanity with the idea that the opponents of the dehumanization thesis are correct in several ways is to follow an argument made by Cedric J. Robinson in 1983 in his research on racial capitalism.

Like later historians of slavery and capitalism, Robinson held that slaveholders knew full well "the enslaved were human beings. But the more authentic question was not whether the slaves (and the ex-slaves and their descendants) were human. It was, rather, just what *sort* of people they were . . . and could be."[34] For Robinson, the key was recognizing that enslaved people became private property, or chattel, a word that shares an etymological history with two others: *cattle* and *capital*. Elaborating upon theories of racial capitalism, Morgan has recently shown how commodification of the bodies of enslaved women, men, and children undergirded European notions of markets and the legal underpinnings of global trade.[35] Their insights build on the ideas of Stephanie Smallwood and Susan Staves, both of whom see the transformation of land and peoples into chattel, and the construction of an English identity around being property-holding owners of chattel, as central to the formation of Atlantic slavery and settler colonialism in the Americas.[36]

How, where, and when did such decisions regarding the chattel nature of human captives take place? And what role did animals play in that process? The core argument of this book is that slaving and slavery relied on and generated complex human–animal networks and relations spanning the British Atlantic world, and that by exploring these groupings historians can gain a deeper understanding of how enslavers worked out the process of turning people into chattel and laying the foundations of slavery by mingling enslaved people with nonhuman animals. Efforts to remake people into property akin to animals involved exchange and trade, scientific fieldwork that exploited curiosity, and forms of labor.

A second key to this story is how enslaved people self-consciously rejected such attacks on their personhood. Slaves, as we shall see, stole, injured, killed, and thought about animals and their humanity in ways contrary to their slaveholders' desires. William Moraley, an indentured servant writing in the 1720s and 1730s, reported that enslaved Africans in Pennsylvania "did not think God made them Slaves, any more than other Men."[37] Decades later, Boyrereau Brinch, an enslaved man taken from the Niger River Valley, characterized the ambitions of a slaver to render the slave "sufficiently subdued, rendered tame docile and submissive," like livestock or pets.[38] These processes were not straightforward and not particularly linear but rather evolved over time and space, and enslaved people resisted them in many ways.

In terms of the book's methodology, the evidence and archives considered will be familiar to students of Atlantic slavery. However, reading this material through the conceptual lenses of human–animal networks and relationships reveals a grounded history of dehumanization. Some of the well-known archival materials discussed include letters written by factors engaged in the castle trade on behalf of the Royal African Company; natural history catalogs, letters, and printed books produced by individuals seeking scientific authority among institutions like the Royal Society; and plantation manuals, account books, inventories, slaveholder diaries, and fugitive slave advertisements published in newspapers. Reading these kinds of sources, which are so common among histories of slavery, for the presence of human–animal relations sheds light on the ways in which Atlantic Africans became less-than-human chattel through a spectrum of activities.

Discussions of slavery, race, and animality in early modern European thought have occupied the attention of historians, anthropologists, and literary critics for decades. One early scholar of the history of racial thinking claimed that English slavers and others turned to the "powerful metaphor" of equating Atlantic Africans and nonhuman animals from their very first forays into human trafficking, beginning in the sixteenth century.[39] English-speaking travelers and merchants in seventeenth-century West Africa likewise "simianized" Atlantic Africans and drew upon the increasingly scientific language and taxonomies of natural history to compare people to apes via physiognomy.[40] Slavers and travelers further used simianization to characterize Atlantic Africans as hypersexualized, and racist tropes of African bestiality spread across the Atlantic world in the early modern period through travelers' tales and natural philosophy.[41]

Comparisons and discussion of slaves and livestock through the business of slaving and the management of plantations grew alongside the legal equation of enslaved people and animals, embedded in the etymological history of the terms *chattel* and *cattle*.[42] These linkages later materialized in eighteenth-century imperial administrative positions such as the Superintendent of all the Negroes and Mules or Horses which are furnished for His Majesty's Service on the plantation island colony of Grenada.[43]

Philosophical justifications for slavery as an institution founded on naturalized human–animal hierarchies reached backwards to the mid-fourth century BCE. In *Politics*, Aristotle asserted that non-Greek-speaking peoples were irrational and lived by habit or their immediate sense knowledge alone and could be justifiably enslaved as natural slaves whose mental capacities placed them somewhere on a spectrum between humans and animals.[44] In manuals for managing slaves and animals on latifundia, or great landed estates, writers such as Cato the Elder, Marcus Terentius Varro, and Lucius Junius Moderatus Columella defined enslaved people and draft animals as belonging to a common category of chattel property, to be treated by managers as functionally equivalent. Aristotelian philosophy and Roman husbandry informed the development of slavery as an institution in early modern Europe, and later in England's colonies in America and the Caribbean.[45] Classical beliefs in the role of climate in determining civilization, namely that temperate climes produce republican-minded polities whereas torrid ones engender naturally servile people, later influenced Enlightenment rationalizations of slavery. Bestialization, or the efforts to reduce a person's humanity to an animal-like status, marks a key difference in the highly racialized form of chattel slavery that developed in the Americas and the Atlantic world, in contrast to its ancient and medieval antecedents in the Mediterranean and Black Sea regions.[46]

To an extent, bestialization is a shared dimension of both Atlantic slavery and settler colonialism in the Americas. English-speaking settlers in North America produced similar kinds of rhetorical equations between Indigenous Amerindians and animals that they could label as either predators or prey. Clothing such as bearskin mantles and tattoo designs of eagles, snakes, and other dangerous animals reinforced among settlers a cognitive link between Indians and alien creatures in seventeenth-century Virginia and New England. Furthermore, settlers carried with them Christian beliefs that assumed humanity's divinely granted power and responsibility to assert dominion over the natural world, including bringing tame animals from Europe across the Atlantic Ocean. Colonist perceptions that Indians did not domesticate animals engendered settler ideologies that justified the dispossession of Amerindian nation's territories.[47] Beliefs about North American dog breeds played a role as well in shaping Anglo-American attitudes toward Indians' lack of civilizational progress in the early republic. Benjamin Smith Barton, a professor of natural history at the University of Pennsylvania in the early republic period, urged colleagues to remember that "the master of the Indian dog is a savage," and that so-called "Indian dogs" were more wolflike than European breeds.[48]

In the early United States, such descriptions of Amerindians as feral and lupine reinforced long-standing racist ideas that originated in Puritan New England. In the seventeenth-century, colonists on the Atlantic coast connected Indians with one predator in particular: wolves. In southern New England, settlers marked the territorial edges of towns with the decapitated heads of Indians and wolves, whom they believed posed the greatest threats to the future of their settlements within the American "wilderness." Solomon Stoddard, the first librarian of Harvard College, described Wôpanâak speakers and Algonquian nations, broadly speaking, as bestial, and opined that "they act like wolves and are to be dealt withal as wolves."[49] Consequently, when praying Indians who had converted to Christianity approached settler towns seeking refuge, they presented themselves as fleeing wolf-like enemies and as similar to "your sheep." Christian Indian self-presentations of docility in an animal register were one way in which Native peoples could appeal to settler values.

Rather than being exceptional to European racist thought, Amerindian nations and cultures developed their own beliefs regarding the animal-like qualities of enslaved people, which predated contact. Before encountering Europeans, Indigenous nations in the Pays d'en Haut and Great Lakes zone transformed human captives taken in raids or low-intensity wars into dogs. Anishinaabe speakers used the term *awakaan* to refer to enslaved captives, and the word can also refer to a dog, prisoner, or pet animal.[50] Tupinambá societies in southern Bahia, Brazil, likewise considered enslaved captives to be dehumanized persons stripped of the recognizable aspects or "prerequisites" for human dignity.[51] During his time in Saponi and Tuscarora towns in Carolina between

1700 and 1709, John Lawson learned, "As for Servant, they have no such thing, except Slave, and their Dogs, Cats, tame or Domestick Beasts, and Birds, are call'd by the same Name: For the *Indian* Word for Slave includes them all. So when an *Indian* tells you he has got a Slave for you, it may (in general Terms, as they use) be a young Eagle, a Dog, Otter, or any other thing of that Nature, which is obsequiously to depend on the Master for its Sustenance" (italics in original).[52] Mvskoke communities likewise likened their captives to "dung-hill fowl," and many Amerindian nations throughout the Southeast thought of their slaves as animal-like.[53] Whether English speakers built upon or incorporated these ideas into their own slaving cultures is unclear. Nonetheless, the existence of autochthonous beliefs about slaves becoming bestial reminds us that these attitudes were not uniquely European inventions.

And yet enslavement as an existential and legal state of being between human and animal was the outcome of Atlantic slavery. Colin Dayan and other scholars have shown that civil law in Anglo-America produced the legal category of the chattel slave that depended on established and agreed-upon ideas of what subjects constituted humans and animals. "Slaves were not simply things," Dayan writes, "nor were they really human. Instead, they seemed to occupy a curiously nuanced category, where animals, humans, and inanimate things juggled for primacy."[54]

Dayan's observations resonate with a petition drafted and signed in 1773 by Felix, a man representing a group of literate and nonliterate enslaved people in Boston and its surrounding towns. In their petition, addressed to Thomas Hutchinson, governor of the province of Massachusetts Bay, Felix and his coauthors emphasized their status as Christians, not unlike the 1723 petitioners from Virginia. And like their compatriots in the Chesapeake, these New England slaves argued for their humanity and against their dehumanization as chattel slaves. Despite being virtuous Christians, the group felt a deep bitterness that they would never "possess and enjoy any Thing, no, not even Life itself, but in a Manner as the Beasts that perish." The group made clear to the governor and to the colonial House of Representatives their existential status, akin to what Orlando Patterson terms "social death," or the condition of bare life described by Giorgio Agamben. As Felix and the group put it, "We have no Property. We have no Wives. No Children. We have no City. No Country."[55]

Scholars working within the tradition of critical race theory further show how animalization and the legal identification of enslaved people with chattel livestock sustained the reproduction of slavery even after the cessation of the

legal Atlantic slave trade in 1808. Female and male slaveholders alike, as Angela Y. Davis, Deborah Gray White, Adrienne Davis, and others have reminded
historians time and again, sought to increase their wealth and property by
"breeding" enslaved people. Documentary evidence of descriptions of women
of African descent as "breeding" material date to at least early seventeenth-
century New England.[56] Again, as Jennifer L. Morgan has reminded scholars,
"the connection between slaves and livestock was always predicated not on
the belief that Africans were animals, but rather in evocation of a degraded but
fully present humanity."[57] Where others, like Dayan, turn to legal and social
history to uncover the processes that led to dehumanization, I see a range of
human–animal networks through trade, science, and labor as no less important sites of contestation where slaveholders staked out the boundaries of the
human and animal worlds.[58] This has spurred my efforts to bring the histories
of slavery and environmental history together in a new conversation.

Historians of early America and the environment have commented on the
entangled lives of enslaved people and livestock animals in Jamaica and other
Atlantic colonies. Entanglement here usefully refers to the ways in which
the predicament of enslavement in practice meant that the lives of people
of African descent were caught up with and compromised by their everyday
relations with nonhumans.[59] Enslaved people on the Vineyard Pen estate in
St. Elizabeth Parish, Jamaica, for instance, fed, nursed, and cared for cattle,
horses, goats, chickens, turkeys, ducks, and pigs. Labor with animals usually
fell along gendered lines, as enslaved men and boys worked closely with cattle
as penkeepers while women and girls cared for herds of sheep, pigs, and goats.
On Vineyard Pen, as on other estates, slaveholders named enslaved men and
women with the same names they gave to livestock animals, such as Cudjoe,
Cynthia, Quash, and Quasheba.[60]

Some enslaved people on Vineyard Pen enjoyed certain privileges with
animals, such as a slave driver named Dick who possessed a hunting dog for
catching wild hogs, and a woman named Phibbah whose animal possessions
included a sow, a boar, and a mare. Phibbah's animals remind us of the para-
doxical nature of slavery: people who were legally considered to be themselves
chattels at times possessed their own animal chattel. Indeed, Phibbah's enslaver's diary contains references to other animals, as entries such as "A fine
land turtle Phibbah sent me" and "18 crabs Phibbah sent me." And we know,
intriguingly, that Phibbah knew how to ride a horse.[61]

Despite the important work of African diaspora scholars like Judith Carney and Andrew Sluyter, environmental historians have made relatively few analyses of human–animal relationships engendered by slavery.[62] One exception is David Lambert's articulation of master–horse–slave, or the human–animal co-mobility arrangement of slaveholders riding horses with the enslaved running behind them, which dramatized the power relations of eighteenth-century British Caribbean slave societies.[63] However, master–horse–slave was only one configuration among many, and the present book builds on this scholarly foundation to tell a new history of slaving and slavery that takes seriously the centrality of human–animal combinations and assemblage in the seventeenth- and eighteenth-century British Atlantic world. Most recently, David Silkenat has shown how the aim to exhaust the labors of people and the fertility of landscapes drove the political ecology of slavery in North America.[64]

The chapters in this book follow the evolution of different modes of interaction, a term developed by Marcy Norton to refer to particular human–animal relationships oriented toward a human end like hunting, and intersections of humans and animals that were constitutive of slaving and slavery in the British Atlantic world from the end of the seventeenth century until the early decades of the nineteenth.[65] While these human–animal relationships are taken in turn, the chapters are organized around networks, power dynamics, geographies, and other thematic points rather than a strict chronology.

Trade in human captives in West Africa in the late seventeenth century, particularly in the Gold Coast and Bight of Benin regions, pivoted on animal bodies. Animal infrastructures of slaving involved cowries, the shells of *Monetaria moneta*, a sea snail endemic to the Indian Ocean, which were used as money to facilitate exchanges among English and Fon, Igbo, Yoruba, and other Atlantic African slavers at trade castles and forts like those built at Ouidah. Canoes and coasting vessels likewise transported cowries and captives along the shoreline. Other animals played spiritual and social roles, like the sheep that Ahanta-speaking traffickers like Captain Nedd offered to Royal African Company factors as gifts, or sometimes as sacrifices, before sanctioning trade at forts like Dixcove and Sekondi on the Gold Coast. Cowries, sheep, and other animals and animal products expedited the castle trade.

Scientific knowledge in early modern England and throughout Europe further depended on slavery as an institution and on enslaved peoples' curiosity about animal forms of life. Anglo-Fante slavers like Tom Ewusi collected faunal specimens at Cape Coast Castle, the headquarters of the Royal African Company on the Gold Coast. Enslaved people, including a man on Nevis named Oxford, who was skilled at diving, furnished marine animal collections destined for the University of Cambridge. Yet slavers mostly discounted or marginalized the skill, labor, and judgment of enslaved naturalists. One such slaver on Barbados characterized the enslaved collector upon whom he relied for acquiring animals as his "Dog."

Plantation labor regimes in the Caribbean and Chesapeake rested on human–animal muscle power and bodily dispossession. Slaveholders conceived of the enslaved "as *Horses* or *Oxen*, to do our Drudgeries," in the words of Cotton Mather, and further placed them alongside horses, cattle, oxen, mules, and other livestock within a plantation anatomy as the bodily "nerves" or muscular "sinews." Drawing from plantation records in the Caribbean and Chesapeake regions, we can further see how slaveholders linked human and animal subjects in their minds and technologies of labor by providing them nearly identical diets and by collecting humanure along with animal waste for revitalizing plantations.

Enslaved people fashioned their own approaches to animals by attacking, stealing, killing, and thinking about animals. The final two chapters follow the decisions made by slaves to use the physical environment of plantations, including ravines and ditches, to injure and kill the livestock animals their slaveholders considered to be their counterparts. Women and men, including people with disabilities, also stole animals, particularly horses, to ride away and flee enslavement and to later reunite with families, lovers, and kin. Flights on horseback engendered rival geographies of power throughout southeastern North America and the Caribbean. Alternative engagements with animals led the enslaved, fugitives, and freed people to think seriously about their relation to the nonhuman world. Some felt profound sympathy with animals, while others elevated their own humanity over animals and animality.

Looking at human–animal histories of slavery does not reveal a straight line from captivity to the ideology of dehumanization. Instead, taking these modes of relation in turn, despite their zigging and zagging, suggests that diverse kinds of human and animal interactions animated and sustained slavery as a transoceanic institution. Indeed, another claim made here is that dehumanization did not occur either instantaneously or in a straightforward, precise fashion. Much like the development of racism and racist thought itself, this history is one that eludes neat starting and ending points. Yet, the Virginia writers of the letter to the bishop of London in 1723 knew full well that their lives had become bound up with animals, that they themselves and their children would be treated like animals, and that the English-speaking slaver-settlers made distinctions between people, animals, and those "in-between" who suffered enslavement. How that boundary line and relationship came to exist out of the interwoven routes of human captives and nonhuman animals is the story we will now follow.

Chapter 1

NOE BOOGES, NOE SLAVES
Animals in the Castle Trade of West Africa

John Carter felt frustration as he wrote to his superiors in the Royal African Company at Cape Coast Castle, the company's chief slaving castle on the Gold Coast of West Africa, in March 1686. For several years, Carter had built a career for himself by exchanging commercial goods in trade for human beings on the Slave Coast, the coastline of the Bight of Benin. He was a factor, or purchasing agent, in the slave trade at the company's factory at Ouidah, sited north of the coastal lagoons. A skilled dealer in global commodities and human captives, Carter served the company and accrued profits for his employers by knowing what goods Fon, Yoruba, and Aja speakers, and traders from other West African polities, desired while bartering for enslaved captives. Raiders and soldiers from the kingdoms of Hueda, Allada, and others plundered captives from northern towns and villages and exchanged their human merchandise for textiles from India, brass kettles and muskets from England, and especially the polished remains of tiny marine sea snails. In his correspondence with Cape Coast, Carter kept his superiors up to date by informing the castle of his recent acquisitions of slaves, the arrivals and departures of coasting vessels loaded with human cargoes, and fluctuations in the demand and prices for different trade goods at Ouidah.

Carter complained in his letter, in a calculating tone, that though "I doe admire that the Affrican Merchant, the Company one ship comeing to" the factory at Ouidah had arrived, the vessel delivered "a great quantity of large bouges, soe much behinde merchantable, that it was 10 slave loss to her cargo in slaves."[1] Carter's Fon-, Yoruba-, and Ewe-speaking clients, among other ethnolinguistic groups in Benin, preferred smaller bouges, the smooth, pale white dorsal shells of the cowry sea snail *Monetaria moneta*. English slavers used the words *bouges,* from the Portuguese *búzio,* and *cowrie,* derived from the Hindi and Urdu word *kauri*, interchangeably to refer to the shells.[2] Carter learned from interpreters, likely Fon, Ewe, or Hueda speakers; his *caboceers*, or local African brokers in the trade; and more experienced factors the particularities of taste and cultural values that made the smaller cowry shells more valuable than the larger kinds sent to Ouidah.[3] By supplying a larger variety of the animals' dorsal shell, and perhaps a different species of cowry altogether, the *African Merchant*'s shipment from Cape Coast had put Carter and his subordinates at the factory at a significant disadvantage in the trade. Moreover, due to their size, consignments of larger cowries reduced the overall quantity of shell money the factory had for bartering for captives.[4]

In his letter, therefore, Carter coolly reminded his employer that future deliveries should contain smaller cowries instead, so that he and his colleagues "may be furnished to purchase a quantity of Negroes reddy against any ships arrivall." In closing, the factor urged Cape Coast to dispatch, along with a shipment of textiles and red coral, "20 barrells bougees" for future trading. Carter again warned his associates in November that if his colleague Captain George Nanter, commander of the African Company's *African Merchant* pink, a kind of small flat-bottomed coasting vessel, "comes downe here without bouges itt will bee troublesome to procure her slaves, butt it shall be done to the best of my endeavor."[5]

One year later, Carter found himself continuing to struggle to emphasize in his letters the importance of sending the right kind of cowry to Ouidah. He notified Cape Coast in 1687 that Nanter's ship carried 230 slaves on board, a disappointing total as it was a diminished shipment compared to the usual capacity of the slaver. "His cargoe falls short," Carter explained, "by reason 6 barrels of his booges proved bigg, whereby was 6 slaves and more lost I thinke." Given the profitability of a slaving voyage and the average mortality rate of a vessel traversing the Middle Passage between Atlantic Africa and the Caribbean, the factors' concerns over the loss of six potentially valuable captives bound for slave markets in Barbados were understandable. Before he folded his letter to send it westward in the care of a canoe pilot employed by the company, he repeated that first and foremost: "The goods I desire are booges."[6] While the *African Merchant* was anchored at Ouidah, Nanter, too, relayed a message to Cape Coast to report that his total cargo fell short of its expected amount, because "severall barrels of booges pranes so large that I am forc't to give the countrey people above a hundred pound for a slave," a frustratingly unfavorable exchange rate for the company's slavers on the ground.[7]

As they considered the size, color, quantity, and weight of the egg-shaped shells of the sea snails in Atlantic Africa, slavers kept in mind their present worth for purchasing captives and the future profits to be made from selling captive human beings at markets in the Americas. Carter and other slavers judged the health and strength of captured men and women in the Bight of Benin and to the west, along the Gold Coast—individuals with names such as Affadoe, Cuffey, Quacoe, Agaba, Bashaw, Mandeloe, and Oldman—as they held on to their shell money. Men like Carter and Nanter performed important skilled labor in the slave trade. They exemplified the necessary judgment that factors and commanders of slaving vessels required to know and predict the value of goods in exchange for captives, including the remains of animals such as red corals and cowries. In addition, their commercial faunal knowledge was not limited to dead animals but encompassed living creatures as well. To succeed in the trade and make a profit for the company and expand their commercial orbit, factors in Atlantic Africa in the late seventeenth century required specific cultural knowledge with regard to animals in West Africa.

Slaving in Atlantic Africa launched the dehumanization and commodification of African captives, and as such the trade should be seen as a set of interrelated markets among many others within the development of early modern capitalism. As one eminent scholar of the trade on the Gold Coast in the seventeenth and eighteenth centuries puts it, the coast became a "stage for a range of activities and practices designed to promote the pretense that human beings could convincingly play the part of their antithesis—bodies animated only by others' calculated investments in their physical capacities."[8] Part of the commodification of enslaved captives involved the methodical evaluation of their bodies, including estimating their future productive labor, against the known value of material objects such as the cowry shells Carter and his partners trafficked at Ouidah. Such evaluations emerged out of complex calculations, cultural negotiations, and the underlying material infrastructure of the trade spanning from England to coastal Atlantic Africa and then across the Atlantic Ocean to England's island colonies in the Caribbean.

Trade depended upon the quantitative methods of accounting and attendant forms of documentary paperwork to render enslaved people—whether shackled in a coffle, bound at a factory sale, or chained in the dungeons below Cape Coast Castle—abstract commodities tied to monetary equivalents.[9] Precise quantities of cowries, whether weighed in barrels, counted on strings, or measured in particular local enumerations, facilitated slave sales between

English and West African traders.[10] By writing in account ledgers, inventory lists, and letters, factors and other agents did the work of "turning people into slaves" through numerical paper records, a process that at every turn depended on knowing the value of cowry shells and other faunal goods like red coral relative to the humans in the trade.[11]

Thus, living and dead animals connected distant English and West African spaces in the slave trade in Atlantic Africa in the late seventeenth century. This chapter investigates two key aspects of slaving related to how English and African agents relied on exchanges of animals to instantiate and reinforce a broad trade in human captives. It does so, first, by examining how a mollusk, the cowry sea snail *Monetaria moneta*, functioned as a widespread form of currency in the castle trade the English struggled to build in seventeenth-century West Africa; and, second, by situating how slave traders used animals, often pastoral farming livestock such as sheep, in ritual sacrifices and as diplomatic gifts to establish political and economic alliances. While these points of intersection in the trade supported commercial networks and expanded the wider traffic in enslaved people, a third section queries how some animals, such as worms and rats, became vermin that interfered with commercial flows by damaging valuable commodities, including trade goods and the health of human captives intended for exchange. Early moderns understood rats to be a "heavy economic burden," as dangerous vectors of disease, especially plague, and by devouring warehoused stores of food and blunting supplies of trade goods.[12]

Using a corpus of letters written by factors of the Royal African Company along with printed accounts of the trade written by other officials, this chapter shows how animals mediated exchanges as the company entered the trade in West Africa in the late seventeenth century.[13] The Royal African Company expanded on the precedent set by Elizabethan slavers like John Hawkins and the Company of Adventurers of London Trading to the Ports of Africa, more commonly called the Guinea Company, which existed between 1618 and 1660. The Royal African Company sought to build more permanent forts and outposts in Atlantic Africa in addition to the forts established by the Guinea Company at Komenda, Kormantin, and Winneba.[14] The company received a charter in 1660 from Charles II, which extended through the loss of its monopoly in 1698 and until its reorganization under James Brydges, the Duke of Chandos, in 1731.[15] After this period, the company turned toward more speculative projects in Atlantic Africa involving agriculture, medicine, and mining—such as indigo and cotton plantations in Sierra Leone, soap and potash manufactories on Sherbro Island, prospecting for drugs at various locales, and gold mining near Cape Coast—as their involvement and profits in the castle trade declined due to competition from separate traders.[16] In 1752, the Company of Merchants Trading to Africa replaced the Royal African Company altogether.[17]

Though these letters were primarily written by white factors, I also read this archive for evidence of the actions taken in the trade by caboceers—West African headmen or brokers, often military or spiritual leaders of communities, who interpreted for and negotiated between factors and local traders—and *curranteers*—rulers of towns, city-states, and larger polities. However, factors frequently confused caboceers and curranteers, making it difficult to precisely identify several African individuals in the archive. And while this chapter strives to recover the enslaved as subjects in the narrative as well, I recognize that the violent commodification and objectification of slaves through the trade led to their fragmentary and mutilated existence in the company's archives.[18]

What emerges from this investigation of the slave trade is a clear picture of the significant cultural, political, and economic roles animals played in connecting or disconnecting sites of exchange across Atlantic Africa. Animals played significant roles in slaving networks, even including the threatening presence of sharks trailing behind slave ships, which became "an integral part of a system of terror" created by captains throughout the Middle Passage.[19] Slave castles, barracoons, and ships deserve a place within a broader environmental history of empire and colonization in the early modern British Atlantic world, and while valuable plants—especially sugar, tobacco, and other botanical commodities—drove the demand from slaveholders in the Caribbean for greater shipments of captive laborers over time, my focus here is on how animals connected spaces of the trade in Atlantic Africa before the peak of the slave trade in the eighteenth century.[20]

Drawing on the methods of imperial environmental historians who question how "interlinked cultural formations, material exchanges, and ecological processes" shaped the expansion of the British Empire and its far-flung colonies and semicolonial spaces in the nineteenth century, this chapter asks how the Atlantic slave trade, which resulted in the unprecedented transfer of approximately 12 million African captives across the Atlantic Ocean from the seventeenth to the early nineteenth centuries, involved, to an appreciable extent, interactions between humans and sea snails, sheep, elephants, guinea worms, rats, cats, and other creatures.[21]

The Royal African Company did not settle colonies in West Africa in the seventeenth century. However, the company performed a significant imperial function in delivering captives to colonies in the Caribbean and to ports in New Spain under the *asiento*—the official license to provide captives from Atlantic Africa to Spain's American colonies via a monopoly contract granted by the Spanish Crown—until the early eighteenth century. These efforts reinforced broader patterns of settler colonialism in the Americas, including the genocide of Indigenous societies through war and disease. Yet before millions of enslaved men and women climbed out of the dungeons of the African Company and passed through the Door of No Return on the shoreline at Cape Coast, animals brought slavers together in Atlantic Africa and shaped the "inhuman traffick" in significant ways.[22] To begin exploring the animals that enabled human trafficking in West Africa, historians must reckon with the cowry.

Animal shells and remains connected the slave trade as forms of currency at the forts and markets where African Company factors and West African traders convened. Among the dead animal bodies traders and caboceers exchanged for enslaved captives were red corals culled from the Mediterranean Sea and the bone-white shells of cowry sea snails transshipped from the Indian Ocean world. *Monetaria moneta,* a species of cowry endemic to the Maldives islands, was most common in the trade on the Gold Coast and Bight of Benin in the late seventeenth century, while to a lesser extent the ringed *Cypraea annulus* species found in coastal East Africa, the Zanzibar Archipelago, and the Red Sea also circulated.[23] Forms of shell money existed in western Central Africa as well, such as the zimbo shell currency prevalent in the Congo.[24]

In the first decade of the sixteenth century, Portuguese traders and navigators, such as Duarte Pacheco Pereira, noticed how merchants in Benin used "money shells" for trade, and they began using the Maldives *moneta* as a form of currency in the region.[25] Forms of shell money, like the shells Pereira noticed around 1508, including Atlantic species of mollusks, had circulated as currency in West and western Central African polities since at least the ninth century.[26] In the medieval era, cowries from the Maldives found their way into West African states such as the Ghana, Mali, and Songhai empires via maritime and overland routes as Arabic traders from Yemen and Oman sailed between ports across the Indian Ocean and shipped cowries through the Red Sea to Cairo and on to other port cities in North Africa.[27] Traders from the Maghreb then transported the cowries south across the Sahara to the western

Sudan.[28] Trans-Saharan trade networks involving the sale of slaves and other commodities, well before the arrival of the Portuguese, involved *moneta* cowries from the Maldives.[29]

Moneta cowries are small marine gastropods found primarily in the Indian Ocean, but as a group of animals, the cowry family *Cypraeidae* can be placed in global history due to the use of their shells as money in antiquity in South Asia, much of continental Africa, China, and Europe.[30] Like other snails, cowries use their muscular propodium to move and to affix their bodies to surfaces. Cowry snails use their tentacles, siphon, and radula to locate and feed on algae and floating bits of detritus. As they develop, their mantle secretes calcium carbonate crystals to produce the enamel of their dorsal shell. Fishers in the Maldives, often women and girls, collected the animals from tidepools along the shore at low tide, either by hand or using nets. After gathering the animals from the shoreline, fishers either piled the animals in the sun to die and rot, after which they could use branches to easily remove the snail carcasses from their shells, or they buried caches of cowries in sand pits to quicken their decay and removal. Next, the fishers washed the shells with freshwater to clean away sand and dirt and any remaining animal matter.[31]

Cowries' value as a form of currency in multiple cultures in North and West Africa derived from the virtual impossibility of counterfeiting the animal's shell.[32] In diverse societies, including those made up of Fante, Akan, Fon, Aja, Ewe, and Yoruba speakers, individuals also valued the snail shells for their political and religious significance as instruments of divination, magical charms, or ornamentation worn by elites, before the arrival of Europeans.[33] Patterned arrangements of cowries were also used as diplomatic objects exchanged among rulers of various West African ethnolinguistic groups in the Bight of Benin, a geographic region that encompasses the present-day nations of Togo, Benin, and western Nigeria.[34] Cowry gifts could symbolically represent social bonds of obligation in early modern Atlantic Africa.[35]

Akinwumi Ogundiran argues that the monetization of these animals did not become absolute or standardized until the proliferation of slave markets developed by Europeans and Africans in the early modern period. Through the expansion of the Atlantic slave trade, cowries gradually became further symbolically associated with wealth, fertility, and high social status.[36] In Benin and Yorubaland, including the kingdom of Oyo, cowries came to be associated with the treasures of a sea deity, Olokun, the "Owner of the Sea." Robin Law cites a narrative from early eighteenth-century Benin that describes how a local king, Eresoyen, struggled with Olokun for control over the flow of the Benin River after the king blocked its passage to the sea. After Eresoyen ultimately bowed to Olokun's might and reopened the passage to the river, the sea god rewarded the king with heaps of "cowries to the sky."[37]

Around 1515, European merchants, beginning with Portuguese traders, began transporting to the Bight of Benin massive shipments of *Monetaria moneta* purchased either directly from the Maldives islands or indirectly from markets in the Indian subcontinent. The Dutch and the English followed the Portuguese precedent in the seventeenth century. In the Indian Ocean, Dutch East Indies Company ships often blocked the rival English East India Company from purchasing cowries directly from the Maldives archipelago. Without regular access to Maldives, English East India Company factors resorted to buying cowries at markets in India—such as Bombay, Calcutta, and Balasore in the state of Odisha—and farther south at Aceh in Sumatra, where the animals were commonly used as currency. In the late seventeenth century, English East India Company officials purchased substantial quantities of cowry shells at Balasore and used the shells as ballast for ships returning to England from their stronghold at Fort St. George in Madras, before selling them at auction to the Royal African Company in London.[38]

Cowries became valuable and vital to the slave trade as an abstract, quantifiable currency form in West African kingdoms, used to trade for gold dust, provisions, ivory, and captives taken from raiding assaults or as prisoners of war.[39] While slavers exchanged cowries for captives in Upper Guinea and on the Gold Coast, the animal shells were most valuable in the Bight of Benin, later known to Europeans as the Slave Coast due to its principal commodity. From the the early decades of the sixteenth century until the early nineteenth century, European merchants shipped approximately 30 billion cowries to the Bight of Benin.[40]

Ships sailing from England to the Gold Coast for the Royal African Company deposited their cowry cargo at the central castle, Cape Coast, where agents then dispersed the shells farther east and west via smaller coasting vessels like the *African Merchant* captained by George Nanter. Company factors at outposts like Offra in Allada, Little Popo, and Ouidah counted and stored the animal shells with local traders, along with trade goods, as money for buying captives. As coastal trade networks involving slaves and cowries expanded outward from the Bight of Benin farther inland, the ubiquity of the Indian Ocean money cowries more fully connected trade networks between coastal West

African and North African slavers via trans-Saharan trade routes that predated the arrival of Europeans by several centuries.[41] In addition to using cowries as money to purchase captives, factors for the Royal African Company paid customary tributes to local rulers and city-states in the form of cowries.[42] Writing from Ouidah in 1682, Andrew Crosbie reported how factors paid "customes to the King" of Ouidah "out of your Honours warehouse in 9 lb of boogees" and other goods.[43]

Coasting vessels like the *African Merchant* connected the Gold and Slave Coasts and sailed to stock the company's forts and outposts with cowries. In a letter from James Fort at Accra, sited east of Cape Coast, Arthur Wendover, a factor, notified his superiors in 1680, for instance, that the captain of the coasting vessel *Bonadventure* requested a typical delivery of "33 3/4 cask of coureyes" to exchange for enslaved captives at Allada on the Slave Coast.[44] "A proper cargo," for purchasing slaves in Allada, wrote one factor, contained first and foremost a necessary quantity of "bougees."[45] In his letters, Wendover complained to Cape Coast that several cowry shipments lately arriving at Accra appeared broken or damaged, which, along with being too large or discolored, depreciated their value on the coast.[46] On their return voyages, coasting vessels transported cargoes of enslaved captives to Cape Coast, where they remained incarcerated in the dungeons below the castle.

Factors and ship captains frequently asked Cape Coast to supply them with transshipments of cowries to successfully carry out the business of slaving. Writing at Offra, the company's factory near Allada and due east of Ouidah, William Cross wrote to Cape Coast in 1681 that the trade in enslaved people continued to accelerate in the region, and urged that "tis very inconvenient for a ship to come here without booges, and if you send none by the next ship, you must hardly expect any slaves." However, he continued, "If you purchase any att the Mina Castle (where I heare there is plenty) you may be sure of slaves in a very short time."[47] Cross's letter suggests how damaged, diminished, or delayed supplies of cowries from England could push the company to turn to its Dutch rivals for assistance and placed the company in an inferior position in the trade.

A lack of cowries stalled the trade. One ship captain, Charles Towgood, complained that without cowries he could not purchase captives while anchored at Adangme, near the Volta River, in 1682, while a "French man had nothing but bouges" and succeeded in buying slaves.[48] James Thorne, a factor at Offra, wrote the same year to Cape Coast while in negotiations with the king of Allada, requesting "booges by the next shipping . . . without them you must expect little to be done, for tis all one their money here, as silver and gold is with us."[49]

In 1686, John Carter continued to complain to his superiors that his base at Ouidah did not receive enough cowries to execute the trade in captives. "I have been so extreamly abussed by the Company," Carter fumed. His letters and advice on what kinds of cowries the outpost at Ouidah required often went unnoticed by his superiors.[50] Carter's knowledge of African aesthetics and values, of course, derived from his interactions with individual Atlantic Africans, including a Huedan *yuvogan*, or trading official appointed by a king, who was known to the company as "Captain Carter."[51] While Cape Coast did respond to factors' demands, men like John Carter and Captain Carter emphasized time and again the necessity of a regular flow of cowries for opening or sustaining economic networks around the bight. One factor summed up the situation by writing that a career "without bowges in these parts here is noe lieving for a whiteman."[52]

In their efforts to track the value of cowries, factors inventoried the company's warehouses at their forts, listed their supply of the shells by weight, and included the current rates of exchange for cowries and slaves in their ledgers. In an inventory of the warehouse at Offra from 1681, James Thorne listed, among the textiles, metal goods, guns, and other trade items at the warehouse, that the fort traded "961 pound of booges att 78 lb per slave." The factor recorded in his account book how the fort paid its caboceers in cowries, paid for repairs to the factory walls and buildings completed by local artisans in cowries, and that he had paid the ransom of a messenger who had been *panyarred*, or kidnapped, at Ouidah "in booges." "I would desire your worship to send booges," Thorne requested in his letter accompanying the updated inventory to Cape Coast, "for I have none for my present use but am forct to borrow of the blacks."[53] Thorne's petition reveals just how crucial the market in cowries and regular access to supplies of the animal shells were for reckoning the value of the enslaved and keeping trade flowing in the bight.

Factors like John Carter repeatedly wrote in frustration to Cape Coast, requesting information on shipments of cowries to the outforts and for information about the changing value of cowries at different markets between the regions of the slave trade. They constantly told Cape Coast that "if you send booges a good quantity, with allmost any other goods you have you cannot want slaves, for they are very plenty" at Ouidah and elsewhere in the Bight of

Benin.[54] While stationed at Appa, near present-day Badagry, Arthur Wendover put the situation frankly to his superiors: "noe booges noe slaves."[55]

Factors often wrote to Cape Coast for updated information on the value of cowries between the Gold Coast and the Bight of Benin. In 1686, Mark Bedford Whiting, a factor at Accra, wrote to Cape Coast "an enquirey for bouges for slaves," requesting to know how the current prices for captives and the worth of cowries differed between the Gold Coast and the Bight of Benin.[56] The following month, Whiting again wrote to Cape Coast that for "bouges and manobut bands we are as yet ignorant of the disposall, not knowing what quantity we must vend for slaves or gold."[57]

Competition from others better equipped with cowry stores frequently frustrated the Royal African Company. In 1681, Daniel Gates reported that a French slaver at Olampo "cleared the towne of slaves, they haveing a great many booges."[58] Writing aboard the ship *Adventure,* in 1687, James Bayly reported that he had purchased "six slaves with such goods as I have" at Ningo, "but theirs twenty gon away for want of goods," especially cowries, which his Dutch competitors possessed in much greater quantities.[59]

Beyond foreign competition, African laborers hired by the company at their factories also posed challenges to the Royal African Company's distribution of cowries. In 1693 and 1694, Thomas Phillips commanded the slave ship *Hannibal,* which sailed from England to Cape Mesurado, the Gold Coast, Ouidah, and São Tomé and Príncipe before crossing the ocean to Barbados. While anchored at the factory at Ouidah, Phillips learned firsthand how difficult it could be to maintain supplies of cowry shells on the ground. In the warehouse at Ouidah, barrels of cowries delivered from coasting vessels were frequently "pilfer'd by the negro porters," who stole cowries using "instruments like wedges" to pry loose barrel staves and pocket handfuls of shells.[60] Phillips and his crew failed to prevent such incidents at the warehouse and failed to successfully catch any of the porters in the act of stealing money cowries.

Factors on the coast likewise faced difficulties in dealing with local workers for the Royal African Company. Josiah Pearson reported from Ouidah in the spring of 1697 on the "rogueryes of the Cabo Corso canoamen" who paddled to the outpost on the Bight of Benin. Tom, a canoe pilot hired by the company, arrived at Ouidah only to quickly loan his canoe to "the Mine blacks to goe to Jacking to take a Portuguze shipp." Later, Tom "took" another canoe pilot hired by Pearson to steal "three caskes bouges" from the factory, which they jettisoned from their canoes "into the sea, and gott them out afterwards in the night." Pearson suspected Tom and his compatriots would attempt to smuggle the stolen cowries to foreign or interloper traders at Grand Popo. Pearson concluded his complaint by condemning "all the Cabo Corso canoamen in generall, they valuing not the English nor the Companyes fort in these parts, but continually side with the Mine blacks" at Elmina Castle.[61]

Captains of coasting vessels wrote directly to Cape Coast to request supplies of shells on slaving voyages as the value of money cowries fluctuated up or down. William Piles, commander of the sloop *Sally Rose,* wrote to Cape Coast off the coast of Teshi, a town east of Accra, in 1697 "a few lines concerning my bouges." Piles asked the factor at Accra to send him the current rates of exchange for enslaved men and women for cowries, and complained that local merchants refused previous prices for slaves in cowries and were now demanding more. After Piles offered seventy pounds of cowries "for a man, they immediately fell a telling them, and return'd back again. I have offered them eighty pound for a man, and they will not take them. . . . I desire your answer," he demanded, "how many pound of bouges you will allow me for a man, and likewise for a woman."[62] Despite factors' regular calculations, the value of cowries varied between places and over time due to their variable size, shape, and relative scarcity. On occasion, the value of cowries could drop precipitously as demand changed. Later that month at Kpone, also east of Accra, Piles lamented that local slavers did "not now ask for any" cowries.[63]

Cowries attracted the attention not only of merchants in West Africa but also of natural historians and specimen collectors interested in improving the company's prospects for accruing wealth in the form of enslaved captives, and by other means. James Houstoun, chief surgeon at Cape Coast Castle, sought potentially valuable plants, animals, and minerals for the "improvement" of the slave trade and the Royal African Company's position in Atlantic Africa on a collecting expedition from 1722 to 1724.[64] James Brydges, the Duke of Chandos and a major investor in the African Company who aimed to diversify the company's activities, appointed Houstoun to the position.[65] Houstoun's itinerary from Sierra Leone to the Gold Coast fit within other speculative missions the company launched in the early eighteenth century, which were designed to adapt expertise in natural history to projects in agriculture, chemistry, medicine, and mining in West Africa.[66]

In 1722, while scouting a "most fertile Island" in the Sierra Leone River, the doctor collected "Cockle-Shells, which very much resemble our Cowries."

These animals, Houstoun reflected, "might have been of considerable Use to me afterwards, as current Money on the Slave Coast. How far these Collections might have contributed to the Rise of *African* Stock, I shall not pretend to determine." In his natural history of West Africa, Houstoun complained that factors on the Gold Coast, including, he alleged, the governor of Cape Coast, undermined the company by illicitly selling cowry stocks to other European competitors, particularly the Portuguese, and he hoped his discovery in Sierra Leone would ameliorate the losses caused by disloyalty to the company.[67] While Houstoun dreamed of translating his knowledge in natural history and medicine to economic proposals for improving the company's position in the trade—such as the substitute cowries from Sierra Leone—his shell scheme never materialized.[68]

While factors for the Royal African Company recorded and negotiated the value of cowries as money for purchasing captives on the Gold and Slave Coasts, enslaved people understood cowries in an altogether different light. As the geography of raiding, war, and slaving expanded throughout West Africa, people living in regions that slavers frequently looted for captives, such as towns further inland from the coastline, like those in present-day Benin, northern Ghana, Nigeria, and Togo, circulated their own stories of how vampiric "cowrie shells feasted on the bodies of captives." Oral traditions in these communities posited that Europeans threw captives overboard from their ships into the waters of the Atlantic to feed hungry cowries underwater and multiply their money, as, they claimed, human blood nourished the creatures in the ocean. Into the nineteenth century, vernacular knowledge in West African communities impacted by slaving held that "the best places to harvest cowries were along the coast where slaves had been murdered or drowned," and that fishermen could become wealthy by salvaging hybrid "human-mollusk" bodies of the trade's numerous victims.[69]

One town elder interviewed in Nigeria in the late twentieth century told of how Hausa slavers captured people and fed their bodies to cowries that then stuck to their skin and "killed the human beings by sucking all their blood."[70] Another elder in northern Togo reported to anthropologists that slavers mutilated captives, tearing their limbs from their bodies to feed cowries in a pool. Similar narratives of ritual human sacrifices in the kingdom of Dahomey involved the blood of captives being spilled to satisfy these hungry animals. The proliferation and durability of beliefs about the vampiric nature of cowries attests to the fact that the enslaved themselves recognized how the trade constituted a deadly entanglement of human and animal life as captives became commodities.

Exchanges of the bone-white shells of cowries for enslaved captives transformed West Africa, especially the Bight of Benin, or Slave Coast, from the seventeenth century onward. Factors purchased slaves using cowries and other goods at outforts in the Gold Coast and at bases along the Slave Coast east of the Volta River. English traders capitalized on the Portuguese precedent of using the shells in the Bight of Benin, and further transformed the cultural significance of the animals from instruments of divination and symbolic power to stockpiles of wealth as the animal currency became loaded with new meaning by the early eighteenth century. However, the English often failed to keep up supplies of cowries, and frequently lost captives to their Dutch, French, and Portuguese competitors.

Cowry shipments thus played a crucial role in shaping the Atlantic slave trade in West Africa. However, other animals likewise took on economic, social, and political meaning in the creation of slaving networks, as gifts, objects of ritual sacrifice, and symbols of bonds of obligation and alliance. Seeing sheep in the slave trade, then, tells us something about the animals that made trade possible.

The Royal African Company's material infrastructure, particularly the forts that defended and facilitated slave trading, developed gradually out of violent conflicts in the late seventeenth century with its major European rivals, the Dutch West India Company. In addition, the company clashed with French, Portuguese, and Danish slave trading firms. On the Gold Coast, English slavers further struggled to adapt to the norms and customs of Atlantic African kingdoms and city-states such as Akwamu, Agona, Fetu, and Eguafo. At their forts and outposts in the castle trade, the company relied on interpreters and caboceers who spoke numerous languages and dialects—including Akan-Twi, Fante, Ewe, and Ga, among others—to communicate with individual slavers and rulers engaged in the trade. In addition to verbal communication, animals played important roles as ritual sacrifices and as diplomatic gifts so secure political and economic alliances between the Royal African Company and West African polities and city-states that shored up their presence on the coastline in the late seventeenth century.

Chartered in 1660, the Royal African Company coordinated the slave trade in West Africa from its heavily fortified central castle on the Gold Coast, Cape Coast Castle, which was captured from the Dutch West India Company by an

English naval squadron in 1664.[71] While officers at Cape Coast reported to the company's headquarters and court of directors at African House in London, the central fort communicated via correspondence with smaller outforts and unfortified outposts to the east and west, spanning more than two thousand miles along the coastline, from the mouth of the Gambia River to the Bight of Benin. As propitiatory offerings used in ritual sacrifice, animals shaped the slaving networks the company struggled to build at these forts and outposts. Examining the development of the company's base at Dixcove, located in present-day Ghana, affords insight into how factors adapted to Atlantic African cultural values and rites involving sheep as sacrificial offerings to forge bonds of trust, commerce, and mutual alliance.[72]

On August 15, 1692, Christopher Clarkson, a surveyor for the company, reported to the chief factor at Sekondi, another outpost sited east of Dixcove, that a party consisting of his men and several company slaves successfully recaptured the site of the company's former outpost near the Ahanta settlement on the Gold Coast. While the company had claimed Dixcove as territory since 1684, it had failed to maintain a permanent fort there until Clarkson's mission.[73] Clarkson seized the space at the edge of Ahanta territory at a crucial moment, as the company feared the rising influence and threatening fortresses to the west, held by the Brandenburg African Company based at Groß Friedrichsburg, and to the east, held by the Dutch West India Company headquartered at Elmina Castle.

Upon landing at Dixcove, Clarkson hoisted a flag and "fired 2 guns to keep of our enimies and encouradge our friends" to approach their camp. Clarkson's ritual of possession claimed the site for the Royal African Company but did not guarantee its long-term security.[74] Aware of their precarity on the coast, Clarkson quickly dispatched messengers to arrange a palaver, a formal negotiation, with an Ahanta headman and the ruler of Dixcove, Captain Dickie, to lay the groundwork for a trading partnership. Prospects of trade with the company and a military alliance against Adom, a nearby city-state, enticed Dickie, who in a gesture signaling his acceptance of the company's terms, sent Clarkson workers to aid a party of company slaves building a fort at Dixcove.

After raising the fort's limestone walls, Dickie, Clarkson, and a group of twelve caboceers gathered for a celebration. In a ritual to seal the relationship between himself and the company, Dickie "layed some gold under the foundation stone and killed a fatt sheep."[75] Clarkson participated as well, and he acknowledged Dickie's sacrificial offering with *dashees* (gifts) of brandy and textiles. Though Clarkson omitted to state whether he and his subordinates ate the sheep's carcass in a celebratory meal with Dickie and his men, it is possible, granted available evidence from early modern West African societies and Dutch materials from this period.[76] In Fante-speaking cultures, and in other ethnolinguistic groups on the Gold Coast, ritual sacrifices of livestock created, or restored, social, economic, and political bonds of obligation among people.[77] Sheep served in proto-Akan and Akan-speaking cultural groups as living instruments for making propitiatory sacrifices, gifts, or payments to resolve disputes and retire debts. Sacrifices of sheep could also serve an apotropaic function to ward off danger.[78] While it is unclear from the records of the company, the animal was likely a breed of sheep indigenous to West Africa, or possibly a breed brought earlier in the sixteenth century by Portuguese merchants.[79]

Rites involving sheep would not have been alien or incommensurable to the English, as families in England and its North American colonies likewise gifted and bequeathed livestock as a form of intergenerational wealth and property.[80] In seventeenth-century New England, for instance, livestock animals were often given as a form of bridewealth. Moreover, in English literature and oral and visual culture, sheep represented social values, including bonds of obedience and trust between servants and masters.[81]

What is crucial to understand here is that in participating in this ritual with the Ahanta headman, Clarkson recognized Dickie's sacrifice of the sheep as an important step toward creating trading opportunities and security for the Royal African Company at Dixcove, embedding the company into a uniquely Atlantic African cultural milieu. Upon its conclusion, Clarkson urged Thomas Johnson, his superior at Sekondi, to send materials to furnish the fort and additional gifts to offer to their new allies. Among the supplies Clarkson requested were bricks, boards, company slaves, and trade goods to offer to Dickie and his caboceers as *dashees*. While Clarkson considered the future profits of trade in enslaved captives and gold dust between Dickie and the company, and the possibilities to enter into lucrative interior trade relations with nearby polities such as the Akan-speaking kingdom of Denkyira, the future of the fort at Dixcove, like others on the Gold Coast, rested upon offering up an animal, the sheep, and the social bonds it represented.

Far from being an exception, sheep became important as ritual sacrifices and diplomatic gifts that shaped alliances between European factors and African actors engaged in the trade. In the mid-seventeenth century, the Dutch dominated the slave trade on the Gold Coast and often frustrated English ambitions to expand the ambit of their activities in the region.[82] From Fort Ruijghaver on the Ankobra River to their outpost at Ouidah, the Dutch manned more than a dozen forts.[83] Since the English first settled their initial fort, Kormantin, on the Gold Coast in 1631, primarily to engage the gold dust trade, continuous fighting with the Dutch West India Company and their allies over influence in the trade had hindered their ambitions.[84]

Despite the station's precarious situation, Dixcove strengthened the company's territorial and commercial expansion among their European competitors on the coast.[85] However, their ultimate success in the trade depended on the company's ability to negotiate and secure alliances with powerful West African kingdoms and city-states, which in part rested on knowing and recognizing the value of animals in diverse cultures. Several of these negotiations, such as the founding of Dixcove, involved accepting, offering, or providing sacrificial sheep. Though Royal African Company officials, and their superiors in Europe, most likely perceived the ritual offering of sheep in Atlantic Africa to be a local fetish—a term referring to deities or other supernatural forces, and the objects that represented their presence or power—and evidence of African irrationality or intellectual degeneracy, factors enthusiastically adapted to these customs and saw them as central to the ongoing work of building out the slave trade.[86]

On April 27, 1698, six years after Clarkson recaptured Dixcove, William Gabb, a factor at the newly reoccupied fort at Sekondi, wrote to the company's headquarters at Cape Coast to report that tensions between the English and the Dutch nearby at Fort Oranje as well as at other outposts, including Butri, Fort St. Sebastian, and Shama, threatened to erupt into war. The Dutch, who obstructed the company's hopes to trade with the kingdoms of Wassa and Twifo, continued to frustrate English entrees into slaving networks. Gabb's fort, Sekondi, lay between Dixcove to the west and Cape Coast to the east. Like Dixcove, the company had claimed to possess an outpost at Sekondi since 1683; however, the English evacuated and abandoned the fort several times in the midst of armed hostilities.[87] From 1694 to 1700, disputes between the Dutch and the English over access to markets in the slave trade; to West African kingdoms and city-states on the Gold Coast, including Adom, Ahanta, and Eguafo; and to the powerful merchant prince John Cabess, at Komenda, broke out in a series of violent conflicts later known as the Komenda Wars.[88]

As West African competitors and their Dutch and English clients clashed, animal exchanges continued to shape the future of the slave trade at the company's Gold Coast forts. In a letter from Sekondi to Cape Coast in the spring of 1698, Gabb informed his superiors on the situation at the fort with regards to the kingdom of Adom. The company had warred with Adom throughout the 1680s and at times found itself drawn into conflict between Adom and Ahanta.[89] As a factor, Gabb attempted to reconcile the company and Adom, but peace between the two proved fragile. Like the foundation of trade at Dixcove, reconciliation hinged upon carefully presenting an animal sacrifice. During a palaver at Sekondi, the "king" of Adom, Gabb reported, "gave the sheep I brought up to the white men that was killed in the Castle, and his fetish [deity] tells him, if he doe not give one for the Castle, it will not doe well, so he desires one of your Worshipps."[90] While the Adom king accepted Gabb's offering of a sacrificial sheep to bind the company to Adom, he also demanded that the company offer a second sheep of its own for him to ritually slaughter in the castle to purify their relationship.

The Royal African Company's assent to providing animals for sacrifice, and the king's demand to properly consecrate this alliance, demonstrates how necessary sheep became for English attempts to solidify their relationships with Gold Coast polities. Gabb immediately requested that Cape Coast send another sheep to assure Adom of their intent for peaceful trading and to ensure their future bonds of mutual support against their Dutch rivals. The company responded promptly to Gabb's missive and forwarded a sheep to Sekondi. Gabb thanked his superiors at Cape Coast the following month for sending the ovine present, which he promptly delivered to the king "and told em all you was pleased to order."[91] The gift of the sheep and other trade goods, including textiles, secured the company's political, economic, and military alliance with Adom and further bolstered its power on the Gold Coast.

In addition to giving sheep as sacrificial offerings, factors understood the sacred nature of sheep in their ongoing negotiations with merchant slavers along the Gold Coast. In the spring of 1681, James Nightingale demanded from his counterparts in the trade at Komenda, a castle sited east of Sekondi, the forfeiture of sheep as the price of loyalty. After Akani traders entered into a palaver with an interloper in the trade, one Captain Been, Nightingale punished their treachery and "made the merchants and Arcanies take this country fetish that none should goe aboard of any ship to trade contrary to your Honours articles, and alsoe prendee'd them three sheep, whereof your Honour will receive two from the transgressers."[92] Nightingale demanded the Akanis pay a fine as well to the caboceers and "fetishmakers" at Komenda, and he sent his dispatch eastward to Cape Coast by way of "Cappusheer Hansico," a caboceer of the castle. While the sheep may have been materially unimportant, Nightingale understood their symbolic value as the cost of disloyalty for the Akani.

Gifts of livestock animals between company factors and African traders, beyond the ritual context of sacrifice, knit slaving networks between forts, towns, and other markets throughout the trade. West African rulers offered animal gifts to the company to keep routes of exchange and relays of communication open. Writing from Komenda to Cape Coast in 1686, for instance, William Cross reported, "The king [of Eguafo] yesterday sent me a sheep for farther sattisfaction about this pallaver, which I have sent your Worship herewith."[93] The king used a gift of livestock to assure his English partners that Eguafo, and the towns subordinate to Eguafo, intended to maintain trade in enslaved captives and other goods with the company's factors at the castle. In later years, Eguafo continued to send animal gifts to the English, who recognized the ovines as valuable promises for ongoing trade, peace, and stability. In July 1698, for instance, Gerrard Gore wrote from Komenda that the king of Eguafo sent the factory a customary gift of "a large sheepe, with severall other things, and likewise [demands] custome of me."[94] Like Gabb at Sekondi, Gore wrote to Cape Coast to send a sheep to Komenda immediately to satisfy the Eguafo king.

Headmen likewise presented gifts of wealth on the hoof to open new lines of trade on the Gold Coast. At Dixcove, Captain Nedd, likely an Ahanta caboceer or curranteer familiar to the company, wrote to Cape Coast informing them of his plans to build a *croom*, or village, nearby the castle in 1698. "My humble service to you all," he wrote. "May it please your worships I have herewith sent you a sheepe, which desire your Worships will be pleased to except off."[95] Nedd intended his croom to profitably trade with the fort at Dixcove, in provisions and occasional captives. Whether Nedd expected that the English would accept the sheep as a sacrifice or simply as a gift of meat, he succeeded in using the animal to insert himself, his kin networks, and his allies into the company's web of trade on the Gold Coast.

Fante caboceers and curranteers continued to leverage four-footed gifts into the early eighteenth century. In the memorandum book of Cape Coast, for instance, entries from 1703 and 1704 record how a local trader, Quomino Coffee, sent the company regular presents of sheep to maintain his connection to the company.[96]

Individuals used animal gifts to influence diplomatic channels established in the trade. Traders plied gifts of livestock, for instance, in exchange for people held in pawnship or taken captive during occasional conflict at the outforts. For example, Thomas Willson, a factor stationed at Komenda, reported in the winter of 1694 that John Cabess, a powerful merchant prince and military ally of the English, had offered a "fatt sheep" as a gift to the company in exchange for freeing "one Peter, a Black, owt of irons."[97] The circumstances of Peter's incarceration are opaque, yet Willson accepted the gift and visited Cabbess's croom a few days later, bringing presents of his own, including casks of beef.[98] In 1695, a messenger of Attabo, "your Cabbosheer att Anguinna," brought with him to James Fort, Accra, a gift of "two sheep" for the company's factor, Edward Searle.[99]

Factors at Cape Coast occasionally found themselves entangled in similar situations. An entry in the memorandum book at Cape Coast from 1704 records that the company redeemed a canoe pilot named Cawera, held in pawn by the king of Asebu, for the price of a fat sheep and three ounces of gold.[100] Further entries in the 1714 fort diary at Komenda document how presents of "fatted Sheep" continued to bind the company to John Cabess and to the burgeoning state of Asante to the north.[101]

Caboceers used animal gifts to ingratiate themselves with curranteers who negotiated with Europeans throughout the slave trade. In 1682, caboceers serving the company at Anomabu brought "3 sheepe" during a palaver with another local headman, Ampeteens, presumably as ritual and diplomatic gifts. Upon seeing the sheep, Richard Thelwall, a factor at Charles Fort, wrote that he "told them that would not doe, I bid them goe to Capo Corsoe" and leave the palaver.[102] The reasons for Thelwall's judgment on this matter are opaque, yet the presence of the sheep indicates the diplomatic nature of this encounter. Caboceers, such as those living around Sekondi, also paid customary gifts of sheep to the factory to maintain relationships with the company.[103] Sheep also existed as common forms of customary payment, as James Walker learned in the fall of 1687. Writing from Sekondi, Walker reported how trade relationships between the fort, their caboceers, and the "younge men" of the *asafo* company, or local militia, at Sekondi deteriorated due to not having "paid their custome," which included three sheep.[104]

Philip Quaque's letters from Cape Coast Castle provides the perspective of a Fante man enculturated into English norms on Gold Coast customs involving sheep. Quaque, or Kweku in Fetu, wrote to Daniel Burton in 1767 on the status of his mission on behalf of the Society for the Propagation of the Gospel in Foreign Parts. Quaque wrote that his "Scholars" were absent one day "as they were going to offer Sacrifice to their chief God, the Goddess Aminsor. A superstitious & Infamous Offering indeed, and that the only Reason I could learn was that this Town lately has been very sickly, but still few died, so that this Custom of sacrificing a Sheep caught by force is on Acct. of the Time & for Her to dispell this Sickness from the Inhabitants or her people." Quaque added that Fantes living near the castle offered ritual sacrifices of sheep to other gods, including Tabarah and his wife, N'eyeer. Quaque himself most often used sheep in his letters as a metaphor to describe his "scholars" and parishioners at Cape Coast, writing of them as his "scattered Sheep" and "peculiar lost Sheep." His own self-description as a "Sheep in the Jaws of so many Ravenous Wolves" reflects his thoroughgoing English education and acculturation as a young adult.[105]

Presents of other kinds of animals, such as those intended to arouse curiosity around the exotic, appeared infrequently on the Gold Coast or along the Bight of Benin. Since slavers often purchased animals such as parrots and monkeys to sell as pets to elites in England who kept fashionable private menageries, it is possible that these occasional gifts reflected Atlantic African savvy in supplying exotic fauna for Europeans.[106] In 1715, for instance, the Royal African Company shipped "a Tyger, 3 Guinea Hens, and the Green Birds" from West Africa via a Royal Navy man-of-war as gifts to be presented to George I.[107]

Atlantic African slavers did offer animal gifts at the company's factories in Upper Guinea. A clerk at the Royal African Company's fort on James Island in the Gambia River, for instance, noted in his journal in 1730 that a Wolof-speaking trader had taken "a young Elephant brought alive as a Present to the Governor" of James Island.[108] While the clerk offered no comment on this animal, or the governor's reaction, perhaps this captive present became a curiosity held at the fort for the amusement of the factors, or was later transshipped to England. On other occasions at James Island, Wolof- and Mandinka-speaking traders presented the governor with "two Porcupines" and an ostrich.

West African slavers in Upper Guinea also offered gifts of curious animals to traders unaffiliated with the Royal African Company, well after the loss of its monopoly and the decline of the castle trade. One slave ship captain anchored at Sierra Leone in 1805, for instance, received presents of "a young alligator, two porcupines, and a crown-bird." In addition, the captain of the slaver liked to show off another gift to travelers he met in Upper Guinea: an enslaved boy named John Favorite.[109] In the early nineteenth century, animal gifts continued to connect merchants in the slave trade. On one occasion, slavers on the Gold Coast furnished live animal specimens for a menagerie at Cape Coast Castle, which included chimpanzees, parrots, and a leopard.[110]

Offerings of animals as propitiatory sacrifices, diplomatic gifts, or curiosities bound for menageries joined English and West African actors together in the late seventeenth century, and over time this forged powerful political and economic networks in the slave trade in Atlantic Africa, which bolstered the Royal African Company's power in the region. Trade in human captives came to be bound up with diverse exchanges in animal flesh that bridged cultural divides between Europeans and Africans and sustained cycles of raiding, war, and routes of trade through which captives moved amid the geography of slavery. Like the value of money cowries, factors needed to adapt to Atlantic African customs and taste to succeed in the trade.

While these two forms of animal exchanges—cowry shell money and animal sacrifices and gifts—sustained commodity flows of human captives for the Royal African Company, other kinds of animals impeded trade. Examining animals classified as vermin or pests complicates our understanding of animals in the slave trade by including more agential and disruptive creatures in the human–animal story of slavery in Atlantic Africa.

Relationships of commerce and trust that English and West African slavers struggled to build across space and over time were vulnerable to animals they understood as vermin, which destroyed valuable goods and commodities, including human captives, across Atlantic Africa. Early modern Europeans considered vermin or pests to be animals that poached food or goods intended for human use and exhibited unusual cunning in eluding humans and avoiding extermination.[111] Pests can also be understood as animals beyond and existing in opposition to the desired modes of interaction that slavers attempted to fashion between enslaved captives and nonhuman animals, like cowries or sheep, for the purposes of exchange.

Vermin in West Africa, in particular worms and rats, exploited and hindered the slave trade in multiple ways by infesting supplies of food and goods, evading plans for their elimination, and endangering the health of the enslaved. At every turn, vermin damaged and imperiled the value of human and nonhuman commodities, and in very material ways limited the expansion and flow of the trade. Reckoning with pests, therefore, is crucial to a deeper understanding of the environmental networks of slaving and adds to a historical awareness of the agency of nonhuman animals in global history.

Shipworms impacted networks in the trade by destroying the hulls of coasting sloops and canoes that moved among castles and outposts while ferrying information, cowries, captives, and other commodities to and from Cape Coast Castle. Factors attempted to counter shipworm (*Teredo navalis*), a saltwater clam that thrives in tropical waters, by sourcing from their partners in the trade particular species of wood that might prevent the animals from damaging the company's vessels. At Anashan, for instance, Arthur Richards wrote to Cape Coast in 1681 that a shipment of timber from the fort, sent by their trading partners, appeared promising for counteracting the creatures: "I am inform'd by the Curranteere itt is a sort of wood that the wormes will not take itt."[112] Richards attempt to source woods that counteracted shipworms represents another form of environmental knowledge that factors of the Royal African Company and their allies sought to obtain. Like Houstoun's search for substitute money cowries, this prospect too appears to have resulted in failure.

Guinea worms (*Dracunculus medinensis*), a species of parasitic nematode that found its way into the bodies of traders and captives through contaminated drinking water, frequently frustrated the company by compromising the health of both merchants and those enslaved. These worms infected people from their habitats in polluted water cisterns at different spaces in the trade, including the "trunks" around Ouidah; the small underground "slave holes" at outforts such as Dixcove; barracoons, "slave yards," or other makeshift holding cells scattered throughout the Gold and Slave Coasts; or the dungeons below Cape Coast Castle, including the central castle's disturbing "Black Hole," where the incarcerated lingered for days or weeks before being sent onward for transatlantic voyages.[113]

In the bodies of their hosts, the worms bred and developed within the intestines, and as they grew they moved outward through the skin, forming blisters that caused their hosts to suffer debilitating pain.[114] Richard Thelwall, a factor at Anomabu, for instance, apologized in a letter to his superiors at Cape Coast in 1681 for not writing or reporting on the status of the trade at the fort for some time. Guinea worms had festered in Thelwall's body, rendering him "very lame, having three wormes in one legg, being in a great paine." As such, the factor failed to regularly write or perform his duties at the fort, including supervising the purchase and transportation of captives.[115] Reporting to Cape Coast in 1687, Thomas Price wrote in desperation from Accra that the factory doctor, gunner, and three other company employees had become "lame with wormes," which impeded the ability of slavers at James Fort to carry out trade.[116]

While guinea worms infested the bodies of English factors like Thelwall, incarcerated captives suffered worse debilitating infections of the worms, at at a much higher rate, due to their exposure to the dangerous, unhealthy environments of barracoons, slave holes, and other carceral spaces on the coast.[117] Worms infected the bodies of enslaved people sold across the Atlantic Ocean and of castle, or company, slaves held in permanent bondage at the forts. Reporting from Dixcove in 1692, Francis Smith complained that a company slave, a carpenter named Quashe, whose skill in repairing fort walls the factor desperately required to fortify the base, became "lame with the wormes." Smith requested that Cape Coast send another enslaved artisan, Bastian, who was known among the company for his skill in carpentry, to replace him.[118] Quashe's pain and the debility caused by the affliction, now known as dracunculiasis, hindered operations at Dixcove.

Pain caused by guinea worms afflicted the health and lives of enslaved people even before they endured the Middle Passage, as the worms often broke out through the skin of captives' limbs while being incarcerated in barracoons. For company factors, whose interests lay in profiting from commodifying enslaved people and dispossessing them of their future bodily labor, worms threatened to undercut profits. Upon receiving notice from Cape Coast in 1693 that an enslaved man sent to the castle appeared sickly and "bursten" with an uncertain disease, Edward Searle at Charles Fort, Anomabu, replied that he "thought soe myselfe at first, but the Negroes told me it was a worme." Searle agreed to take the man back from Cape Coast as a company slave at Charles Fort "if hee bee not passible" for sale.[119] In 1694, Searle continued to write to Cape Coast on the problems worms posed at Anomabu by rendering captives held there incapacitated and entirely unfit for sale, which led to significant losses for the company. Searle warned that the worms also weakened the ability of company slaves to function as laborers in fortifying and manning Charles Fort: "The slaves wee have here are not sufficient to finde the Fort in wood and water, they are soe disabled with wormes."[120]

While guinea worms infested the bodies of factors, captives waiting to be taken aboard ships, and castle slaves held at the forts, other kinds of worms, and perhaps other insects such as crickets and cockroaches, chewed through valuable provisions and trade goods and frequently ruined factors responsible for purchasing and overseeing enslaved people on the coast. In an inventory of the warehouse of James Fort, Accra, from 1681, Ralph Hassell recorded that among the provisions he received from a coasting vessel that month were fifty-six pounds of "wormeaten stockfish" that were absolutely useless as a foodstuff.[121] Later that year, Hassel complained that the barrels of corn delivered by another coasting vessel were "soe bad" from worms and rot "that the slaves will not eate it nor scarce the hoggs."[122]

Worms also damaged cloth textiles used as trade goods at the factories. In 1682, worms forced Richard Thelwall to sell "broken and wormeaten" textiles at deep discounts to Akani traders arriving at Anomabu.[123] Writing in 1686 from Mumford, an outpost sited between Tantumkweri and Winneba, Hugh Hilling complained that there were "slaves plenty here but I want some good sayes [a fine worsted wool cloth used for barter], these I have are worm eaten" and worthless for exchange.[124] Later that year, Henry Wood, commander of the sloop *George*, wrote from off the coast of Axim that he too faced challenges while slaving, due to problems caused by worms. While negotiating for captives with slavers on the Grain Coast, Wood noted that his "carpitts proves bad, here is 24, all worm and rott eaten and not worth one ounce."[125] Worms interrupted the progress of coasting vessels as they sailed as well. William Piles, commander of the sloop *Sally Rose*, reported in 1697 that worms had eaten through his stock of yam provisions intended for the captives, necessitating the ship's return to the coast to resupply the ship before sailing onward to Cape Coast.[126]

Elusive nests of rats further evaded and troubled English slave traders at their forts along the Gold Coast. Rats in astonishing numbers gnawed at trade goods stored in warehouses, rendering valuable textiles for barter worthless. In Hassell's inventory of James Fort, Accra, he also reported that every bolt of the twenty sayes delivered by Captain Samuel Rickard of the coasting sloop *Blessing* was "ratt eaten" and useless for trade.[127] Another factor, at Mumford, found that nearly all of the twenty bolts of sayes he received from a sloop captain were "much rat eaten, ten of them we found a dead rott in the case."[128] At Charles Fort, Anomabu, William Cross complained that casks of valuable tallow for use at the fort and for trade were "eaten quite up by the rates" after being neglected by company officials and castle slaves tasked with supervising the warehouse.[129] Three years later, another factor at Anomabu, John Rootsey, continued to complain to Cape Coast that trade goods improperly maintained at the fort and nearby at Anashan appeared "much eaten by the ratts," temporarily halting exchanges in captives between both forts and their partners while the outposts waited for new supplies.[130]

Unable to endure the plunder caused by rat attacks, some factors attempted to eradicate the pests by introducing a predator, cats, into company warehouses. In 1686, Thomas Bucknell wrote to Cape Coast that the fort at Sekondi was "most intollerably trobled with rats in the warehouse. They now begin to damnifie the goods, I haveing found severall things knawed per them. . . . If any man in the Castle," he pleaded to Cape Coast, "can advise me how to distroy them, to advise me of the means; niether can I gett a catt any where."[131] Bucknell and his subordinates desperately sought after a cat at Sekondi for weeks without success.

The following month, Bucknell wrote again to Cape Coast that the warehouse continued to suffer from vermin: "I know not what to doe with the rats, they damage so much good that would make one mad to se, especially the woolen good." The rats ate "wholes in the boysadoes, Welch plains and blankets" so large that the factor could "run my fist in them." Bucknell attached to his letter an inventory of the goods "damagd per the rats" and wrote despondently, "How to remidy it I canot tell." He tried moving the textiles onto scaffolding above the warehouse floor and in the process moved a nine-hand canoe that had sheltered "eight ratts of a great biggness," which he and his men killed, along with "two nests of six young ones apeice, but some escap'd our hands doe what we could." Bucknell then "spoild their harbors and made all passages free that they cannot secure themselves from a good cat." Bucknell eventually found a cat for the warehouse, yet he discovered his proposed predator to be "to little, soe I humbly desire your Worship to send me a bigger if it can be procurd. Here be rats almost able to deal with catts."[132]

Bucknell's encounters with rats were not exceptional, and neither was his failure to eradicate the pests. The company warehouse at Anomabu faced a similar problem in 1687. Ralph Hassell wrote apologetically to Cape Coast that "I am sorry to write of dammage done by ratts, which is verry much, especially in the allejarrs: we are so pester'd with them that they are not easely destroyd, although keep three catts in the warehouse."[133]

Rat attacks compounded the duress English slavers faced from other European competitors and from warfare in Atlantic Africa. Thomas Willson described his station at Komenda in 1696, during the Second Komenda War, by writing that people "here live pend up" in fear of the Dutch and their "abundance of blacks alwaies in arms about their fort." Willson added that he and his companions "are all so lame with our late journey that wee are hardly able to stir." That spring, the factory's "towns people," including their caboceers, also deserted the English. In his conclusion to the letter, the factor wrote that it "is almost incredible to report the abundance of rats we have, that wee cannot lye in our cotts a night but with sticks in our hands to kill them."[134] The following month, Willson pleaded again for support from Cape Coast, requesting supplies for the factory, including "one or two hour glasses, the rats haveing broke ours, that wee have none to stand sentry by."[135]

Rats continued to pester slave traders and endanger the health of enslaved people in Cape Coast Castle, and later belowdecks aboard transatlantic voyages. James Houstoun described the dungeons of Cape Coast, where enslaved people languished before being taken on ships, as perilously unhealthy and "swarming with Vermine."[136] One trader recalled that in addition to the "hot and corrupted air" aboard a slave ship, the crew and their "cargo" suffered from the presence of rats that "have done a great deal of damage, we being quite over-run with them."[137] Rats attacked the crew and the enslaved stowed below and devoured the ship's meager stores of provision foods like corn, oats, and barley.

By damaging trade goods, including slaves, and preying upon provisions, vermin animals, including multiple species of worms and rats, placed real material limits on opportunities for English factors to purchase captives from their West African counterparts. These animals could significantly impinge upon the mercantile networks that slave traders labored to produce through exchanges of money cowries, ritual animal sacrifices, and animal gifts. The power of predatory vermin to curtail trading networks and exploit the vulnerabilities of factories and their warehouses indicates how the production and maintenance of human–animal networks in the slave trade in Atlantic Africa was never all-encompassing or permanent but rather limited, assailable, and fragile.

On the ground, the slave trade in Atlantic Africa involved the production and maintenance of human–animal networks of exchange by English and West African slave traders who mobilized fauna as political, cultural, and economic actants in the late seventeenth century. First, we have seen that the cowry sea snail, *Monetaria moneta*, became a valuable form of currency that facilitated transactions in captives between the Royal African Company and their partners in Atlantic Africa. Focusing on supplies and the status of money cowries reveals how tenuous could be the relations people created with the shells over long distances, and how the monetization of the cowry depended on joining together overseas systems of trade between the Indian Ocean, Europe, the Atlantic Ocean, and West Africa.

Second, this chapter illuminated how trading relations between European and African groups, as evident in the founding of Dixcove, oftentimes involved ritual propitiatory sacrifices of sheep. Sheep and other animals, such as elephants or ostriches, like the ones given to the governor of James Island in the Gambia River, also became valuable as diplomatic gifts to open new trading connections, as offerings to mediate political alliances, as payment for the redemption of pawns, or as curious faunal specimens for collections or menageries.

Slavers built out commercial networks with money cowries, sheep, and animal curiosities, which enabled the expansion of the slave trade in early modern Atlantic Africa. Yet, simultaneously, traders also created the conditions for vermin to thrive, and these animals, including worms and rats, frequently unmade or impeded such networks by damaging valuable commodities, disturbing provisioning supplies, and infecting the bodies of enslaved people.

Focusing on the commodification and valuation of captives and of animals like the cowry, and the instrumentalization of animals as either commercial instruments or ritual objects, reveals the roles that animals played in the Atlantic slave trade, indicating human–animal encounters that are quite different from established narratives in environmental history, such as the familiar "portmanteau biota" that sparked ecological imperialism.[138] Looking at animals in this context further illuminates the process by which the captured became commodities. The coconstitutive commodification of human captives and money cowries enabled the trade to flourish on the coast, and their combined valuation is evident in the ledgers and inventories that listed their equivalent value. Turning people into slaves depended on turning animals into money. Factors like John Carter and others performed skilled labor to keep cowries—evaluated by weight and shape—useful for the trade. On the other hand, factors learned and appreciate the value of other animals, as evident in their prompt responses to the demands of their counterparts for offerings of animals especially sheep, for sacrifice, as when William Gabb told the king of Adom the company was "pleased to order" another ovine to sacrifice to his fetish.

This chapter has mostly focused on English factors, particularly because the fragmentary archival existence of Atlantic African caboceers like Captain

Nedd or of the enslaved themselves places significant interpretive limits on a fuller understanding of how captives themselves perceived different kinds of animals in the trade. Indeed, the archive of the Royal African Company itself enacted the commodification of people as abstract figures existing only between the pages of a ledger book.[139] The enforced anonymity of thousands of enslaved men, women, and children deepens our collective inability to know what individuals who witnessed sacrifices of sheep from behind the bars of a barracoon thought of these episodes, or if they watched, while bound together in a coffle, as slavers calculated their price with money cowries.[140]

Seeing human–animal networks such as those discussed in this chapter deepens our understanding of the environmental and cultural foundations of relations among imperial metropoles, colonies, and semicolonial commercial sites created by the agents of joint-stock companies, local rulers, and merchants in the early modern world. The Atlantic slave trade taking place at the outforts and castles of the Royal African Company involved rapidly increasing transfers of human captives, exchanges of sheep, deliveries of cowries, and other interactions between people and fauna. Along the Bight of Benin, a trader equipped with "noe booges" often found "noe slaves" for purchase. "To get a cargo of flesh, bone, and blood" in Atlantic Africa, as one nineteenth-century writer later put it, English slavers needed to know and act on the value of animals.[141]

Yet even as some animals in the slave trade enabled human agency, others circumscribed such plans. Animals, whether livestock, sea snail shells, or rats, could extend human networks or break them apart. Although this chapter focused on commerce and commodification in the slave markets of Atlantic Africa, other kinds of human–animal relations also emerged out of the slave trade, including relations that increased scientific knowledge. As we will see in chapter 2, slavers and enslaved people produced global knowledge of Atlantic world fauna by collecting animal specimens at slave castles, aboard slave ships, and on plantations in the Caribbean, New Spain, and North America.

Chapter 2

SHOWING THEIR SLAVES HOW TO COLLECT

Enslaved People and the Origins of Early Modern Science

I n 1681, the Reverend John Banister proposed to his patrons among the Royal Society of London for Improving Natural Knowledge "a way which I believe may be very satisfying to you" to prepare a "Naturall Hystory" of Virginia.[1] An Anglican minister and resident of Bristol Parish on the southern banks of the James River, Banister collected plants, animals, and minerals and conducted observations of Appamatuck and Pamunkey towns during his time in the colony, between 1678 and 1692.[2] Reading Banister's proposition raises questions about the foundations of scientific knowledge of animals, within the discipline of natural history, during a tumultuous period spanning the Restoration and the English Revolution of 1688.

In his letter to his supporters in London, Banister underscored that he expected to rely heavily on enslaved Atlantic African laborers and the Atlantic slave trade to collect animals and compile his natural history. "Supposing that some member of your Society (which I fancy may be no great difficulty to do)," he suggested, "can prevaile so far with the royall affrican company & bestow on me 4 or 6 young negroes it will be but a small matter to them yet with which flock I can procure my selfe may in time make me a pretty livelyhood and to tell you that I am as willing to give any token encouragement to the carrying on so gradual and so copious a work."[3] James Delbourgo, Kathleen S. Murphy, Susan Scott Parrish, and others have shown how requests like Banister's were commonplace among those engaged in producing and circulating botanical, mineral, and faunal specimens in the seventeenth-century Atlantic world.[4]

My intent here is to expand on this foundational scholarship. What kinds of knowledge about animals was produced by men and women like the "4 or 6 young" people that Banister and his contemporaries depended on in their collecting endeavors? How did their own scientific and aesthetic judgment shape early modern science, museum collections, and even theoretical questions at the heart of natural philosophy into the period of the Enlightenment in the eighteenth century? If we take seriously the idea that enslaved Atlantic African men and women identified, selected, collected, and preserved animals from a diverse range of environmental settings, does the history of science in this period begin to look decidedly more African than European? This chapter explores how enslaved people and the geography of slaving, between slave castles in Atlantic Africa, depots in New Spain, and plantations within England's colonies in the Caribbean, shaped the development of knowledge about animals in the period between Banister's proposal and the networks that developed during the Enlightenment, as so-called Linnaean science matured before and after the American Revolutionary War.

Natural history and natural philosophy flourished across routes of slaving that spanned the Atlantic world. The founding members of the Royal Society, several of whom offered Banister their patronage, conceived of their society at its founding as the "Twin-Sister" of the Royal African Company. Charles II granted a royal charter to both corporations in 1660, and overlapping memberships and investments bound the organizations together. "In both these *Institutions* begun together," an English historian wrote, the Stuart crown "imitated the two most famous *Works*" of King Solomon of Israel, "who at the same time sent to *Ophir* for *Gold*, and compos'd a *Natural History*, from the Cedar to the Shrub."[5] By the time Banister began studying Virginia's natural history, the Royal African Company had begun to pivot away from bargaining for gold dust and instead pursued its fortunes in human trafficking. From its inception in the late seventeenth century, its "Twin-Sister," the Royal Society, frequently relied on reports from slaveholders in the American colonies, such as the slaveholder and silkworm experimenter Edward Digges of York County, Virginia.[6]

The fate of Banister's appeal for slaves to assist him is unclear. In 1690, the minister held two enslaved Africans as his chattel property and acquired a 1,735-acre plantation in the parish along the Appomattox River.[7] Francis Nicholson, the lieutenant governor of the colony, gave the minister the plantation, situated near Hatcher's Run. In his unpublished natural history fragments and published letters in the *Philosophical Transactions*, Banister never acknowledges either of these enslaved people, or the wealth and privileges he derived from his plantation. Yet it is very likely that one or both of these enslaved people collected animals for the minister, given that many naturalists in this period employed slaves as collectors in the field. Perhaps one of these men or women gathered the "10 or 12 *Species*" of land snails, mussels, and insects Banister shipped across the Atlantic to his clients in London between 1689 and 1692.[8] What is certain is that Banister accrued wealth from their labor on his plantation and gained status as a propertied landowner and slaveholder in the colony.[9] Banister further benefited from the friendship and support of other enslavers, including his neighbor and colleague William Byrd I.[10]

Banister's conjoined plans for becoming a slaveholder and natural historian in Virginia either inspired his contemporaries to follow his lead or reflected an established, connected world of slaving and natural history in North America. John Clayton, rector of nearby James Town Parish in Virginia from 1684 to 1686, and a contemporary of Banister, likewise relied on enslaved people to collect animals. In a letter to the Christian natural philosopher Robert Boyle, Reverend Clayton described lizards unearthed from a drained swamp and how he learned about it from enslaved men, who "mentioned they digged up a Creature wch one of them cald a blew ground Lizard." Desiring to impress Boyle and his colleagues, Clayton "profered six pence" to the enslaved workers to "skin it for me," yet the men found the animal "so loathsome" they refused the clergyman's offer. Clayton further discussed a species of "land frogg," which he learned about by witnessing a "Negro child" catching and eating them, after being "starved by the overseer" of a plantation.[11]

Banister's efforts to become a slaveholder and Clayton's discussion of enslaved collectors provides a starting point for considering the role of displaced Africans and people of African descent in producing knowledge about animals in the early modern world. Banister's request to his patrons, and his subsequent status as a slaveholder and naturalist, requires historians of science to reckon with what Annette Gordon-Reed terms the "enforced anonymity of slavery" and Stephanie Smallwood's claims that slavery's archive is defined by "silences and disavowals" that constitute "an active epistemological gesture that leaves in its wake a trace of its own processes and maneuvers."[12]

Whether Banister intended his enslaved "flock" to labor on his plantation or to collect specimens for his "gradual and so copious" natural history is unclear, but what is probable is that the two slaves he did possess labored both as plantation workers and as collectors gathering freshwater and land snails, mussels, wasps, and other insects in Bristol Parish. Their judgment, skill, and curiosity constituted a crucial foundation of natural philosophy, yet, like other invisible technicians, their presence in the archive is in fragments and ghostly traces.[13] Likewise, Clayton's brief mention of enslaved collectors tells us that slaves did occasionally refuse to participate in the plans of naturalists. Moreover, Clayton's knowledge of the "land froggs" was not the product of African curiosity but rather the result of suffering and abjection, mental states not often associated with early modern science.

Natural history originated in the castle trade discussed in the chapter 1, along the Gold Coast and above the dungeons at Cape Coast Castle, even as it developed in rural counties in southern England like Oxfordshire, Surrey, and Wiltshire.[14] While antiquaries, clergy, and others turned to the countryside to collect and categorize England's environs, slavers in Atlantic Africa followed their own intellectual pursuits through correspondence and shipments to the metropole.

Thomas Edward Barter, or Tom Ewusi, an Anglo-Fante factor at Cape Coast Castle, divided his career in the slave trade between trafficking captives and collecting marine animals and insects. Barter's mother hailed from a prominent Fante family of Anomabu, and around 1690 or 1691, when he was a young man, the Royal African Company sent Barter—also spelled Bartar—to England to learn about the company and his father's homeland. In 1693, Barter returned to West Africa and became a powerful figure in the company, responsible for collecting debts held by the king of Eguafo, negotiating the company's settlement at Fetu, serving as a diplomat to Akwamu and Allampo, and acting as an interpreter for the company and its Fante- and Akan-Twi-speaking partners at Komenda and other outforts.[15] A Dutch merchant in the region during the late seventeenth century described Barter as holding the "greatest Power on the Coast, than all the three *English* Agents together" at Cape Coast Castle.[16] Barter commanded his own asafo, or military company, for his personal defense, and he became a slaveholder in addition to a being a slaver.[17]

While in England, Barter may have met with the apothecary and naturalist James Petiver, who urged him to collect Atlantic African plants and animals upon his return to Cape Coast. From his apothecary shop in London, Petiver collected collectors for the purpose of amassing specimens from across the globe. He later cataloged his global natural history collections in "centuries" that painstakingly listed each object.[18] Barter forwarded small animals from the Gold Coast to London, including a limpet snail, a butterfly, and an "elegant hairy Catterpillar."[19] Animals appeared in these encyclopedic catalogs alongside plants and drugs gathered from the empire's margins, and from trade outposts beyond England's territorial limits. Petiver intended that in their totality his lists could provide useful knowledge for commercial development within the empire and insight into the heavenly order of nature.[20]

Barter's Atlantic African collections appeared alongside those produced by other slavers, including John Smyth, the chaplain of Cape Coast; John Kirckwood, who gathered butterflies from Ouidah to Cabinda; and Richard Planer, a surgeon who gathered plants and animals at Montserrado on the Grain Coast.[21] In printed and manuscript directions for collectors like Barter, Petiver advised that they equip their subordinates with "2 or 3 quires of brown paper & Insect books to have filled by their servants or slaves," who they should encourage to collect animals. In a set of directions to another collector, Petiver instructed his contacts to "Procure Correspondents for me wherever you come, and take directions how to write them, and procure something from them you stay, showing their Slaves how to collect things by taking them along with you when you are abroad."[22]

Petiver's numerous collector-correspondents also included prominent colonial slaveholders such as William Byrd II.[23] In 1709 or 1710, Petiver urged Byrd to "employ some of yr own Servants or Negroes to make collections for me" of insects, shells, and fossils from Virginia. Petiver desired "wtever I can obtain," and his correspondents hoped that their efforts would lead to their names being credited in printed catalogs and that their newfound patron might introduce them to advantageous contacts. However, because Edward Barter was already a powerful merchant slaver and diplomat in the region, his reasons for collecting animals on the Gold Coast are opaque.[24]

Thomas and Rachael Grigg, slaveholders and the proprietors of Parham Plantation, a sugar estate on Antigua, joined Petiver's "philosophical Parlour" sometime around 1700.[25] Petiver first wrote to Thomas in December, requesting "wtever Plants Shells Insects &c as yr Island affords."[26] On Antigua, the Grigg family held more than one hundred enslaved people as their chattel property on Parham, situated in St. Peter Parish on the northern coast of the island.[27] As he advised other collectors, Petiver suggested that the Griggs direct enslaved men and women on Parham to gather animals for his collections whenever possible.[28] In addition to these enslaved collectors, the sugar fortune that the Grigg family accumulated afforded the leisure and opportunities for women like Rachael Grigg to oversee the enslaved as they collected small insects, butterflies, and shellfish. In addition to Rachael Grigg, Petiver benefited from Rachael Chapman—who sent him "red Beam'd Jamaica Muscle" and a "Carolina Egg-Cockle"—and the efforts of one "old Mrs. Rawlins."[29]

Plantations like Parham, where enslaved people toiled at planting and harvesting sugarcane, fit seamlessly into an Atlantic geography of slaving and natural history that bound the colonies to the metropole. Military spaces installed to defend England's colonial plantations and merchant slaving fleets also proved to be valuable sites for producing natural history. In his correspondence to Petiver, Captain Thomas Walduck discussed overseeing enslaved collectors while stationed in Barbados between 1710 and 1712. Walduck resided at Rupert's Fort in St. Peter Parish, one of several fortifications placed on the western coast to safeguard the colony's merchant traffic, including slavers, as ships arrived and departed from the port at Speightstown.[30]

Walduck initially wrote letters containing "a little Naturall History" of Barbados to his nephew, John Searle.[31] Hoping to gain notoriety for his scientific abilities, the captain requested that his nephew refer his services to "some Gentlemen of the Royall Society" to promote his role as a correspondent on the animals and environment of the Caribbean.[32] Walduck possessed several enslaved African men and women, who labored as his domestic servants in the fortress. After Searle introduced the captain to Petiver, Walduck boasted in one letter to the apothecary that "I have Negros and other opportunities to Imploy" for acquiring animal specimens for English naturalists. In 1711, Walduck forwarded to Petiver specimens and descriptions of "Shells, Fossils, Animals, flyes" that the enslaved had collected in the environs surrounding Rupert's Fort, and he mentioned several plants whose medicinal properties he had learned through conversations with slaves. Further, the captain forwarded three bottles filled with "a worme I found under a stone in the sea att Low water," another containing "wormes and Crabs" and other unidentified marine animals, and a specimen of "a poyson Lizard speckled with white and yellow upon a Brown skin." Along with the lizard, Walduck packed in several spiders, including a "fly catcher or the Hunting Spider."[33]

Included in this shipment, Walduck added a specimen and narrative of a "sea hedgehoge," which he detailed in an account explaining how he had acquired the animal from his enslaved collectors. "This sea urchin," he explained, "my Negros took out of the sea stuffed it and brought it home when I was about and hung it up in my Chamber." After they carefully suspended the animal in the air, Walduck returned to his quarters and fell asleep until "I was surprised to see alight or rather a 1,000 lights in my Chamber motionless" emanating from the animal's body. Startled, Walduck rushed to grasp the urchin, and hurt his hand as the light "caused by the salt particles" slowly vanished.

While the captain made no mention in his letter of punishing his slaves for their mischief, he related to Petiver that on the following day he ordered the slaves to return to the shoreline, dip the urchin in the water, and attempt to replicate the visual effect.

Walduck's urchin story and mention of his enslaved collectors perhaps struck Petiver and his circle as a comic anecdote. However, slavery underpinned his collections in darker ways. Alongside his descriptions of marine life, Walduck added notes on medical "curiosities" from Barbados that pointed to the violence implicit in his natural history. Set between sketches on plants and animals in Barbados, Walduck mentioned seeing "a Negro woman the last yeare in the parish of St. Thomas delivered of two Children att one birth, the one as white as any European, the other as black as any Negro, both Boyes."[34] For Walduck, and presumably his audience in London, this woman and her children, and their differing skin colors, became objects for study and collection and lost their humanity in the pages of a natural history letter. Granted that enslaved women faced rape and sexual violence from slaveholders like Walduck, it is very possible that another soldier or planter raped this woman.[35] In another passage, Walduck described an enslaved woman and her child who both died during her labor while in St. Michael Parish. Morbid medical observations described in a detached way fit within a wider circum-Atlantic discourse of anatomical descriptions that positioned enslaved people as natural historical curiosities for abstract consumption by scholars in England.[36]

Walduck continued to send Petiver letters on natural history and animal specimens for several years, including descriptions of ambergris, sea tortoises, and sea urchins, until their correspondence ended in 1716. His letters illuminate two important aspects of the intersection of slavery and animal knowledge in this period. First, the judgment and playful approach of the enslaved certainly shaped what animals were collected by English naturalists. Second, as the enslaved collected animals, they became specimens to be consumed, as is evident in the captain's scientific discussions of the woman who gave birth to infants with different skin colors and his detailed description of a slave woman who died during childbirth.

Petiver's correspondents did not see any conflict between the violence of plantation slavery and pursuing their interests in natural history. Mary Stafford, a slaveholder in St. Peter Parish, South Carolina, wrote to her cousin in England in 1711 to "give my humble service to Coz. Petiver & tell him" that she remained prepared to serve him as his accomplice in the colony. "Pray tell him

I often think of him when I am in the Woods and meet with such swarms of Insects and some very troublesome, there is great quantitys of Snakes allsoe." Stafford intended her cousin would share her letter with the apothecary and hoped to reinforce her role as one of his colonial contacts. Knowing he would read the letter, Stafford did not hide that she believed South Carolina to be "a good Country for many things," where a settler could "get a few slaves and can beat them well to make them work hard, here is no living without."[37] Stafford's mention of collecting snakes and assaulting slaves, not unlike Walduck's discussion of enslaved women, underscores how natural history and knowledge of animals depended on the ongoing, everyday war between the enslaved and their enslavers.

Beyond England's trade outposts in West Africa and colonies in the Caribbean and North America, Petiver turned to other imperial settings within the Atlantic geography of slaving to accumulate animals. In the first decades of the eighteenth century, slave ships owned by the Royal African Company crossed the Atlantic to port cities in the Caribbean and New Spain. Surgeons hoping to gain recognition as naturalists traveled along with captive human cargoes. Medical officers for the South Sea Company, a joint-stock company that engaged in the asiento slave trade and contracted with the Royal African Company, further used their positions at company outposts in the Gold Coast, Bight of Benin, and Spanish Main to collect faunal specimens and observations.[38]

After the War of the Spanish Succession, in 1713, the English state awarded the South Sea Company the rights to the asiento, a thirty-year contract to supply slaves to Spain's American colonies.[39] The London-based company originated in 1711 as a mercantile interest intended to reduce the English national debt through economic projects in the Atlantic world, including whaling in the North Atlantic and slaving in the South Atlantic.[40] The terms of the asiento granted the firm the privilege to deliver a cargo of 4,800 enslaved Africans annually to entrepôts in the viceroyalties of New Spain, New Granada, and Cuba, after the Treaty of Utrecht.[41]

Using ships leased from the fleet of the Royal African Company, and escorts from the Royal Navy, the South Sea Company delivered captives purchased from trading castles in West Africa across the ocean to depots at Caracas, Cartagena de Indias, Havana, Portobelo, Veracruz, and other ports.[42] In each of these cities, the company operated small, marginal factories staffed by two factors, a bookkeeper, a surgeon, supercargoes, and a few other employees.[43] In addition to this network of slave trading terminals, the company operated provisioning stations at Port Royal, Jamaica, and Bridgetown, Barbados, where separate traders under contract and company officials, often surgeons, fed and cared for the captives who had survived the Middle Passage, before transferring them to ships bound for Spain's American colonies.[44]

Upon docking at slave depots in New Spain, Spanish officials often forced company captains and officials to accept agricultural commodities from New Spain—usually cacao, balsam woods, sarsaparilla, and various drugs and dyestuffs—in exchange for captives rather than paying for slaves with silver bullion.[45] In these arrangements, which often resulted in the unprofitable exchange of slaves for unfamiliar plants, company officials recognized the necessity of employing surgeons trained in natural history who would be capable of evaluating whether the "fruits" the company received could be adapted as profitable drugs or agricultural products.[46] In addition to their botanical duties, surgeons used their status and position in the company, and their relative mobility through the geography of Atlantic slaving, to collect specimens of the faunal environments of New Spain for Petiver. David Patton, a surgeon serving aboard the man-of-war turned slaver *Elizabeth*, for instance, retrieved a "large lizard" from Veracruz, which he "fed by the way on cockroaches, came alive to England where it lived till killed by the cold in January."[47] Notes on animals like this lizard fill Petiver's correspondence.

William Toller, a surgeon who traveled to Buenos Aires in 1715, wrote a manuscript natural history of his "Diurnall Observations" during a voyage from England to the South Sea Company's entrepôt on the southern banks of the Río de la Plata estuary, intended for Petiver. Toller used opportunities on land and sea to observe animals for his own "singular improvement & Satisfact Curiosity" and to impress his metropolitan patron.[48] At Buenos Aires, the southernmost station the company operated in New Spain, South Sea Company officials assumed the business of the trade at El Retiro, a building complex of warehouses previously leased and operated by the prior holders of the asiento, the French Guinea Company.[49] The slave warehouse sat in the present-day Retiro barrio on the eastern edge of the city. Provisions for the factory's captives and employees came from a nearby farm sited on the river and farmed by company workers.[50] Among the promised annual total of 4,800 captives, company ships transported eight hundred to the depot on the Río de la Plata, beginning in 1715.[51] Among the captives the company purchased for the markets at Buenos Aires were slaves from Angola and Madagascar.[52]

After arriving in the city, English and Spanish slavers inspected the enslaved through official appraisals, or *palmeos*, and then branded those who had survived the journey and were neither diseased or disabled.[53] Much like the castle dungeons of Cape Coast, enslaved people lingered in underground cellars at El Retiro and other *casa de negrerîas* in New Spain before being sold as *fardos racionales*, or "rational bales," of chattel property.[54] Some enslaved people at Buenos Aires were sold and taken overland to the north to labor in the silver mines at Potosí.[55]

Due to the relative dearth of documents, such as letters between factors, it is difficult to locate individual enslaved captives within this colonial context. As in plantation inventories, enslaved people frequently appear in South Sea Company records as anonymous figures, such as the "Venta de Negros" and "Negros Indultados" listed in the account books of the factories at Portobelo, Panama between 1718 and 1722.[56] Similar records for Cartagena reveal that the enslaved who did survive the long voyage from continental Africa to New Spain frequently arrived missing toes and eyes, infected with ringworms, losing their sight or altogether blind, afflicted with sores across their skin, or suffering from scurvy.[57]

Thomas Dover, the chief agent of the company base at Buenos Aires, hired Toller to serve as physician for the depot.[58] Dover, also a physician by training, established himself as a surgeon serving ships in the Bristol slave trade in the first decade of the eighteenth century, then as a surgeon for the South Sea Company, and later became an independent slaver in his own right.[59] In Buenos Aires, Toller's duties as a surgeon ranged from prescribing medicines and pharmaceutical supplies to stock slave ships, to diagnosing and treating endemic diseases associated with the Middle Passage, such as those that resulted from overcrowding, malnutrition, and exhaustion and frequently led to premature death, to certifying the health of the enslaved during each palmeo, in conjunction with a Spanish physician.[60]

Embarking from Plymouth in February 1715, Toller traveled aboard the company's ship *Warwick*, sailing first to the Atlantic islands, anchoring at Madeira and Cape Verde for provisions, before making the transatlantic voyage.[61] As the *Warwick* sailed for Buenos Aires, its sister ship, the *Angelsea*, embarked for the company's factory in Cartagena. In June, the *Warwick* landed at the Bay of Castillos, situated near present-day Maldonado, Uruguay.[62] While the *Warwick* itself did not serve as a slave ship, the company permitted Dover to personally transport ten enslaved people on the voyage.[63] When their ship arrived at Buenos Aires, Toller noted in his journal the simultaneous arrival of several "Guinea Ships," likely Royal African Company ships, sailing into port. In the pages of his journal, the surgeon, like others, did not acknowledge his own financial and professional benefit from the slave trade, yet his status and position in the trade afforded him numerous opportunities to collect fauna throughout the Río de la Plata estuary.[64]

During their voyage and expedition in New Spain, Toller penned a manuscript, *The History of a Voyage to the River Plate and Buenos Ayres*. Though he never published his book, the surgeon presumably intended that the text would impress Petiver and his circle of natural philosophers in England. In his book, Toller described numerous animals he collected and observed while sailing to the Atlantic islands, and later afield in Río de la Plata, at the Bay of Castillos, Isla de Lobos, and the Río Santa Lucía.

In early June, the *Warwick* reached the easternmost mouth of the Río de la Plata estuary.[65] Toller immediately set out to collect animals on fishing and hunting excursions, during which he drew sketches directly into his manuscript, between scribbled lines of text. Whether the ten enslaved people Dover transported joined the party is unclear, though it certainly is possible. While fishing in a stream near the Bay of Castillos, Toller caught corvina, mullets, flounders, and other fish. Teals, plovers, swans, flamingoes, and other birds filled the sky overhead, which the surgeon carefully drew in his book. In his journal, Toller drew more than a dozen species of birds he observed in Buenos Aires, in flight and at rest.[66]

For Toller and his crew in the Río de la Plata, collecting animals in New Spain intersected with fishing and hunting trips. Further, beyond his singular reference to seeing "Guinea Ships," Toller avoided discussing either the lives of enslaved people or their assistance in the field during his time in Buenos Aires. Other employees of the South Sea Company saw their efforts to collect animals as embedded within and akin to the objectification of captive people that buttressed Atlantic slavery.

John Burnet, a Scottish collector for Petiver and later for the Chelsea physician Hans Sloane, moved across New Spain through his position within the South Sea Company to assemble collections of animal and human specimens for clients in England. Burnet studied medicine at the University of Edinburgh and entered the service of the company as a surgeon examining captives on the Gold Coast aboard the slave ship *Wiltshire*. After probing the bodies of the human merchandise his employers sought, Burnet traveled to company factories in Nueva Granada, taking up surgical posts at Portobelo and later

Cartagena de Indias between 1716 and 1728.[67] From his station in Panama, Burnet forwarded to Petiver cargoes containing specimens of shells, fish, and appendages, including a shark's jaw.

Burnet's enthusiasm for collecting blurred the boundaries between people and animals as objects for consumption, satisfying curiosity, and delivering intellectual pleasure. On one occasion Burnet sent Petiver the remains of a stillborn fetus taken from an enslaved woman who had suffered a miscarriage, or who perhaps had self-induced an abortion.[68] Either Burnet or Petiver described these remains as "Taken out of the Hands of a Negress," a note that underscores how natural history and slaving were so entangled and dependent on violence against people of African descent. Burnet further sent a "worm of about 4 foot long" removed from the leg of a person on the Gold Coast while the *Wiltshire* anchored there.[69] However, there is no mention of the pain the worm afflicted on the captive, or the pain she endured as they removed the animal.

Animal specimens and human remains filled the shipments Burnet forwarded to his London correspondents. In 1716, Burnet sent an assemblage of items to Petiver containing "three polipus taken out of the heartts of two negroes," two fishes, "the bill of a fish taken out of a shark's belly almost dissolved," and "the shell of an ostrage egg from Buenos Ayres." When the company relocated the doctor from Portobelo to its outpost at Cartagena in 1722, Burnet entered into local networks of information, which included a Franciscan at Santa Fe and "one of the *oidores* of Charcas," an important judge within the Real Audiencia of the Viceroyalty of Peru. That year he wrote to the company's court of directors requesting permission and funding to lead an expedition across New Spain to produce a "Naturall History of these Countreys."[70] To his frustration, the court denied Burnet's proposal.

Despite this rejection, Burnet continued to send Petiver and Sloane animal and human specimens in the hope of using slave body parts to gain praise for his skill in natural history, and to parlay recognition from these contacts into a promotion in the company from surgeon to factor.[71] Burnet continued to send butterflies, a wingless cockroach, a marine caterpillar, an armadillo, and a scorpion from Portobelo to London during his residency.[72] In 1722, Burnet sent Sloane two taxidermied sloths, a mother and her offspring, from the Cartagena factory. Burnet hoped to keep the animals alive to send as living specimens, but after they perished, he sent the doctor "the old ones skin stuffed & the young one in spirits."[73]

Recorded in Sloane's catalogs are specimens Burnet sent from Buenos Aires in 1723, during an expedition to the company's depot in the Río de la Plata, such as "a white swallow from Buenos Ayres. Feathers made up to fright the slaves" and an "ostriches egg from Mr. Burnett from Buenos aires much lesser an Condors a smaller sort of Ostridge, whose feathers are of no value."[74] Perhaps Burnet came into possession of the "white swallow" feathers following conversations with slave ship crewmen or the factors who policed the cages of the company's depots. Or perhaps he confiscated the feathers from enslaved people during his coercive inspections of their limbs, mouths, and other orifices. Burnet and others suffused their observations with racialized language, as is evident in Sloane's catalog descriptions of a "fowl whose feathers," a collector in Cartagena opined, "resembled the skin of a negro."[75]

Interloping independent traders who operated in competition with the Royal African Company also used slaving ventures to collect animals. The London-based slaver Richard Harris, a long-standing opponent of the Royal African Company's monopoly over the trade, instructed his "Ginny masters" to collect, preserve, and ship to Harris's friend Hans Sloane fauna taken from slaving voyages to the Gold Coast and the Bight of Benin in the 1720s.[76] While anchored and negotiating for captives, captains put together animal collections—some perhaps given as gifts by Atlantic African slavers—which they later sent to Chelsea after their vessels delivered and auctioned slaves at markets in Barbados, Buenos Aires, Caracas, Jamaica, and Puerto Rico. Among the creatures Harris's slavers forwarded were a hawksbill tortoise, the tooth "of a monstrous Sea horse," guinea fowl, "large black shining beetles with 2 horns," a "Guinea Sheeps Skin," deer, lizards, "a Cameleon from Angola," and a gazelle.[77] Harris's collecting efforts boosted Sloane's accumulation of global fauna and in turn reinforced his own political standing with the Board of Trade and with Parliament as an expert on commerce, trade, and natural history in Atlantic Africa, New Spain, and North America.[78]

Individuals pursued the gathering of faunal specimens as a form of leisure and of sociability, to imbricate themselves within intellectual and slaveholding networks. In the Caribbean, slaveholding clergy intent on improving their status and connections to elite scientific circles coerced enslaved people to locate, identify, acquire, and transport animals in the field as part of their own bids for greater recognition. Members of the priesthood justified their enthusiasm for natural history as being complementary to their studies in natural theology, or the scientific inquiry into nature for evidence of divine order and Providence.

Reverend William Smith, rector of St. John Parish, Nevis, for instance, used his position as a minister from 1716 to 1721 to study fauna, among other subjects, while being accompanied on multiple collecting excursions by "my Negro Man Oxford."[79] Smith exploited and relied upon Oxford's labor and judgment, and the labors of other enslaved people who toiled on sugar plantations in St. John Parish. Enslavers in the parish paid the minister an annual salary of "sixteen thousand pound weight of Muscovado" sugar. After Oxford and others plucked fish and marine fauna from the shoreline, or from beyond the surf, Smith sent collections of cockles, "Groopers, Rock-fish, Old Wives, Welchmen" and other species across the Atlantic, from Nevis to Charles Mason, Woodwardian Professor of the University of Cambridge.[80]

Writing about fish and other sea creatures from Nevis and Saint Christopher, Smith described in detail how enslaved divers, including Oxford, collected fauna for slaveholders who mostly indulged in natural history as a pastime. To collect shells and other small marine animals, enslavers ordered slaves using baskets to sift through "sandy Bays" for colorful or unusually shaped specimens of mollusks.[81] Slaveholders further instructed enslaved collectors in "Fish-hunting," a kind of sport that combined the pleasures of collecting, curiosity, and sociability. Clusters of slaveholders assembled on the beaches to watch enslaved fishers and divers swim, plunge beneath the waves, and capture underwater prey.

On the shore, Smith and his friends would "send each of them a Negro Slave to the Woods" to first gather supplies of dogwood bark. After crushing the bark with stones and packing tree pulp in sacks, slaves dipped the bundles into the surf until the satchels excreted a dark "Juice." As the bark secreted its ooze, the juice colored the water "with a reddish hue; and being of a poisonous nature" slowly rendered the fish "so drunk or intoxicated" that they swam heedlessly toward the surface. At this point, Smith watched the men collect the fish by "both swimming and diving."[82] Oxford and other enslaved swimmers on Nevis identified numerous specimens for Smith ,including corals, crabs, crayfish, and sea urchins, which, the reverend added, "prick the Feet of such Negroes as dive to take them up."[83]

The precise species of dogwood used on Nevis is unknown. However, the "reddish hue" of the bark pulp poses an intriguing possibility. In several West African societies, poisonous plants—including calabar bean, "red water bark," and sasswood—figured in judicial ordeals wherein a person accused of a crime would be subject to consuming the poison.[84] It is certainly possible that if Oxford or others on Nevis hailed from Asante towns or communities on the Gold

Coast or from Kru towns and states on the Windward Coast, they may have had prior knowledge of the ordeal tree bark. It's also possible that they had knowledge of plants such as fish-poison bean, a plant used to poison waters before fishing.[85]

In addition to swimming and diving underwater for fish, enslaved naturalists on Nevis shot and caught birds for Smith's fauna collections. While on an expedition from Nevis to nearby Saint Christopher, across the tidal strait, Smith tasked "a sharp-sighted and nimble Negro" with shooting local birds, including kites, screech owls, noddies, spoonbills, pelicans, boobies, and hummingbirds. Smith further relied on this person to shoot and retrieve bats flying overhead at dusk.[86] Smith himself lacked any skill in collecting animals, and his natural history endeavors would have floundered without the labor of these enslaved naturalists.

Returning from Nevis to England in 1721, Smith began writing and revising a series of letters addressed to Mason on the natural history of the Leeward Islands, including Saint Christopher and Montserrat. In 1745, Smith published *A Natural History of Nevis,* an epistolary natural history, which introduced Oxford in print as a significant figure in the reverend's collecting treks. Smith described Oxford as a skilled diver, collector, and preserver of animal specimens, and briefly noted that he was born in West Africa, captured as a child, and taken aboard a slave ship to Brazil before being sold to Smith on Nevis.

Natural history fulfilled Smith's intellectual and spiritual desire to understand the cosmos as an ordered totality. The reverend studied the "Animal World" on Nevis as a microcosm of "the great Creator's Wisdom and Magnificence."[87] Collecting animals to improve the soul and mind entailed compelling enslaved people such as Oxford to expose their bodies to dangerous risks, especially drowning. Moreover, collecting led clergymen like Smith to objectify and dehumanize enslaved people as both sources and objects of scientific knowledge. Like Walduck and Burnet, Smith enjoyed discovering human "curiosities," such as "a Negro Boy, as soon as born; he looked of a dark Red colour; and I also visited a Mulatto Child, about half an hour after his Mother was brought to Bed of him, and I do sincerely declare, I could not have distinguished him from a White Woman's Child." On another occasion, Smith scrutinized an enslaved woman who gave birth to two children, one "Coal Black" and the other "Mulatto," and speculated about how parentage determined skin color.[88] Anatomical queries turned enslaved women and children from fully human beings into objects of curiosity for philosophical consumption.

The judgment of enslaved naturalists on occasion involved their specula-tions about the deep past. Mark Catesby conducted an expedition to research the natural history of North and South Carolina, Florida, and the Bahama islands from 1722 to 1726, and like Banister, he planned to rely on enslaved people as assistants. During his travels, Catesby purchased for £20 an enslaved man to assist him in collecting animals, plants, and minerals from the south-eastern colonies.[89] Shortly after arriving in South Carolina, Catesby learned to appreciate the knowledge of enslaved collectors, particularly after learning that several men at "a place in *Carolina* called *Stono*" had unearthed "three or four teeth of a large animal, which, by the concurring opinion of all the *Negroes*, native *Africans*, that saw them, were the Grinders of an Elephant."[90]

In addition to enslaved people, Catesby collected the patronage of slavehold-ing families in England and South Carolina, including James Brydges, the duke of Chandos and a major shareholder of the Royal African Company, and the Chel-sea physician Hans Sloane, an absentee Jamaican slaveholder.[91] While in South Carolina, and later Virginia, Catesby called on William Byrd II, who introduced him to wealthy planter clans—including the Moore, Bull, Johnson, and War-ing families—who hosted him and his enslaved assistant during their travels.

Clerks and factors on the margins of the Royal African Company pursued natural history in Atlantic Africa much like their peers in either the South Sea Company or the Church of England, as a means of promoting their own intellectual status in the Atlantic world. Francis Moore, a clerk who later rose to the position of factor for the Royal African Company at James Island in the Gambia River, compiled a journal of notes on fauna during his residence in Upper Guinea from 1730 to 1735. Similar to the way captives at Cape Coast were circulated, Fort James, on James Island, received captives from smaller outforts at Bintang, Cabata, Colar, Cuttejar, Geregia, Joar, Juffure, Samy, and Wally.[92] While cannons surrounded Fort James, cane palisades defended the smaller outforts, or "lodges," the company established in the Senegambia.[93]

Moore intended his journal "to improve myself, and keep in my Mind the Things worth Notice."[94] The range of observations Moore assembled reflect how information from natural history, including animals and geography, could be useful for individuals and the institutions they served. After returning to England, Moore revised his journal into a travel account, which he published in 1738.[95] Moore's book included ethnographic observations on Senegambian societies, notes on economic botany, and a geographic account of the Gambia River as a waterway for trafficking enslaved captives and other commodities.

Moore's descriptions of Senegambians differentiated between Arabs and "Negroes," whom he argued were "a Race of People who appear to be different from the rest of Mankind," possibly an entirely distinct species of humans.[96] Moore's biblically unorthodox claims were not exceptional in this period. John Atkins, a naval surgeon who moved between West Africa, Brazil, and the Caribbean from 1721 to 1723 on a mission to suppress piracy in the region and defend Britain's merchant slaving fleets, circulated similar arguments regarding West Africans. In his career aboard the ships *Swallow* and *Weymouth*, Atkins became "persuaded that the black and white Race have, *ab origine*, sprung from different-coloured first Parents."[97] Moore's racial ideas developed in tandem with his animal collecting efforts.

Moore observed animals in towns and villages along the Gambia River upon his arrival in 1730. While meeting with Fula, Mandinka, and Wolof slavers, he witnessed the king of Demel offer a camel as a gift to the king of Barsally.[98] "Sea-Horses" and crocodiles swimming below the waterline of the river struck him as "Matters of Curiosity," as he believed the animals could be evidence that the Gambia, Senegal, and Sierra Leone rivers fed into the Nile. In his journal, Moore noted previous writers' assertions that these animals could be found at each river, and he imagined their presence meant that the waterways connected at some juncture.[99]

Moore hoped that several animals in the Gambia would be his unique discoveries, and he intended to furnish specimen collections for naturalists in England to bolster his own credibility and career as a source of information on Atlantic Africa. While at Joar, a town and trading outpost on the banks of the river near Ballanghar, the factor collected and wrote in detail about several chameleons. Correcting previous authors who "think [chameleons] live upon the Air only, and that the Object before them makes them change their Colour," Moore watched the animals feed on flies and change their coloration "as they please. . . . I thought that the Tongue and Eyes of this Creature had been observed only by myself," he added, yet "after I return'd to *England*, going to see the Collection made by that Learned Gentleman Hans Sloane, I found nothing had escaped his Curiosity, and that the Tongue of a Cameleon had been by him preserv'd in Spirits." Despite his disappointment over being unable to impress Sloane, Moore used the animal as an example of harmonious design within nature, noting of its tongue "that Nature has wisely provided the Cameleon with a Weapon" for preying on flies in the same manner as an elephant uses its trunk.[100]

While at the company's outpost at Yamyamacunda, Moore watched Mandinka fishermen net a number of fish from a nearby lake.[101] In his book, Moore frames the men as his assistants, and one fisherman warned him that one of the fish, which resembled a gudgeon, would "suffer me to come near it, telling me that it would kill me." Intrigued, the factor watched as the men used sticks to touch the fish from the safety of the shore until reaching out to probe its body with their hands. "At last," the factor noticed, "when they touched it with their Fingers, they could not bear it the twentieth Part of a Minute." Moore concluded that the fish was not a mere gudgeon but a "Torpedo, or Numb-Fish." Summoning enough "Curiosity" to touch it with his fingers, Moore felt a shock travel instantly through his body as his arm became "dead quite up to my Elbow." Moore touched the animal again a few more times, using his body as an instrument for conducting and observing electric charges. As the ray's body continued to produce shocks after it died, out of the water, Moore ordered one of the fishermen to touch the animal again, and he wrote that its shocks derived from its skin, "which, when dried, had no Effect at all."[102]

Slavery's dehumanizing orientation gradually influenced the way naturalists discussed their collecting efforts with enslaved people. From 1736 to 1748, Reverend Griffith Hughes served as rector of St. Lucy Parish, Barbados, and pursued Caribbean animals while under the aegis of the Society for the Propagation of the Gospel in Foreign Parts. Though the society had charged Hughes with proselytizing to both free and enslaved people on the island, the minister mostly neglected his pastoral duties and instead filled his time on the island collecting flora, minerals, and faunal specimens, especially sea creatures, for a planned natural history.

In 1743, Hughes promoted his book project to Hans Sloane and Martin Folkes in London, and as a preview, he offered Sloane "some worms and Reptile" for his collections.[103] Seven years later, in 1750, with the support of Sloane and slaveholder subscribers such as Landon Carter, Richard Bland, and William Fitzhugh, Hughes published *The Natural History of Barbados*. In *Natural History*, Hughes described how an enslaved man collected an intriguing sea creature on Barbados. While scouting the northern cliffs of St. Lucy, Hughes spied a rare mollusk, a murex, clutching a distant rock. Murexes are carnivorous marine mollusks with spiny, spiraled shells. Hughes immediately saw the animal as an opportunity to distinguish himself as a naturalist in Europe and to denigrate his enslaved assistant.

In his narrative of the murex that caught his attention on the cliffs, Hughes recalled that after sighting the animal, he quickly "ordered a Slave to fetch" the creature.[104] This man, whom the parson first referred to in his account as his "Lad," hurried to collect the sea snail. In his rush, he "grasped it with so much Roughness" that the murex's shell broke in his hand, staining his arm in the bright hues of Tyrian purple, known to dyers in Europe and throughout the Mediterranean world as imperial purple.[105] Disappointed, Hughes recalled how the accidental damage to the specimen repeated the mythical discovery of this natural dye by the ancient Greek hero Hercules and his loyal dog. In his *Natural History*, Hughes cast himself as an ancient demigod amassing knowledge of animals in the Caribbean, aided by his "Dog."

Ministers like Hughes with ties to slaveholding also used animal collecting opportunities to support future evangelical missions. Thomas Thompson, another clergyman of the Society for the Propagation of the Gospel, collected fauna on the Banana Islands during his transatlantic journey from New Jersey to Cape Coast Castle. In 1752, the society approved Thompson's request to relocate from his parish in Monmouth and take up the post of chaplain at Cape Coast to "make a Trial" of introducing the doctrines of the Church of England in Africa as well as to minister to the factors and other servants of the Company of Merchants Trading to Africa.[106] While the society ministered to enslaved people in North America and the Caribbean in the early eighteenth century, by the time of Thompson's mission, the society had become an intellectual and institutional supporter of chattel slavery.[107] On plantations and in slave castles, Thompson and his fellow ministers taught the compatibility of enslavement with Christianity within Britain's Atlantic empire.

Thompson arrived at James Island in the Gambia River in January 1752. From the Gambia he sailed south to the Banana Islands and Sierra Leone before arriving at Cape Coast Castle. Throughout his journey, Thompson recorded notes on birds, fish, insects, and livestock. In his journal, the reverend wrote a lengthy description of an arachnid species he encountered while traveling to Cape Coast.

While anchored at the Banana Islands, an archipelago within Yawri Bay, Thompson hired several Indigenous men, likely Temne speakers affiliated or familiar with English slavers, to collect tarantulas for him. The reverend exchanged a flask of rum for each specimen the men gathered. One collector brought the missionary several live tarantulas, along with "a Bag that they are bred in, very much like a Sheep's Bladder whilst it is green." While examining the specimens, Thompson cut open the egg sac and watched as several young spiderlings crawled out. Thompson's tarantula observations served as an instructional memorandum for future missionaries in identifying and avoiding venomous creatures. He described the animal's body, including its legs, abdomen, and back, which he likened to a "Shell resembling that of a Crab." Thompson cautioned that "in the shelly back, standing forward, are two large Claws, armed with each a Sting, very sharp, and crooked shutting in like a Cat's Nails." Thompson conversed with his collectors on the Banana Islands and learned from these anonymized naturalists that "this Enemy, that it attacks unprovoked, springing out into the Paths as they go along; and they say, that Oil cures the Poison of it."[108] Thompson intended this Atlantic African materia medica would prove to be useful knowledge for future missions the society launched on the Continent.

Naturalists continued to rely on slaving networks in the late eighteenth century, after the decline of the Royal African Company and its subsequent transformation into the African Company of Merchants in 1752. Metropolitan naturalists with ties to independent slavers drew on their contacts to maintain steady supplies of animals from Atlantic Africa. Dru Drury, a silversmith with an interest in insects and arachnids, relied on slavers to furnish his vast entomological collections. Drury and his collaborator Moses Harris assembled a circle of insect enthusiasts in 1762 to establish the Aurelian Society of London.[109] This group esteemed science as a fundamentally ennobling endeavor. Drury held that natural history improved one's mind by refining an individual's "Standard of Judgement."[110] For improving the nation and society, Drury further praised natural history as an enterprise "of no small importance to mankind, since it may not only promote trade, arts, and sciences, but be conducive to the immediate happiness and safety of men's lives" by accumulating, classifying, and experimenting with economically and medically valuable plants and minerals.[111]

Drury began collecting insects in the 1760s by hiring collectors embedded in the slave trade in West Africa. The silversmith built up epistolary networks of exchange with slavers and slaveholders that led to further contacts in the Caribbean and North America as slave ships moved between mercantile and colonial spaces across the Atlantic world. Drury corresponded with naturalist-slaveholders in the Caribbean, particularly in Antigua and Jamaica. Tesser Samuel Kuckhan, a slaveholder in St. Andrew Parish, Jamaica, corresponded with Drury about his collections of African and American insects. Drury hoped the planter would play host to one of his collectors in America, John Abbot.[112] In Bath and Dinwiddie County, Virginia, Drury maintained correspondence with two slaveholders, Reverend Deveraux Jarrat and James Greenway, both of whom held a keen interest in natural history.[113] In 1772, Drury expanded his network of collectors significantly by publishing a short instructional pamphlet titled *Directions for Collecting Insects in Foreign Countries.*

Slave trading routes and the transit of slave ships from England to Atlantic Africa, and further onward to American plantations, presented the foundations for Drury's collections. In a letter to Mr. Hugh, likely a surgeon aboard a slave ship, who was "going to Africa with Capt. Johnson" in 1762, Drury requested that he collect "Locusts and Grasshoppers" from the environs where his ship anchored in both Atlantic Africa and Jamaica. The silversmith specified that the surgeon collect insects that appeared "being just like leaf and branch of a tree, others like half a dozen straws joynd together."[114] Drury supplied another slave trader, Captain Mayle of the sloop *Hound*, with boxes, cork, nets, pins, and other instruments for collecting insects in West Africa on a voyage in 1766.[115] Writing to one Mr. Richards, a surgeon aboard the slave ship *Tartar* bound for West Africa in 1769, Drury entreated he collect "insects from Princess Island," referring to Príncipe in the Bight of Biafra.[116] In 1770, he wrote to a ship's chief mate, Mr. Stewart, with instructions for transporting the collections made by Richards at Príncipe from Whitstable to London upon the *Tartar*'s return to England.[117]

Drury used his contacts in the trade to obtain not only novel specimens but also rare insects already well known to entomologists. Learning of a slave ship bound for the Bight of Bonny, Drury sent the ship's captain, Richard Cowley, a print of a Goliath beetle and asked that he "show this print to some of the natives both at Calabar and Princess and if it is possible to get such a one" for his collection.[118] Drury became interested in the Goliath beetle after a merchant ship captain presented to a naval surgeon, David Ogilvie, a specimen of *Goliathus goliatus* that he had found floating in the Gabon River in 1766. Returning to England, Ogilvie offered the insect as a gift to the Scottish anatomist William Hunter. After seeing the beetle in Hunter's collections, Drury coveted a specimen of his own and printed an image of the animal in his *Illustrations of Natural History,* the print which he later sent to Cowley.[119] While Drury found success in these frequent requests to individual slavers and mariners in the trade, he also began to consider the prospect of organizing and funding a long-term collecting expedition to Atlantic Africa.

In 1771, Drury and a group of wealthy naturalists—including John Fothergill, Joseph Banks, and Margaret Cavendish Bentinck, Duchess of Portland—financed an expedition to send a naturalist, Henry Smeathman, to collect animals in West Africa. Before his voyage, Smeathman worked in London occasionally as a carpenter and insurance broker. He immersed himself in studying natural history when he could, and he gradually became a respected entomological collector in his own right among the members of the Aurelian Society in London. During his four-year residence in West Africa, from 1771 to 1775, the "flycatcher," as he styled himself, acquired numerous animal specimens for his patrons, including corals, locusts, moths, tarantulas, butterflies, snakes, lizards, shells, birds, a pair of African king monkeys, and a sizeable collection of termites.[120]

Smeathman's ability to collect animals on the ground hinged upon the ongoing support and friendship of slave traders at Îles de Los in Guinea, Bunce Island, and the Banana Islands, and of slavers based along the coast and rivers of Sierra Leone. Smeathman cultivated and maintained an expansive network with slavers, including Miles Barber, a Liverpool factor who established his own trading fort at Îles de Los; James Cleveland, a slave trader in the Banana Islands and a member of the powerful Cleveland family; John Aird, one of several traders whom he befriended at Bunce Island; Zachary Corker, an Afro-European slaver in Sierra Leone; and Alexander Grant, a trader residing at an outpost on the Sierra Leone River.[121] While collecting African animals, Smeathman planned to become a slave trader himself and even tried to persuade Andreas Berlin—an apostle of the Swedish taxonomist and agronomist Carl Linnaeus who joined him on the Banana Islands—to partner with him as a ship surgeon in a slaving venture.[122] When he did return to England via the Caribbean, he wrote to his chief patron, Drury, to request he "be so good as to insure for me on slaves & my collections, books, drawings, philosophical instrument, cloaths &c £500."[123]

Smeathman further relied on Atlantic African slavers he met in Sierra Leone to conduct his collecting work, particularly Temne men and women, whose firsthand knowledge appeared in his later termite essay, in which the flycatcher discussed the practice of collecting the animals in situ and recorded their Indigenous names for his European readers.[124] Moreover, Smeathman inserted himself into Temne kinship networks through marriage to gain status on the Banana Islands and further access in the region.[125] One of Smeathman's wives in Sierra Leone, for instance, was the daughter of a powerful "King of a Country up the River Sherbro."[126] Smeathman's research into termites and territaries involved learning from Atlantic Africans in Sierra Leone, though few individual enslaved naturalists like Oxford or the "Lad" mentioned by Griffith Hughes on Barbados appear within the shared archive of slavery and natural history.

One exceptional figure in this overwhelming archival silence raises questions about the Africanness of Atlantic natural history and animal collecting during the Enlightenment. Examining this person's collecting endeavors and expedition draws our attention to how Atlantic African scientific judgment and technique formed the basis of animal knowledge in Europe. In the summer of 1770, an enslaved man traveled from the port city of Charleston, South Carolina, to Isla de Providencia, the "island of Providence," a small Spanish Caribbean island situated 120 miles east of the Miskito Coast of present-day Nicaragua.[127]

Settlers had been interested in the natural environment and natural history of Providence Island since the seventeenth century. Individuals scoured the island for useful plants, animals, and minerals from its initial settlement by the Providence Island Company in 1629 until its capture by the Spanish in 1641.[128] It is unclear how this man, whose name and identity are irrecoverable from the archive, traveled to the island. Moreover, it is unclear whether he was accompanied by an overseer or an associate of his enslaver, Dr. Alexander Garden. It is possible he carried letters of introduction identifying the slaveholder who held him as their chattel property in South Carolina, explaining his mission between the two colonies—and two empires—perhaps along with directions to support his efforts toward collecting animals.

During his interimperial expedition and his time collecting animals on Providence Island, the man, referred to by Garden in a letter as his "black servant," obtained specimens of chigoe fleas "preserved in spirits of wine."[129] To portray the parasitic insect's life cycle, the man collected multiple specimens of the animal, including "some full grown, others younger and smaller, others in the little bags in which they conceal themselves, while they wound the skin of the feet, or other parts of the human body, for the sake of depositing their eggs there."[130] Given his ability to identify and collect specimens of chigoe fleas at different stages of development, the man demonstrated an eye for entomology and insect anatomy. How he collected the animals remains obscure. Perhaps he removed the fleas from his own feet or the feet of enslaved people on the island, using the bodies of others to carry out his natural history.

In addition to the chigoe fleas, the man "collected and preserved some fishes amongst other things" from the island, including "Goat Fish," "Spanish Hog Fish," "Pork Fish," "Schoolmaster," "Parrot Fish," and "Leather coat."[131] Other animals this "black servant" collected were a "Potato Louse," "some Fire-flies," a "coleopterous insect," an insect known in South Carolina as "a *Smith*," an "unknown animal" in a glass bottle, and another fish called a "*Fat-back*."[132] This man's enslaver later sent specimens from the Providence Island expedition and South Carolina to the Swedish botanist and agronomist Carl Linnaeus, in 1771.

Garden never named this man in his letter to Linnaeus, yet, as Whitney Barlow Robles has shown, his labor and skill are apparent in the astonishing variety of specimens he collected and the few he successfully preserved in transit on his return to South Carolina. Moreover, the man's ability to collect animals in the Spanish Caribbean likely hinged upon contacts with others he encountered in his travels. Perhaps the man caught some of these specimens while fishing on the coastline around Providence Island. It is possible he conversed with other enslaved men and women who caught fish for food, or perhaps exchanged goods for specimens of fish or information about where to find rare kinds of fish that naturalists would find appealing. Undoubtedly, his work to accrue animals required persistence and the skill in taxonomy and specimen preservation that white natural history enthusiasts valued in the enslaved collectors to whom they turned for assistance.

Returning to South Carolina, the man packed and stored the animals from Providence Island aboard the ship he sailed on. Exposure to tropical weather, both heat and rain, destroyed most of the specimens in transit—an unfortunate, though common, outcome of many collecting expeditions in the eighteenth century. While Garden chided the man for having "neglected all his specimens," plant and animal collections often withered, rotted, and decayed on ships sailing between the colonies of North America and the Caribbean.[133] Rats and other vermin frequently chewed through boxes for preserving specimens and ate animal remains intended for scientific displays. Moreover, while aboard the ship on the turbulent surface of the Atlantic seascape, the man later reflected, he often feared "immediate shipwreck." The man's fears underscore the dangerous, risky labor to which colonial naturalists like Garden exposed enslaved collectors, both above and below the waterline, while gathering animals.

Despite his losses, Garden forwarded to Linnaeus the "whole stock" of what remained from the man's voyage.[134] Garden's correspondence with his

Swedish client began with their initial exchange of letters in 1755 and continued until Linnaeus's death in 1778.[135] As one node in the global network of collectors assembled by Linnaeus from his home outside Uppsala, Garden embedded himself in natural history networks as a means to gain botanical and zoological knowledge and specimens and to join elite circles of scientific research as a naturalist in Europe. In 1763, Linnaeus nominated Garden for membership in the Royal Academy of Uppsala, propelling Garden to eventually be elected a fellow of the Royal Society, in 1773, and later in other societies, including the Royal Society of Arts, the Philosophical Society of Edinburgh, and the American Philosophical Society.

In South Carolina, Garden practiced medicine as a physician and reaped the profits of a plantation he purchased from John Moultrie in 1771, named Otranto, in St. James Parish.[136] He used the fortunes of his plantation and his medical practice to fund his collecting interests, and by 1785 he possessed seventy-six enslaved people, among them the "black servant" who traveled to Providence Island.[137] As a correspondent of European taxonomists, Garden accrued further credit by corresponding with and supplying specimens to English naturalists like John Ellis and Linnaeus. Linnaeus rewarded Garden for his efforts by immortalizing his name with the genus *Gardenia* in the twelfth edition of *Systema Naturae*. What became of the career or life of the "black servant" is unknown. However, his judgment and skill shaped the natural history collections of Linnaeus.[138]

Slavers engaged in the purchase of enslaved captives in the late eighteenth century also produced natural histories of coastal West Africa filled with observations on animals. After serving as a lieutenant in the Royal Navy, John Matthews entered the trade in Sierra Leone as a factor for a Liverpool firm in 1785.[139] While serving the company, Matthews wrote a natural history of the region spanning from the Rio Nuñez, in present-day Guinea, to Cape Saint Ann, off Sherbro Island. Matthews's book included descriptions of creatures ranging from sharks to leopards, civets, chameleons, manatees, and alligators.[140]

Matthews's career in the trade first began at a slaving factory on Îles de Los. Later, he resided in the Banana Islands, the earlier base of Henry Smeathman, where he met with and lived alongside the Cleveland family until his departure in 1787.[141] After returning to England, Matthews published an account of his career in Sierra Leone, in 1788, including his natural history and an extended defense of the slave trade as an endeavor that supported the "welfare of the nation at large."[142] Matthews's natural history reveals his interest in West African fauna, derived from reading Smeathman and from extensive interactions, conversations, and exchanges with slavers and enslaved people. Matthews learned the West African names for animals in Sierra Leone from conversations with his partners in the trade. Descriptions of two species of snakes—tenné and finyacki-amoofong—appeared in his natural history. These names reflect Matthews's reliance on local contacts, which likely included enslaved people.

Wild chimpanzees who assembled in troops in trees near the firm's factories on Îles de Los and the Banana Islands caught Matthews's attention early in his residency. He learned from other traders, who warned him about fierce attacks by chimpanzee troops if a slaver shot at a pack for sport. Unlike wild chimpanzees, Matthews wrote how traders and West Africans, likely Baga or Temne speakers, captured and domesticated young "Japanzees, or Chimpanzees" in Sierra Leone, who became "very tame and familiar." Matthews and his associates observed how chimpanzees kept as pets grew to be "extremely fond of clinging" to humans and were "very sensible of good or ill treatment."[143]

Matthews's observations and behavior toward chimpanzees is unsettling, given that the slave trade itself relied upon slavers simultaneously acknowledging and denying the humanity and sensibility of captive people. For instance, Matthews experimented on a "young one in my possession" by teaching the chimpanzee to come by calling its name. He added, "If I push him from me, or strike him, or even do not regard his advances by shewing him encouragement," the ape became "sullen or sulky" and despairing. In his natural history, Matthews combined cruelty and racist condescension by describing the chimpanzee as resembling "an old negro, except the hair on their heads is straight and black like an Indian's."[144] By the 1780s, this description fit a familiar narrative trope that readers in Britain consumed, which frequently compared Sub-Saharan Africans to primates.[145]

Matthews used his descriptions of West African fauna, and the ethnographic text embedded in his narrative, to defend the slave trade and slavery as legally and morally beneficial for Britain's Atlantic empire.[146] Moreover, he aimed to establish slavery as a natural consequence of human difference. In the conclusion to his book, Matthews argued that "man, of created beings, holds the first link" in a divinely ordered hierarchy of life. Yet, he claimed, "there are different degrees of excellence in the human race, as there are in every other animal, or descending link, of the great chain of nature." In Africa, he elaborated, "experience fully authorizes our assent to this" fact. "Trace," he instructed his readers, "the manners of the natives, the whole extent of Africa from Cape Cantin to the Cape of Good Hope, and you find a constant and almost regular gradation in the scale of understanding, till the wretched Cafre sinks nearly below the Ouran Outang."[147] Matthews's book—published during debates surrounding the abolition of the slave trade—defended the interests of slavers and slaveholders.[148] However, his natural history relied on scientific knowledge generated by slavery and the enslaved.

Enslaved people and the networks of slaving and slavery furnished animal specimens for collections throughout the Atlantic world, and this knowledge changed early modern science. Enslaved people's collecting efforts and labor influenced scientific debates over the boundaries of plant and animal life in the late eighteenth century. In letters appearing in the *Philosophical Transactions* of the Royal Society, John Ellis—a textile merchant and royal agent for West Florida and Dominica who resided in London—persuaded his peers at the Royal Society and throughout continental Europe that various forms of marine life, including corals, corallines, and polyps, exhibited the anatomical and physical qualities of animals. These creatures possessed observable musculature and tendons, unlike plants or minerals, and, he argued, ought to be categorized as such taxonomically.[149] In his correspondence with the Swedish naturalist Carl Linnaeus, Ellis challenged the positions held by natural philosophers on the Continent, especially Peter Simon Pallas and Job Baster, who claimed that these marine creatures were either flora or minerals.[150]

Ellis, with the aid of his collaborator Daniel Solander, an apostle of Linnaeus, and others, collected, described, and cataloged in his numerous letters and scientific publications hundreds of species of marine fauna acquired from sites around the globe. These writings later appeared in a collected volume, *Natural History of Many Curious and Uncommon Zoophytes*, published by his daughter, Martha Watt, in 1786. Correspondents across the planet sent animals to Ellis, who listed in his book the provenance of the animals gathered from locations near and far, including Aberdeen, Algiers, Ascension Island, Cornwall, Mauritius, and even a "Sea-Feather" and a "Shagg Sponge . . . sent from our factory at Cape Coast Castle on the coast of Africa, where it grows in plenty on the rocks."[151]

John Greg, Ellis's most prolific collector, fashioned a career for himself as a planter and slaveholder in the Caribbean. Greg begin his career as a land surveyor in Dominica, and in 1765 purchased and managed two sugar plantations on the island, Hertford and Hillsborough.[152] He sent Ellis dozens of specimens from Dominica: various "animal flowers," or sea anemones; a "pipy sea mat," a species of bryozoan; a kidney-shaped purple sea pen; eight species of gorgonia; "Trident" and "Cylindrical jointed" corallines; and an alcyonium with "little Eyes."[153] While visiting Charleston, South Carolina, Greg collected a "Spanish Broom Gorgon" and a sea pen, which Ellis discussed at length in a letter published in the *Philosophical Transactions*.[154]

Whether Greg solicited the assistance of enslaved collectors to assemble these animal specimens for Ellis is unclear. Yet, given the cases forming the narrative here, it is highly likely that Greg sought the aid of Atlantic Africans to collect, assemble, and transport specimens. Greg's investments in slavery in the Caribbean certainly furnished the collections Ellis later mobilized in London to defend his zoological claims in print that zoophytes belonged within the kingdom Animalia.[155] Even without the clear evidence of individual enslaved naturalists in either Greg's letters or Ellis's book, a question remains: What does it mean for the history of science, here in particular the collection of animal specimens, that Atlantic African labor and knowledge undergirded the scientific endeavors of Britons in the Atlantic world?

When early modern naturalists like Petiver or Drury urged their peers to collect animals by "showing their Slaves how to collect," they implicitly acknowledged how allegedly English or British science rested on Atlantic African foundations. It was the curiosity, taste, judgment, and expertise of enslaved people like those held by Captain Walduck and Reverend Hughes in Barbados, and men like Oxford on Nevis, that undergirded the expansion of specimen collections and knowledge about animal life in the long eighteenth century.

Slavers and slaveholders played a role in this process, including figures like Tom Ewusi at Cape Coast and the "Ginny masters" sent by Richard Harris to ply the trade in the Bight of Benin. Just as slaveholders like Mary Stafford routinely turned to physically assaulting the enslaved "to make them work hard" and acknowledged that there was "no living without" slaves, violence permeated the labors of enslaved naturalists and those whose bodies became the sites of natural history itself. Recall how a South Sea Company surgeon collected the remains of a stillborn fetus "Taken out of the Hands of" an enslaved woman in Cartagena, along with fish, shells, and other curios. It's possible that this woman felt real anguish and psychological shock from the surgeon's extractive attitude, knowing full well that the fetus would later be gawked at by physicians and natural philosophers.

Yet slavery's archive denies our desire to more fully know Atlantic African figures like the "black servant" sent to Providence Island to collect marine life. This man's efforts, and likely the efforts of others enslaved, formed the basis of global collections like those of the Swedish taxonomist Linnaeus. These men and women made the foundations of early modern science possible, yet the aftermath of their enforced anonymity—and their afterlives here, as subjects of this narrative—haunts the history of science and empire in our present.

Chapter 3

WE FLESH BELONG TO BUCKRA

Human–Animal Labor on American Plantations

Upon returning to Antigua from England in June 1750, Samuel Martin found his family's plantation, Green Castle, "all tumbling down" and "ten fold worse than it was naturally."[1] Since the Christmas Day 1697 murder of his father, Major Samuel Martin, by enslaved people armed "with the hoes they had been using in the cultivation of his sugar-canes," the five hundred–acre sugar estate sited in St. Mary Parish on the western side of the island had been overseen by managers for nearly four decades.[2] From atop a high hill, Martin could stand on the grounds of his family's manor and gaze downward at the slave cabins lined up to the west of the house.[3] From this vantage point, Martin began to conceive of how to reassemble the material basis of his family's wealth and plantation enterprise. In the process of reconstructing Green Castle, Martin discovered that in addition to physically restoring the plantation fields, buildings, and agricultural machinery, he needed a new language to imagine how to order and discipline the estate's human and nonhuman animal laborers.

In a letter to his son eight years after his arrival, Martin computed that a catastrophic decline in the population of enslaved people and cattle, and other disastrous mismanagement owing to the ineptitude of their managers, had cost the family dearly, as sugar production "dwindled from 300 to 100" hogsheads yielded annually in the decades between his father's death and Martin's return to the ruins of Green Castle.[4] "I have good reason," he said, "to believe my two last Managers cheated me most abominably."[5] Martin learned from his subordinates' deception, or sheer incompetence, the acute challenges that a planter transitioning from absenteeship to management on the ground faced in controlling both human and nonhuman actors at a distance. For Martin, grappling with how to coordinate humans and animals as productive tools proved foundational to his ambitious restoration.

Through instructions to overseers and enslaved people, including drivers, Martin immediately set about rebuilding Green Castle, and after the better part of a decade he had succeeded in restoring his family's plantation to its former condition. He explained to his son that with a "Stock of Cattle & Mules [which] do the [labor] of" sixty enslaved men and women in spreading dung across the crop fields, and with the muscular toil and skilled labor of 270 enslaved men, women, and children who drudged in hoeing soil, dunging the earth, gathering fodder vegetables and grasses, and planting, weeding, tending, harvesting, crushing, refining, and carting row after row of sugar cane, by 1758 Green Castle began to produce an average of 250 hogsheads of sugar, which was packed into caskets to be shipped to markets across the British Atlantic world.[6] By focusing an innovative scientific bent on controlling patterns of human–animal labor already existing under slavery, Martin achieved the total reconstruction of the plantation.

In a treatise on the subject of "plantership," composed sometime in the early 1750s, several years into his efforts, Martin circulated the insights he had gained from repairing Green Castle to advise his slaveholding peers. He intended his book to serve as a comprehensive manual for new planters, especially others transitioning from absenteeism to directly overseeing their estates, by providing detail on the techniques necessary at each stage of sugar production.[7]

At the outset of Martin's *Essay Upon Plantership*, after urging that planters inspect their estates with their "own eyes" rather than become dependent on managers, he emphasized that, above all, slaveholders in the Caribbean must hold fast to a fundamental principle: that enslaved people, "cattle, mules, and horses are the *nerves* of a sugar-plantation" and required expert attention in their management.[8] John Pinney, an absentee planter-merchant based in Bristol and a contemporary of Martin, who owned a similar sugar estate on Nevis, likewise emphasized to his overseers in correspondence that "slaves and stock" are "the sinews of a plantation and must claim your particular care and attention."[9] When enslavers like Martin and Pinney used this anatomical language to describe enslaved people and livestock as vital "nerves" and "sinews," slaveholders who read their advice manuals or written instructions further elaborated their existing conceptions of the fundamentally interconnected labor and equivalence of slaves and animals in the colonial British Atlantic world. Enslavers understood the bodies of both human captives and animals as instruments operating within networks to be systematically disciplined to secure future profit. Moreover, their instrumental rhetoric coexisted alongside dehumanizing, and in many cases simianizing, rhetoric, such as that of one of Green Castle's aristocratic visitors, who perceived slaves on Antigua to be "monkeys."[10]

African men, women, and children toiled with draft animals at Green Castle and on other plantations, such as those of Martin's neighbors on Antigua. Among those who labored at Betty's Hope, the sugar estate of the Codrington family in St. Peter Parish on the eastern side of the island, were Ebbo Nan, Pappaw Mary, Fibbah Creole, and Collomante Quaw. Their names reflect their likely origins from Igbo-, Fon-, Fante-, and Akan-speaking states from the Gold Coast and Bight of Benin regions of West Africa, and their birth as enslaved children in the Americas. Slave ships such as the *Pearl*, owned by the Codrington family, transported cargoes of hundreds of human captives from across Atlantic Africa—including the Bight of Biafra, Bight of Benin, Gold Coast, Windward Coast, and ports in western Central Africa—to Caribbean islands such as Antigua in the early eighteenth century.[11]

Plantations like Betty's Hope and Green Castle were not isolated sites of agricultural production but commercial spaces in the Caribbean that were interconnected with other slaveholder investments in land and trade elsewhere in the Atlantic world. Consider, for instance, the holdings of Shute Shrimpton Yeamans, a slaveholder who owned land in New England, a sugar plantation in Antigua, and shares in the South Sea Company, whose slaving voyages terminated in Buenos Aires, Cartagena, and other ports throughout the Spanish Main.[12] Slavery united this Atlantic-wide commercial geography.

Almost three decades after he wrote his *Essay*, Martin wrote in a letter to an associate in 1776 that "the profits of a Plantation consist not so much in great works, as in the fertility of soil, & strength of Negroes, Cattle, and Mules."[13] In these discussions of nerves, sinews, and muscular strength, Martin's and Pinney's anatomical terminology raises questions that lie at the core of the environmental history of slavery in the Caribbean and beyond: How did slaves and animals come to be considered as interrelated subjects through such bodily rhetoric?

For early moderns, nerves functioned as connective tissue through which signals moved from the mind to the brain and then to distant parts of the body, such as the limbs and muscles, and relayed sensory impressions from the limbs back to the mind.[14] "Sinew" denoted the material substance binding muscle to bone, enabling motion and connecting flesh to the skeleton.[15]

Nerves and sinews in human anatomy linked the mind's capability to exert physical power over the body. This language raises questions about how planters like Martin came to understand slaves and animals to be the "nerves" and "sinews" of a dualistic plantation body in which the enslaver took on the idealized role of the mind and the enslaved served as their real somatic appendages. What grounded realities did this language derive from? And to what extent did labor relationships between enslaved people and livestock in the Caribbean, where Martin began his career, resemble or diverge from other plantation regimes on tobacco or wheat estates to the north, in regions like the Tidewater Chesapeake?

Questioning how and why enslaved people and animals came to be understood, valued, and employed as the "nerves" and "sinews" of slaveholders on plantations in the Caribbean and southeastern North America in the second half of the eighteenth century presents opportunities to analyze how modes of plantation labor and the wider social and ecological contexts of slavery shaped the kinds of interactions that took place between enslaved people and nonhuman animals. Slaveholders aimed to yoke slaves and livestock into productive labor relations to cultivate profitable agricultural commodities, especially sugar, tobacco, and wheat, destined for transatlantic markets. These human and animal relations, like those found in the routes of the Atlantic slave trade in Atlantic Africa, produced environmental and cultural networks binding enslaved people and animals on plantations to markets and colonies across the British Atlantic world. While there existed real ecological and environmental differences between Caribbean islands and Chesapeake plantations, the concept of plantation zones helpfully draws into focus similarities between these two regions with regard to slaves and livestock.[16] In both temperate and tropical climates, plantation environments depended on the entanglement of human, animal, and botanical life with soil, winds, rain, and other nonhuman forces that slaveholders hoped to control in their agricultural endeavors. Efforts to discipline people and nonhuman life led to the further production of colonial racial hierarchies.

Burdensome tasks imposed upon slaves and animals by the slaveholders who adopted plow culture in the eighteenth century ranged from plowing fields with draft oxen before a planting season to carting loads of crops or barrels of plantation products.[17] Enslaved children labored as well, performing such tasks as worming tobacco plants, and in one scheme proposed by John Archdale in his promotional book on the Province of Carolina, they were set to carefully feed silkworms.[18] Into the late eighteenth century, as Ben Marsh has shown, South Carolina Lowcountry slaveholders conceived of linking the labors of enslaved children and elderly women with the lives of silkworms in their sericulture efforts.[19] Beyond such speculative plans, enslaved people's everyday lives involved caring for animals in livestock pens, horse stables, domestic settings, and plantation fields.

To understand the logic developed by Martin and other enslavers, this chapter will focus foremost on enslaved people and the kinds of livestock outlined in his *Essay Upon Plantership*. Plantation labor arrangements in both the Caribbean and southeastern North America buttressed a broader political economic system that spanned Britain's Atlantic colonies and constituted a settler-planter empire founded upon slavery, agricultural commodities, and slaveholders' treatment of people of African descent in the Americas as mere things, akin to animals.

Between 1650 and 1680, the fruits of plantation agriculture from the colonies in the Caribbean and the Chesapeake supported the colonial architecture of the English Empire that emerged out of the economic profits of sugar and tobacco in these two geographic regions.[20] Economic historians characterize England's Atlantic empire of the late seventeenth century as a "plantation empire" due to the extensive networks of intercolonial trade and shipping that connected the Tidewater plains of Virginia and Maryland to the volcanic and coralline island arcs of the Caribbean Sea, including Martin's seat in Antigua, linking the northern and southern basins of the ocean.[21]

While economic historians use receipts, account books, and ledgers of planter-merchants to plumb the centrality of agriculture for Britain's plantation empire, the analysis here shifts the focus from that foundational quantitative scholarship toward discussing the laboring experiences of enslaved people and livestock on the ground in a more qualitative mode. Across plantation fields, warehouses, mills, quarters, pens, and stables, enslavers like Martin and Pinney aimed to transform the enslaved and livestock into vital "nerves" and disciplined "sinews" through everyday tasks, punishments, and material linkages that bound the two together.

Slaveholders themselves did not consider such language to be dehumanizing. Rather, Martin himself repeatedly avowed the humanity of diasporic Africans in his essay. In a passage on the use of dung baskets, Martin warned his peers of "degrading human nature to the toil of brutes" and claimed his advice would ameliorate the conditions of slavery in the Caribbean.[22] An earlier generation of historians even framed Martin and his meliorist contemporaries as effectively "humane."[23] By contrast, I claim that examining human–animal relationships on plantations reveals how slaveholders crafted a political ecology that produced a racial hierarchy, one founded on dehumanization, in which enslaved Africans and animals became inextricably entangled as and imagined to be the energetic appendages for enacting a white planter's will.[24]

Taking Martin's principle as my starting point, this chapter turns to three modes of interaction between enslaved people and livestock in both the Caribbean and Chesapeake regions. The first section examines the muscular labor involved on plantations, such as plowing fields, harvesting plants, caring for animals, and hauling commodities, which the enslaved carried out with livestock. Turning from drudgery to diet, the second section looks at how and why enslavers prescribed malnourishing diets of foods for enslaved people—often foods that either in whole or in part could also be used as fodder for livestock—to reduce the will of the enslaved through near starvation and to further manage and equate their bodies with those of animals. A third section moves to how slaveholders imagined and at times aspired to routinely accumulate and mobilize excreta from the bodies of both slaves and animals to transform bodily waste into energy for revitalizing plantation fields.[25]

After considering these three material forms of interaction, a fourth section shows how planters' comparisons of the enslaved to animal forms of life existed in documentary forms of paperwork, especially inventories, wills, and indentures. In sum, this chapter argues that slaveholders aimed to fully dispossess enslaved people of their bodies through labor, diet, and even waste, and that enslavers enacted bodily dispossession by enmeshing the lives of the enslaved with those of animals. The story of these human–animal networks begins by following captives from the auction block to the plantation field to understand plantation regimes of labor and to see this enmeshment in action.

Martin's analysis of the intertwined labors of enslaved people and livestock on Antigua in the mid-eighteenth century emerged from a deep history of plantation slavery on estates in the Lesser Antilles, reaching back into the seventeenth century. English settlers had begun colonizing Barbados in 1627, after merchants funded a settlement on the island.[26] In 1650, the traveler and historian Richard Ligon observed how newly arrived planters on the island colony invested a significant portion of their wealth in purchasing enslaved people as well as "Horses, Cattle, Assinigoes, [and] Camels" to furnish their operations on the island. Ligon also witnessed how the geography of slavery drew on diverse sites to relocate people and animals for plantation labor regimes. Before the planters Ligon discussed even arrived in the Caribbean, would-be settlers stocked transatlantic ships with enslaved people taken from the Senegambia, Windward Coast, Gold Coast, and Bight of Benin, along with horses, cattle, pigs, sheep, goats, and fowl purchased from markets at the Canary Islands, Cape Verde, and Madeira.[27] Slavers from Atlantic Africa carried livestock and captives together across the Middle Passage.[28] Caribbean planters also imported workhorses such as the Narragansett Pacer from as far abroad as New England, New York, the Netherlands, and Virginia to labor on plantations.[29]

Labor regimes involving animals developed alongside racial attitudes among Europeans who equated people of African descent and livestock. While residing at the five hundred–acre sugar plantation of William Hilliard, in St. John Parish on the west coast of Barbados, Ligon sought "to improve my self, in the knowledge of the management of a Plantation" by studying the kinds of labor taking place in Hilliard's fields and sugar mills. Hilliard's plantation works included a sugar *ingenio*, or mill, livestock stables and pens, storerooms filled with provisions of corn, and "Houses for *Negroes* and *Indian* slaves, with 96 *Negroes,* and three *Indian* women, with their Children; 28 Christians, 45 Cattle for worke, 8 Milch Cowes, a dosen Horses and Mares, [and] 16 Assinigoes."[30] Ligon's list, like other inventories and wills from this period, lumped enslaved people and animals into the same economic and social categories, namely as labor and chattel property. And Ligon's notes reflect the coexistence of both African and Indigenous slavery in this period.

Enslavers like Hilliard frequently compared enslaved people with animals as commodities and sources of labor. As slave ships laden with captives from Atlantic Africa arrived in Bridgetown, Ligon observed that planters "choose them as they do Horses in a Market; the strongest, youthfullest, and most beautifull, yield the greatest prices."[31] Captives brought by Royal African Company slavers and independent traders waited on the auction block at markets in Bridgetown and other port cities as potential buyers examined their skin, eyes, limbs, and frame before making their offers, and enslaved people felt and understood the moment of being sold as a crucial, demoralizing stage in their animalization.[32]

Ligon set out to study plantation labor in action by observing combinations of human workers and animals in Hilliard's fields. He watched enslaved people's efforts at harvesttime as they cut off the tops and blades of sugarcane plants with hand bills, a kind of small agricultural knife, and piled up the remnants, known as cane trash, to be used later as fodder for cattle, horses, donkeys, and pigs. Without cane trash to eat, Ligon warned aspiring planters, "our Horses and Cattle are not able to work, the pasture being so extream harsh and sapless."[33] Enslaved people's toil at cutting sugarcane and making cane trash fed the bodies of the draft animals they further labored with on plantations.

After cutting the plant's tops and blades, enslaved men and women bound together piles of sugarcane stalks and loaded them on to "the backs of *Assinigoes*" equipped with small pack saddles. Next, these donkeys—a breed from the Senegal River Valley, named by Portuguese traders after their encounters with North African Berber Azenegue traders and imported to multiple European colonies in the Americas—carried the plants from the fields to the ingenio.[34] "So understanding this little beast is in performing his duty," marveled Ligon, that after delivering bundles of sugarcane stalks to enslaved workers at the mill house, the animals returned to the fields without a guide. Donkeys, he reflected, "may not unfitly be compar'd to Bees; the one fetching home honey, the other sugar."[35]

Enslaved people labored with animals in sugar mills to transform the plant stalks into marketable sugar. In cattle mills—the most common ingenios in the seventeenth-century English Caribbean—enslaved people drove teams of five oxen or horses to power grinding machinery to crush the juice from cane stalks.[36] "This work," wrote one author, "continues from Monday morning till Saturday night, without any intermission, day and night, with fresh supplies of Men, Horses, and cattel."[37] In an index accompanying diagrams of an ingenio he had observed, Ligon marked the precise radius that livestock treaded as slaves drove them on to power the rollers of the mill works.

Hazardous mill works exposed enslaved people to incredibly dangerous risks, including risk of mutilation or death. Cattle mills proved durable machines in the Caribbean, and wind- and water-powered mills did not entirely replace human–animal ingenios until the early nineteenth century.[38] After tallying up the mechanical costs of a sugar ingenio, Ligon calculated that "there is yet more to be added: for though we breed both Negres, Horses, and Cattle; yet that increase, will not supply the moderate decayes which we finde in all those."[39] Deadly and exhausting plantation labor necessitated a regular influx of captives from Atlantic Africa to the Caribbean, which slavers supplied in increasing quantities in the final decades of the seventeenth century as the

Royal African Company expanded its trade networks in West Africa and as interloping separate traders entered into the slave trade.

After extracting and processing sugar in the ingenio, human laborers and nonhuman livestock transported barrels of crystallized sugar from the mills to shipping docks and small boats. In Barbados, enslaved people arranged convoys of camels to lug hogsheads of sugar from plantations to ships in the port in Bridgetown. Enslavers valued camels as "very usefull beasts," yet Ligon remarked that "few know how to diet them." In addition to sugar, camels transported "hogsheads of Wine, Beer, or Vinegar, which horses cannot do, nor can Carts pass for Gullies, and *Negroes* cannot carry it" on other islands in the Caribbean beyond Barbados, until the late eighteenth century.[40]

Entwined patterns of human and animal labor even led enslavers to consider the spatial boundaries of their estates with both subjects in mind. Samuel Clarke reported that slaveholders on Barbados cultivated a species of "*Lime* tree [that] is like a thick Holly-bush in *England,* and as full of prickles." Clarke added that slaveholders "make a Hedge of them about their houses, [and] it's an excellent fence both against the *Negroes,* and Cattel."[41] While it is unclear how many enslavers in Barbados or elsewhere in the Caribbean adopted the practice of planting lime trees to limit the movement of enslaved people and livestock, Clarke's description furthered the link between the two for his audience.

Forms of human–animal labor that Ligon described persisted into the eighteenth century. Evidence of slaveholders' dependence on and equating of the labor of enslaved people and livestock can also be established from legal records such as indentures made between absentee planters and managers. In 1746, for instance, William Hollyer signed an indenture with James Gordon for the lease of his three hundred–acre plantation in St. Paul Parish, Antigua, which included control over the enslaved people, horses, and mules in Hollyer's possession. Numerous indenture contracts from Antigua and other colonies in the Caribbean included clauses specifying the lessee's right to a plantation's "negros, horses, mules, asses, bulls, oxen, cows, sheep, and other live stock."[42] Contracts reflected the real and legal conflation of these plantation nerves and sinews.

Court of Chancery records from Antigua further demonstrate how the social and economic status of enslaved people and livestock became bound together as chattel property and fixed capital under English law in the Caribbean. Chancery courts adjudicated legal disputes involving private property.[43]

John Gray, Master in Chancery for Antigua, for instance, ordered the sale of a plantation in St. Mary Parish in 1787 to one John Rose upon the death of another planter, Thomas Hawes, as payment for debts Hawes had incurred to Rose. Hawes's estate contained twenty-five enslaved people, two cows, three mules, and six horses.[44]

Very few slaveholders in the Caribbean used draft animals for plowing fields before a planting season and instead ordered the enslaved to dig and prepare soil by hand with hoes. However, among his proposed "improvements" for ameliorating the labor of the enslaved, Samuel Martin advised planters to adapt a small breed of cattle for plowing fields. The cattle's horns, he recommended, could be bored with "gimblet holes" to loop a "ligature" that connected a team.[45] Among the "Working Negroes" recorded in the inventory of Green Castle were enslaved men who drove teams of cattle over the topsoil to prepare fields for planting.[46] After receiving instructions from an overseer, drivers worked to train cattle to "walk before [horses] as a leader" in straight, uniform lines. Martin recommended planters implement pairs of "a man and a boy" with two horses or mules connected to a Dutch hoe or a triangular horse–hoe–plow setup for plowing.[47] Several elite slaveholders in the Caribbean, including the Jamaican slaveholder Bryan Edwards, followed Martin's advice.[48]

Letters between plantation managers and absentee owners discussing the status of enslaved people and livestock also offer evidence of their shared economic status. James Stothert's managers and overseers wrote to their employer about the condition of his family's sugar estates and pens, or grazing farms for raising livestock, in Hanover, St. James, and Trelawney Parishes, Jamaica. Writing from Dundee in Hanover Parish, James Alexander, one of Stothert's managers, recorded in his letters the health and labors of the enslaved, cattle, and mules on the plantation.[49] In 1787, another of Stothert's managers, at Dundee, recommended "selling the sheep from Dundee, it will save two Negroes who attend them and also save grass."[50] Stothert's managers likely reassigned these two enslaved shepherds to either further labor with draft animals on his sugar plantation or in another livestock pen. Writing from Salt Marsh and Stonefield, two grazing pens near Martha Brae in Trelawney Parish, John Fowler wrote to his employer to report on recent livestock deaths in the pens, including "Several of the Old Mules [that died] in Crop," and on the poor health of several enslaved people, such as Susan, Tom, and Bella, who the penkeeper described as "all weakly."[51]

Maps of plantations offer another way to understand the proximity of enslaved people and animals in the Caribbean. Manuscript maps of four estates held by the Jarvis family in Antigua—Harts, Royals, Thibou, and Blizards—indicate the closeness of slave quarters to animal spaces such as horse stables, cattle pens, and mule pens at each site.[52] Maintaining proximity between enslaved people and animals supported the efficient operation and surveillance of a sugar plantation labor regime. Moreover, the visual and spatial closeness of slaves and livestock further encouraged enslavers to conceive of the two in their minds as connected subjects.

Descriptions of enslaved people and animals on plantations in letters between enslavers further conflated the two. Writing in a letter to another slaveholder, Mary Trant, the Antiguan slaveholder Thomas Jarvis expressed apprehension about a gang of enslaved men and women he rented from her in 1791. "I am entirely concerned," Jarvis wrote to Trant, "of the declining state of the Gang. The Men & most of the Women are far advanced in Years and only two of them have bred during their abode with me, namely Nanny & Bess, and each of them have only scared me & this the only increase."[53] In accordance with the terms of his lease, Jarvis replaced six of Trant's fifty enslaved people, who died while he rented their laboring bodies as chattel. However, it is clear from his letter to Trant that Jarvis sought to exploit Nanny, Bess, and other women from the gang to "breed" more children rather than be forced to purchase new captives.

Jarvis's use of rhetoric akin to animal breeding to describe Nanny and Bess was not exceptional among slaveholders in the Caribbean. Overseers and managers kept up monthly estate records to provide absentee planters with rates of "increase" and "decrease" among the enslaved and livestock. As several historians argue, slaveholders' numerical valuations of slaves and animals were bound up with future aspirations for accumulating and bequeathing these forms of animate capital. Tables of increase and decrease, then, can be seen as intellectual efforts to rationalize slavery in the Caribbean, which involved a hierarchy of fully human white slavers, animal-like enslaved Africans, and animals.[54] Calculations and quantification further obscured the violent reality of slavery, namely that slaveholders and overseers raped enslaved women and that inventory tables hid ongoing sexual violence behind numerical data.

Quantifying the "increase" of enslaved people and animals became an intellectual pursuit of improvement-minded enslavers inspired by Martin. In 1804, a circle of slaveholders in Barbados, including Reverend Henry Evans

Holder and Philip Gibbes, formed the Society for the Improvement of Plant-ership based on their Antiguan peer's recommended rubric for study and ex-periment in plantership—especially arrangements of human–animal labor.[55] During a meeting in 1805 at Malvern Estate, in St. Joseph Parish, for instance, the society began a discussion on "the quantum of labor which will be re-quired to perform each respective" task involved in operating a plantation.[56] Among the tasks the society identified, and attempted to quantify, were clear-ing land, cutting cane tops, and making, turning, throwing, and bedding an-imal dung. On other occasions, the society discussed techniques for plowing fields, methods for treating diseases that afflicted livestock, and "the practical advantages of keeping horses on plantations for the purpose of husbandry."[57] Out of these discussions surrounding labor came further questions over the topic of population.

Enslavers in the Caribbean continued to worry over "the subject of popula-tion" on plantations, and particularly asked each other "what causes prevented the more rapid increase of" enslaved people. William Grasett, one of the founders of the Society for the Improvement of Plantership, introduced the topic during a meeting in March 1805. Grasett and his colleagues discussed how "promiscuous intercourse," "the suckling of the children an improper length of time," the "unwholesomeness" of provisions on plantations, and the alleged polygamy of enslaved men and women hindered slave population growth.[58] In May 1806, the society voted to continue investigating the topic, and in January 1807, Grasett passed a motion for the members to record and share information on the "annual increase and decrease of" enslaved people on the estates of the members.[59]

Grasett's peers likely kept records of "increase" and "decrease" well before his proposed investigation. In inventories and other plantation account books, slaveholders often included lists of both their human and nonhuman chattel property with titles like "Increase of Negroes," "Increase of Cattles," "Increase of Donkeys," and "Increase of Horses."[60] Since the seventeenth century, plant-ers in the Caribbean had kept track of the number of livestock animals—in-cluding pigs, poultry, sheep, cattle, and horses—and of enslaved people under the same rubric of "increase" in inventory lists.[61]

In the spring of 1810, Grasett shared his findings and thoughts on the "best mode of increasing" the population of enslaved people. Grasett began by em-phasizing "the importance of the present question to a colonial agriculturalist," particularly for enslavers in the Caribbean, who legally could not acquire new captives from Atlantic Africa since Parliament's passage of the Slave Trade Act in 1807. Citing the population studies of Thomas Malthus, Grasett advised his fellow slaveholders that "it would be good policy in us not to suffer our breeding women to perform the most laborious work of a plantation." While Grasett believed provisions on plantations to be sufficient, he suggested improving housing and medical treatment for the enslaved, limiting enslaved people's consumption of liquor, and allowing enslaved men and women to marry.[62]

Similar regimes of human–animal labor existed under plantation slavery in Britain's North American colonies in the seventeenth and eighteenth centuries. In the Chesapeake Bay area, tobacco and wheat planters in Virginia and Maryland relied upon combined forms of agricultural labor involving enslaved people and livestock that their peers in the Caribbean would have recognized.[63]

Traces of enslaved people's labor with animals can be found in documents like probate inventories that reflect the lived experience of numerous enslaved people who tended to livestock animals in the southern Chesapeake in the late seventeenth and early eighteenth centuries.[64] Even if most enslaved people did not labor with animals through plow culture, the inventories document daily forms of labor that bound enslaved people to nonhuman creatures through animal care. Inventories from York County, on the northern edge of the Virginia Peninsula, for instance, include frequent references to enslaved people and livestock, such as the inventory of Colonel William Digges taken in 1698. Digges's estate included several cows and calves, steers, heifers, yearlings, "barren Cowes," an old mare, and enslaved men and women named Dick, Oakey, Bob, Mary, Kate, Billey, and Betty. Like the animals listed in the inventory, several enslaved women are not named but simply listed as "1 Negro Woman and Sucking Child" and "1 old Negro Woman."[65] Even very small-scale planters and slaveholders in southern Virginia typically owned one or more enslaved people along with livestock such as cattle, pigs, and a horse.[66] Men like Dick and Bob may have cared for and driven the cattle to pasture, and women like Mary and Kate kept and fed cattle, sheep, and pigs in their pens. While most probate inventories recorded the monetary values of the enslaved and livestock, some simply listed them together, as in the inventory of William Blaikley, who at the time of his death in 1736 owned "Negroes about the house Nanny Lucy and hannah a Cow a horse."[67]

Reconstructing the lives of enslaved people like Hannah and their interactions with animals on these small estates is difficult. One of the earliest narratives involving an enslaved person in early eighteenth-century Maryland, Ayuba Suleiman Diallo, a Fulbe man from Bundu, offers insight into the entangled lives and labor of slaves and animals in the Atlantic world.[68] Before his enslavement, Diallo profited as a slave trader himself, trading captives with Europeans from Senegal to the Gambia.[69] In 1730, a West African slaver captured and sold Diallo along with "a Servant, and about twenty or thirty Head of Cattle" on the Gambia River.[70] The slaver sold Diallo and his servant to an English slave trader, a man named Pyke, whose ship *Arabella* sailed from the Gambia across the ocean to Annapolis on the mouth of the Severn River. After being sold to a tobacco planter on Kent Island, on Maryland's Eastern Shore, Diallo labored at planting until he "grew sick" and his enslaver "therefore put him to tend the Cattle." Diallo came from an elite Muslim family in Bundu, and he was not unfamiliar with herding. Yet Diallo "would often leave the Cattle" under his supervision to pray alone in the woods near the plantation.[71] It is possible that Hannah and Dick likewise brought cattle herding techniques with them from Upper Guinea to Virginia, as many Senegambians from diverse ethnolinguistic societies introduced cattle ranching techniques to the Americas, from the Rio de la Plata to North America.[72]

Reading fugitive runaway advertisements, such as those printed in newspapers like the *Virginia Gazette*, gives a sense of the spectrum of work enslaved people carried out with animals in the Chesapeake. In newspaper announcements, slaveholders solicited the arrest of enslaved men and women they depended upon as dairymaids, cattle drivers, plowmen, farriers, grooms, postilions for leading coach horses, and stablemen. In 1768, for instance, an advertisement from a slaveholder in Stafford County offered a reward for the arrest of Peter Deadfoot. The newspaper copy described Peter as a skilled plowman and carter and noted that he "understands breaking oxen well . . . he is so ingenious a fellow, that he can turn his hand at anything."[73] An advertisement regarding an enslaved man, David, who ran away from his enslaver's estate in Northumberland, in the Northern Neck of Virginia, noted his skill as "a good driver, ostler . . . can work at the plough."[74] Another planter, in Louisa, Virginia, advertised that a man named Jacob, valuable for his "great skill in farriery," had fled his estate.[75] Dozens of other advertisements appeared in newspapers in the late eighteenth century, written by planters seeking the arrest of runaway slaves valued for their abilities as hostlers, cockfighters, and jockeys, whose worth for slaveholders derived from their experience and skill in laboring with and caring for animals.

The centrality of slaves and livestock for agricultural labor on Tidewater Chesapeake plantations is further visible in advertisements announcing the sale of slave lots by auction. One advertisement from 1773 for the sale of a group of enslaved people born in Virginia at Williamsburg noted that many of the men were skilled in plowing with cattle and caring for horses, likely as coachmen and stablemen.[76] In addition to the slaves, four bay coach horses were part of the auction lot, and it is likely the men worked with these horses in their daily labor. In 1777, one slaveholder in Charles City County announced the sale of their total estate, including one hundred "*Virginia* born *Slaves*," for sale to the highest bidder. Among them were skilled dairymaids, along with a "stock of horses, cattle, and sheep, and some very valuable high blooded horses."[77]

While few Chesapeake slaveholders relied upon the skilled agricultural labor of enslaved people and livestock for plowing fields to cultivate crops of tobacco and wheat, enslaved plowmen on some plantations labored by leading teams of draft animals, which required skill and patience for managing teams of stubborn creatures.[78] One of the few diaries kept by planters in eighteenth-century Virginia offers a unique window onto this kind of labor. Landon Carter, a tobacco and wheat planter who held five hundred acres of land in Richmond County on the southern banks of the Rappahannock River, relied on the labor of several enslaved plowmen, such as Manuel, Peter, Simon, and Joe, who drove teams of oxen, mules, and on occasion horses, to prepare soil before the planting season.[79]

While Carter's diary is exceptional, given its level of detail and the scale of his estates, the kinds of labor that Manuel and his fellow drivers performed did exist on the estates of other improvement-minded planters in Virginia and Maryland, such as Richard Corbin and Francis Jerdone, in the second half of the eighteenth century.[80] Elite slaveholders also occasionally invested in new technologies that enmeshed the labor of enslaved people and animals. On the Dogue Run farm of his tobacco and wheat plantation in Mount Vernon, George Washington ordered enslaved carpenters to build a sixteen-sided wheat-treading barn.[81] In the barn, enslaved people guided horses on to the treading floor to crush seeds out of wheat stalks before winnowing the grains from the straw.[82]

On the farms surrounding Carter's estate of Sabine Hall, enslaved plowmen drove animals yoked to plows to dig furrows into the soil, crush weeds, and turn the earth. In his diary, kept between 1752 and 1758, Carter entered brief entries on the labor of his slaves and livestock, such as how the planter

"Left Manuel plowing my Fork Land for Wheat."[83] In the diary, he noted how groups of slaves and livestock worked together, like "Peter and two horses in his light plow" ripping up fields designated for barley, oats, and tobacco in the late spring of 1772.[84] Men like Manuel and Peter drove livestock for plowing, and their control over the animals indicates enslaved people's ability to discipline livestock for agricultural labor. Moreover, Carter expected the same people to care for the animals' welfare, which was frequently a point of contestation and resistance between enslavers and enslaved people.

Elite Virginia slaveholders encountered friction in putting their plans involving human and animal laborers into action. Carter, a well-read planter like Martin and his peers in the Caribbean who embraced English husbandry techniques, complained that using mathematical calculations for planning plowing, sowing, and harvesting during a crop season could be useful but was often frustrated by real difficulties and limitations. "Castings up by arithmitic" in plowing, he complained, rarely proved accurate. In 1772, he noted how "Manuel's Oxen does 32 rows in the day. Peter has 90 rows to come to his ditch which finishes that field. Certainly 4 horses can do more then 4 oxen." But Carter doubted the plowing could be done reliably with such precise and timely standards.[85]

At harvesttime, the same drivers and draft animals carted wheat and tobacco plants gathered from the fields to storehouses across the plantation. Diary entries record that Manuel and others led teams of oxen to cart crops from the fields to the slaveholder's warehouses, and their labor resembled the kinds of carting and hauling performed by enslaved people in the Caribbean.[86]

Other enslaved people on Carter's plantations, such as a man named Talbot, performed different tasks with animals, such as shearing sheep for wool.[87] Another man, Robin, watched over hogs at the Fork Quarter, one of Carter's surrounding farms.[88] Enslaved women supervised livestock on Carter's plantations as well. Two elderly women, Sukey and Betty, cared for geese, ducks, chickens, and turkeys in Carter's henhouse.[89] Sukey reported to Carter on the health of the birds he entrusted to her care, especially when the animals laid eggs or when their eggs hatched. Carter tasked two other women, Rose and Sicely, with keeping cattle from trespassing into his fields and damaging his plants.[90] In addition to these burdensome tasks, Carter trusted at least one enslaved man with another form of plantation labor: veterinary medicine.[91] Carter relied on an enslaved man whom he referred to in his diary as "Dr. Nassaw" to care for his livestock when they gave birth or became ill, and to administer therapeutic bleedings. In a diary entry from 1771, for instance, Carter recorded how "Nassaw cut and marked 16 piggs, marked and turned out 2 black Cows, [and] mark one sow pigg at the Fork." Nassaw also inspected the health of Carter's horses and often treated the animals for worms.[92] Nassaw's skilled work exemplifies the productive and reproductive labor enslaved people carried out on plantations.

As entanglements involving the labor of enslaved people and animals on Tidewater Chesapeake plantations intensified, slaveholders increasingly drew upon and developed racialized rhetoric that characterized enslaved Africans as akin to animals in their minds, bodies, and sexuality. In his diary, Carter justified his status as a slaveholder by questioning the humanity of people of African descent. Carter wrote to himself that the enslaved could "as little be humanized as bears," and that Africans represented "nothing but a brute in human shape."[93] In his natural history treatise *Notes on the State of Virginia*, Thomas Jefferson, a slaveholder in the Virginia Piedmont and a peer of Carter, suggested that Africans were akin to animals. In his book, Jefferson repeated the racist trope that "Oran-ootan" apes sought after African women for sexual intercourse in Atlantic Africa.[94] Jefferson declared that he considered the physiology and mental abilities of Africans to be comparable to that of "our horses, dogs, and other domestic animals."[95] While he did not describe enslaved people as nerves or sinews, his rhetorical conflation of slaves and animals is strikingly similar to the language in Samuel Martin's book on plantership. Dehumanizing people in theory, however, is a theoretical exercise that necessarily relies on material realities, including the political uses of food, to support such ideas in practice.

Slaveholders further entangled the lives of enslaved people with livestock by provisioning slaves with malnourishing diets of foods that also could be used for fodder.[96] Food and fodder, or provender, are socially constructed categories, not natural kinds, and it is important to bear in mind here that their very porousness could be one way that slaveholders exploited the bodies of the enslaved. Feeding enslaved people and animals nearly identical diets supported a wider ideological structure and cultural perception among enslavers that the bodies of the enslaved and animals could be understood as functionally equivalent. In his scholarship on slavery and provisioning in the early republic, Thomas Andrews argues that enslavers self-consciously created a caloric gap between whites—whose diets included regular portions of protein-rich meat—and enslaved people—whose nutrient-deficient diets consisted mostly of fodder grains—to support an ideology and material reality that reduced the enslaved to the status of livestock through food inequalities.[97]

The framework of the caloric gap is also useful for understanding diets prescribed by enslavers in the colonial Caribbean and Chesapeake worlds of an earlier period. Nicholas Crawford has shown that abolitionists and proslavery apologists clashed over the diet of enslaved people, and debates surrounding what constituted a humane approach to feeding a laboring person revolved around disputed quantities of foods like corn, beans, oats, peas, potatoes, and yams.[98] Moreover, as Anya Zilberstein has shown, enslavers used foods that were culturally recognized in Europe as fodder, or food primarily suited for animals, especially cereal grains, to feed enslaved people.[99] Rather than being unique to plantation slavery, Zilberstein shows that eighteenth-century experiments in nutrition for dependent populations in Europe included the poor, soldiers, sailors, and incarcerated people. Contests surrounding provisioning and self-provisioning are therefore as much a site of conflict within the political economy of food as they are a conflict over humanity, about whether one is being perceived as human or as less than human.[100]

Like forms of human–animal labor, dietary regimes designed to minimize a planter's costs emerged in the seventeenth-century Caribbean. In a set of instructions to his overseers, written around 1670, the planter Henry Drax ordered his manager, Richard Harwood, to direct the enslaved on his estate to plant provision crops, especially potatoes, "Guny Corn or rather bony biss"— referring to sorghum and bonavist pea—and plantains, in small grounds on his Drax Hall and Hope plantations in St. George Parish, Barbados.[101] The cultivation of sorghum, along with rice and millet, on Caribbean plantations reflects the transfer of Atlantic African agrarian technologies to the Americas, which slaveholders relied upon for provisioning and self-provisioning via grounds cultivated by people of African descent themselves, on Sundays and in whatever time they could find for growing food.[102] Drax stressed that "Most be Care takne to plantt all the ground you Can with Corn without Enough of which neither horses nor Cattle will be able to perform theire work and when theire is no wantt of thatt Every thing in the plantation will be fatt[—]itt being also for Change wery good for negros."[103] Drax and his peers valued sorghum in particular as cheap food for feeding both livestock and slaves.

Enslavers and others recommended that planters adapt cheap diets for slaves and animals in England's southern colonies in North America as well. In 1700, John Lawson, the surveyor-general for the Province of Carolina, reported that during his expedition he learned that "*Indian* Corn, or *Maiz,* proves the most useful Grain in the World and had it not been for the Fruitfulness of this Species, it would have proved very difficult to have settled some of the Plantations in *America*. . . . And this Assertion is made good," Lawson continued, "by the *Negro*-Slaves, who, in many Places, eat nothing but this *Indian* Corn and Salt. Pigs and Poultry fed with this Grain," he added, "eat the sweetest of all others."[104] Lawson lavished praise upon corn, a plant he speculated could "refuse no Grounds" and might be adapted for distant soils for the purpose of expanding slavery from New England to the Caribbean.

Hugh Jones, chaplain to the Virginia General Assembly, likewise heaped praise upon corn as a food for "great Increase and most general Use" for provisioning enslaved people, "Cattle, Hogs, Sheep, and Horses." Agricultural labor involving the enslaved and animal diets overlapped on Chesapeake plantations, Jones observed, as enslaved people raised "*Hogs* and *Cattle,* and plant *Indian Corn* (or Maize) and Tobacco for the Use of their Master." The enslaved simultaneously furnished for slaveholders the labor to plant, raise, and harvest fodder crops for livestock and for themselves. Fields in Virginia and elsewhere, Jones recommended, could fruitfully alternate between seasons of tobacco, corn, and wheat with "wonderful Increase" as the enslaved raised commodities for market and food crops.[105] Jones's use of the word *increase* to describe the fertility of the enslaved, livestock, and agricultural commodities fit within the discourse of Caribbean enslavers, who similarly accounted for "increase" and "decrease" on their estates.

In the same intellectual vein as his contemporaries, Jones defended slavery as a natural and healthy institution, alongside his praise for corn provisions. The chaplain assured aspiring planters that enslaved Africans in Virginia "are not only encreased by fresh Supplies from Africa" but were "very prolifick" in the Tidewater Chesapeake. Like others, such as the planter and would-be natural philosopher William Byrd II, Jones justified slavery in Virginia by claiming that Africans "are of a more servile Carriage, and slavish Temper" and "by Nature cut out for hard Labour and Fatigue." The chaplain argued that "Chimerical hard Slavery" on Virginia plantations "is not very laborious." Moreover, he added, Africans worked with "delight" in laboring under "violent Heat" or wet weather.[106] Jones's phrase "Chimerical hard Slavery" is indicative of how slavery generated notions of human–animal mixtures, like the Chimera of classical antiquity, and how those ideas surfaced in the rhetoric of slaveholders and their associates.

Natural historians likewise underscored the value of corn on plantations in Virginia and in the Carolinas, which were divided into North and South Carolina in 1712. The naturalist Mark Catesby wrote how planters in South Carolina ordered enslaved people to cut corn blades, like the leaves of sugarcane plants, as "winter provender for horses and cattle." Here again we can see the simultaneity of food and fodder: slaves, and other people, ate the kernels of *Zea mays*, while animals ate the blades and stalks. The easy culture of corn, Catesby wrote, "adapts it to the use of these countries as the properest food for" enslaved Africans.[107] While traveling in Virginia, Catesby discussed with the naturalist and slaveholder William Byrd II experiments in feeding slaves diets consisting entirely of wheat or maize.[108] Diets for slaves and livestock continued to occupy the attention of naturalists in North America into the second half of the eighteenth century.[109] In 1767, for instance, the physician and geographer John Mitchell reported to the London Board of Trade that planters fed enslaved people on Tidewater plantations "entirely on Indian Corn."[110]

While slaveholders in the Chesapeake used maize, enslavers in the Caribbean more frequently resorted to sorghum to provision the enslaved and as fodder for livestock in the mid-eighteenth century. Many West African societies had cultivated sorghum as a staple crop for centuries before the Atlantic slave trade, and enslavers found the grain to be especially useful for provisioning slave ships and plantations.[111] One missionary for the Society for the Propagation of the Gospel in Foreign Parts, who resided in St. Lucy Parish, Barbados, between 1736 and 1750, observed that planters on the island primarily fed enslaved people bread made from "*Guiney* Corn."[112]

Though enslaved people's diets did not solely consist of fodder foods, cereals and other cheap vegetables made up the bulk of slave diets on plantations in the Caribbean. In his plantership essay, Samuel Martin recommended that planters feed enslaved people "Guinea corn, yams, or eddas, besides potatoes growing in regular succession."[113] Planters in Jamaica likewise fed the enslaved rations of sorghum and maize.[114] Edward Long, a slaveholder in Clarendon Parish, described sorghum as the "principal part of the food" for enslaved Africans, horses, and hogs, and maize as "wholesome food" for slaves as well to feed "horses and mules, instead of oats, and to sheep and poultry, in order to fatten them."[115] Writing in a meliorist tone, Martin advised planters that diets consisting only of "New England corn" would be insufficient, yet he and other planters prescribed malnourishing diets for the enslaved, made up primarily of cereals and few vegetables.[116]

Enslaved people did possess their own animal livestock in their provisioning grounds, but it is difficult to ascertain how common this was or how many animals an enslaved person or community might own. In his unpublished manuscript written in the 1740s, James Knight, a Jamaican slaveholder operating a plantation and a livestock pen in St. Andrew Parish, noted that enslaved people on the island "have indeed some Cattle, sheep, and Horses which they dispose of" through local trade.[117] Despite their humanist pretensions, enslavers relied on conceiving of the bodies of the enslaved and of animals as functionally interchangeable.

Plantation manuals inspired by Martin and written in the second half of the eighteenth century recommended that enslavers implement nearly identical grain-based diets for enslaved people and livestock. In his unpublished manuscript manual on plantership written in 1774, the Jamaican slaveholder John Dovaston included a chapter on "Planting of Grass, Corn, and Provision for Cattle and Slaves."[118] The centrality of corn and other grains for plantations also can be found in records kept by overseers. An overseer at Somerset Vale, a coffee plantation in St. Thomas Parish, Jamaica, for instance, kept a journal from 1776 to 1780 to record the weekly labor of the enslaved. Entries from the journal list the tasks of enslaved men: tending yam hills, "Breaking in Corn in old Negro Ground," "Cleaning new Ground Corn and plantin walk," planting sorghum, and harvesting other fodder crops.[119] The enslaved at Somerset Vale lived and worked alongside livestock animals, for which they built pens and hog sties, and ate diets nearly identical to that of their animal charges.

Grain-based diets implicated slavery within a wider Atlantic world of projects surrounding scientific agricultural improvement. In Barbados, planters implemented corn-centered diets adapted from natural philosophers including Benjamin Thompson, Count Rumford.[120] In an essay, Thompson advocated the many virtues of corn for feeding "negro slaves," "fattening hogs and poultry," and "giving strength to working oxen."[121] Philip Gibbes, a planter who held the estate of Spring Head in St. James Parish and studied Thompson's work closely, printed directions for making cheap soups for the enslaved from corn and other grains, in his *Instructions for the Treatment of Negroes*, published in 1797.[122] Adapting Thompson's research, Gibbes stressed to the manager of his plantation that the portions of food, mostly corn, provided to the enslaved should be "more than sufficient." Large amounts of food, he claimed, would lead to greater rates of "increase" on plantations. In the recipes for cheap soup described in his *Instructions*, which used corn, sorghum, and oats—"the food of man and beast"—Gibbes promoted a dietary regimen for providing large quantities of food, yet the soups proved malnourishing for the enslaved.[123] Later manuals inspired by Gibbes continued to suggest slave diets primarily made up of sorghum, another "food for both man and beasts."[124]

Plantation doctors likewise prescribed grain-centered diets in the Caribbean. In his plantation manual appearing in 1803, David Collins, a physician in Saint Vincent, discussed using soups made from corn or sorghum to feed enslaved people.[125] Horse beans, another food Collins recommended, could be equally useful for feeding the enslaved, hogs, and horses on an estate.[126] Planters valued cereal grains as durable supplies of food in moments of crisis such as hurricane strikes, and Caribbean planters, Collins warned, must prepare for moments of chaos, and particularly slave revolts, caused by food shortages.[127] "Nothing is better for that purpose then the Indian corn of America," he counseled, "because, if wanted, it will afford a good food to the negroes, and, if not wanted for them, it may be given instead of oats, to the horses and mules." Though some enslaved people did receive an "animal part" of their diet, Collins and others pointed out that it was typically "small indeed," and that fodder grains, by far, made up most of their food on plantations.[128] Meager diets of fodder exposed enslaved people to frequent suffering and persistent ill-health.[129] Among the diseases caused by malnutrition that plantation doctors like Collins identified among enslaved men and women were "dirt-eating," "yaws," and infectious worms.[130]

While slave diets in the Chesapeake were meager compared to that of whites, enslaved people in the Caribbean faced far greater privation related to dietary malnutrition, due in part to the agricultural labor demanded by different plantation commodities.[131] The effects of physical and psychological violence caused by malnourishment in the Caribbean can be seen most clearly in cases of "plague hunger." Griffith Hughes, a missionary for the Society for the Propagation of the Gospel, for instance, observed as enslaved men and women suffering from painful starvation in Barbados unearthed the corpses of perished cattle and horses to consume as food. In his description of a "very contagious and pestilential" disease afflicting livestock on the island, Hughes described how animals "feeding heartily" and appearing otherwise well would "without any Symptom of a previous Disorder, drop down and die." Planters immediately buried the animals and appointed watchmen to guard their graves and prevent newly bought captives arriving on the island from West Africa, and other enslaved people, from "digging up the Carcasses, and feeding upon them." Hughes learned that enslaved people who ate the liver or entrails of buried livestock quickly became sick and died.[132]

Abolitionists testifying before the House of Commons in 1790 and 1791 added to their brief against the slave trade plague hunger, as evidence of the brutality of slavery. Though this testimonial evidence may have been calculated and scripted to shock the nation by political campaigners, the attesters included white plantations laborers with direct experiences bearing witness to planter's overt uses of malnourishment. Mark Cook, an overseer in Jamaica who worked on multiple plantations between 1744 and 1790, testified that enslaved people in the Caribbean "have not sufficient food." On Jamaica, Cook observed, "Africans and *Creoles* eat the putrid carcases of animals, and is convinced they did it *through want*." John Terry, an overseer and plantation manager in Grenada, witnessed enslaved people, "on estates *where they have been worse fed than on others,* eat the putrid carcases of animals also." Another Jamaican overseer, Henry Coor, who served on plantations in Westmoreland Parish, recalled how planters burnt dead "mules, horses, and cows" to prevent such occasions. "Had they been buried," he claimed, "the negroes would have dug them up in the night to eat them *through hunger.*"[133]

Plague hunger disturbed planters in the Caribbean. In 1795, John Gay Alleyne wrote in a letter that three enslaved people on his plantation, Turners Hall Wood in St. Andrew Parish, Barbados, had "been destroyed on the Estate with Plague hunger, the Effect of their Eating putrid Cattle."[134] Instances of plague hunger reflect how white slaveholders used food and near-starvation in the formation of the caloric gap as weapons to attack and undermine the health and will of enslaved Africans in the Caribbean.

Enslaved people did not passively accept the malnourishing dietary regime of slavery. Slaves fished and hunted for animals inside and beyond the limits of a plantation and the formal self-provisioning in the gardens and yards surrounding huts and cabins. In Jamaica, the naturalist and physician Patrick Browne, who practiced medicine on the island from 1746 to 1755, saw enslaved people catch and eat the supposedly poisonous mangrove crab found in lowland marshes, and fish for young sharks on the shoreline. Further inland, Browne observed, enslaved people hunted for yellow snakes and feral cats.[135] In the Bahama islands, another naturalist observed enslaved divers and fishermen catching green turtles, land crabs, and other fish.[136] Enslaved people also made use of fishing traps and pots to catch shrimp, crawfish, and on occasion alligators in rivers, creeks, streams, and bays.[137] A few enslaved people, such as a mulatto man named Dick on Vineyard Pen in St. Elizabeth Parish, Jamaica, possessed dogs for hunting game.[138] Fishing, trapping, and hunting afforded some enslaved people the means to diversify their diet and bolster their health with animal protein. By acquiring food through their own clandestine movements away from the plantation, enslaved people defied the will of slaveholders who aimed to equate their bodies with animals through diet.

Cooking food and preparing meals also can be seen as not only a form of resistance to the caloric gap but also an even more meaningful intellectual refusal to be treated or seen as less than human. Cooked food and shared meals, or feasting, are hallmarks of humanity, what some anthropologists refer to as "cultural universals."[139] Beyond the universality of commensality, or eating together, scholarship on food in the African diaspora attests to the intellectual history embedded in foodways, which preserved knowledge, technology, culture, and ideas among enslaved people.[140]

Many enslaved fishers and hunters ate their game to fortify the malnourishing diets of fodder grains they endured. However, enslaved people in the Caribbean occasionally sold at Sunday markets the animals they caught.[141] A colorful lithograph print from 1806 depicts *Negroes Sunday Market at Antigua*. In the center of the foreground, an enslaved woman sits on the dirt ground. Animals for sale—ducks, chickens, geese, and other birds—encircle the space around her. To the right, an enslaved man drags a reluctant pig by a rope. Behind him, Black men and women with goats, pigs, and deer for sale sit and engage in conversation. In the lower right-hand corner of the image, a man of African descent sits with a pair of fowls. Behind him, a woman with a basket loaded with pigeons stands in the distance. In the far left corner of the image, a man of African descent appears to be selling an iguana, while to the right a small boy carries a lamb over his shoulders. Throughout the image are scattered several dogs and deer, possibly belonging to one of the marketers or perhaps one of the few white planters in the background. This image and others like it indicate the economic decisions made by some slaves to sell their quarry at market, using the animals to purchase other valuable goods, such as clothes or tools.

Diet and dietary costs continued to occupy the attention of planters interested in "improving" or ameliorating slavery in the Caribbean. The members of the Society for the Improvement of Plantership in Barbados, for instance, met often to discuss dietary advice on plantations. In 1805, the society met on several occasions to report on various experiments in planting potatoes, yams, and eddoes as cheap provisions for the enslaved.[142] In February 1808, the planters, led by Henry Evans Holder, began correspondence with Alexander Anderson, the superintendent of the royal botanical garden on Saint Vincent, on the subject of a species of rice "planted in Sierra Leone," which they hoped could become a plantation provision crop.[143] In October, Anderson replied by sending the society specimens of "Upland Rice" for experiment.[144] Anderson expected the rice would become "a useful acquisition" for slaveholders and offered to send future specimens of rice from South and Southeast Asia.

Enslaved people in the Caribbean understood that the food they received from their enslavers was intentionally malnourishing and differed from that which whites enjoyed. One enslaved man on Bloxburgh, a coffee plantation in the Port Royal Mountains of Jamaica, explained to an overseer that their diet consisted almost entirely of "raw corn." In conversing with the overseer, Benjamin M'Mahon, the man emphasized "we flesh belong to buckra, and no more; we bones belong to we self." M'Mahon, who found employment on multiple plantations on the island, repeatedly during his career observed emaciated, skeletal enslaved people "who looked more like phantoms then human beings," suffering from malnourishment. Another enslaved man, on Harmony Hall in St. Mary Parish, told M'Mahon that their enslaver treated his slaves worse than his cattle. While employed at Passley Garden in Portland Parish, M'Mahon discovered to his astonishment that the enslaved did not receive any rations of herring, even on holidays like Christmas and New Year's Day, when planters customarily provided slaves with meals of fish. M'Mahon learned that the enslaved "chiefly supported themselves by night-fishing" in their efforts to close the caloric gap slaveholders embedded in their diets.[145]

Slavery's foodways, the malnourishing diet of fodder foods that enslavers prescribed for enslaved people and livestock, existed to support a material and ideological equating of slaves with animals that emerged from human–animal regimes of labor. As dietary limitations—what Andrews terms the caloric gap—followed from labor, so too did further schemes to extract energy and to more fully dispossess the enslaved from their own bodies.

After exhausting the muscular labor of enslaved people and livestock, while feeding both groups diets of fodder foods, slaveholders in the British Atlantic continued to "improve" plantations and dispossess the bodies of the enslaved through highly aspirational schemes to restore the fertility of their lands by collecting the waste of slaves and animals. Enslaved people's labors in accumulating, storing, and distributing human and animal manure became crucial for revitalizing sugar and tobacco plantations in the Caribbean and the Chesapeake as soil depletion in both regions worsened in the second half of the eighteenth century.[146]

As Lois Green Carr and Russel Menand show, seventeenth-century Chesapeake slaveholders in colonies like Maryland did not collect or use animal manure because they lacked sufficient amounts of fodder or forage.[147] Lorena S. Walsh argues that efforts to mobilize manure, among other techniques, "dominate the story" of Virginia's eighteenth-century tobacco plantations' attempts to replenish exhausted fields.[148] Yet the constraints imposed by available forage and limited pasturage severely blunted such efforts until the early nineteenth century. In his research on Mount Vernon, Justin Roberts likewise points out that slaveholders there struggled to use on their fields the amounts of manure that their Caribbean peers used.[149]

Enslavers' interest in profiting from waste during this period emerged from a wider context of scientific agriculture in Europe. Enslaved people toiling alongside livestock animals in both regions labored at gathering, hauling, and casting dung at greater rates for planters who increasingly promoted dunging as a crucial material foundation for plantations. However, enslaved people's exposure to manure through the dirty, dangerous, and exhausting work of dunging increased rates of illness and disease. Hauling pounds of manure tore people's muscles, damaged tendons, and strained joints to the breaking point.[150] Enslaved people's backbreaking labor with dung further encouraged descriptions of the enslaved as animal-like drones, as in the narrative of one enslaver on Barbados who observed "*Negrees* work at it like Ants or Bees" while lugging animal waste and humanure across plantations.[151]

Planters approached manuring in a similar fashion to their approach to labor and diet, by treating the bodies of slaves and animals as functionally interchangeable. Scholarship using close reading from literary theory reveals how enslavers built out on plantations networks of animals and humans connected by excreta and ordure. Samuel Martin wrote that a Caribbean planter intending "to grow rich with ease, must be a good oeconomist; must feed his negroes with the most wholesome food, sufficient to preserve them in health and vigor." Furthermore, "it is nature's oecnomy so to fructify the soil by the growth of yams, plantains, and potatoes, as to yield better harvests of sugar by that very means."[152]

For the most part, agricultural historians examining Martin's essay usually overlook this passage of the text. However, Anna Foy, a literary historian of

Augustan poetics, interprets this passage as an instance of circumlocution—the rhetorical use of a series of related words to indirectly discuss a topic generally considered beyond the boundaries of polite discussion.[153] Through close reading of Martin's advice on preparing soil, organizing plantation space, and planning crop harvests; by reading the essay in its historical context alongside agricultural improvers such as Francis Home and Arthur Young; and by reading contemporary travel accounts by writers including Janet Schaw, Foy argues that Martin's essay used circumlocution to propose that planters use human excreta, specifically the excreta of the enslaved, as fertilizer to replenish the land of their weakened estates.[154] Though Martin did directly discuss using animal dung on plantations in his essay, focusing on the exploitation and extraction of humanure from enslaved people, and slaves' labor with dung, deepens an analysis of the entanglements of humans and animals. Planters sought to capture the vitality of slaves and livestock at every turn, first by exhausting their muscles through work and then by seizing their waste.

In print, Martin expounded on the problem of soil depletion with his peers in Antigua, Barbados, Saint Christopher, Jamaica, and Britain's other Caribbean colonies. While rebuilding Green Castle, he learned when "soils are exhausted of their fertility, by long and injudicious culture, they may be restored by any kind of dung well rotted."[155] Situating sheepfolds on fallow fields could improve soils; however, he added, "this can be practised only where there are extensive pastures," an unlikely prospect on small island colonies such as Antigua. Systematically collecting and mixing the waste of humans and animals solved a pressing ecological problem originating from the exhaustive nature of monocropping and the limited space of island colonies.

In addition to mixing the combined excreta of enslaved people and livestock, Martin advocated the "art of caving," or mining marl—lime-rich mud, which planters added to manure as fertilizer—from hillsides. Mining for marl transformed the landscape of the islands as the enslaved excavated vertical layers of earth to restore plantation fields. "Ten mules or horses" driven by ten enslaved men equipped with mattocks to dig out the marl, Martin calculated, could produce "more dung, than sixty able negroes can do in the present methods."[156]

Slaves dug out marl pits from the downward slope of hillocks until they became "caved." After removing the marl, enslaved men piled the material onto cattle carts, "from whence it may be carted into cattle-pens" to be combined with animal manure and, presumably later, with human ordure. Martin estimated from his calculations that a team of slaves "with the assistance of cattle-carts" could provide enough marl for seventy or eighty acres of land. Caving, he judged, would be an "improvement highly worth every planter's consideration, when negroes, and feeding them, are so expensive." In his essay, Martin further recommended that planters direct the enslaved to spread dung across fields using cattle carts or wheelbarrows, and in keeping with his meliorist tone, judged planters who ordered slaves to toil with "dung by baskets, and by spreading it with dung-forks" as unenlightened by the scientific principles of English husbandry.[157] In his observations on marl, Martin displayed the range of his reading by citing the scholarship of the Dutch chemist Herman Boerhaave as an influence on his improving techniques.[158] Unlike their "improving" peers in the Caribbean, slaveholders in the Chesapeake did not experiment with employing slaves at mining for marl until the nineteenth century.[159]

Innovating schemes for maximizing human and animal dung, marl, and cane trash appeared in Caribbean plantation manuals published after Martin's essay. William Belgrove, a planter who read Henry Drax's instructions and likely Martin's essay, advised planters in his 1755 manual to "know to a Certainty the Quantity of Dung you'l require" for a plantation. Drax's 1670 instructions included an entire section devoted to "ways to provid dung every Yeare." Belgrove emphasized that planters recognize dung's crucial role as "the Article upon which the success of a Crop almost intirely depends." Enslaved people, he advised, should routinely collect manure from cattle and mule pens, sheepfolds, and horse stables, and mix piles of animal excreta with the soil of the fields they turned for the "Improvement of the Dung."[160]

Belgrove included examples of calculations in his book for computing precise quantities of dung, using the number of animals in the pens, the square footage of each pen, and the acreage to be planted. He further recommended that planters site "Dung-Heaps most convenient for the Carriage" and, as other meliorist planters wrote in manuals, should not overtax the bodily labor of their slaves. "The want of a sufficient Stock of Cattle and Horses, to make the Dung within due Time," he cautioned, "is attended with many Inconveniences, and a manifest Loss. And I not only recommend a proper Quantity of those, but a sufficient Strength of Negroes; whom I would employ on a Work, which though of much Consequence, has been very little thought of."[161]

Edwin Lascelles, another Barbadian planter, likewise dedicated attention in his manual to the "improvement of dung," cautioning planters to be "accurate in your calculation" of dung produced and applied. Like Martin, Lascelles imagined himself as an ameliorating improver, and he cautioned his slave-holding peers that slaves should not carry more than seventy pounds of dung during a day's work, which "is surely as great a load as any negroe should be made to carry."[162] The work of manuring was not exclusive to adults, as child gangs on sugar plantations also labored at spreading manure.[163] Through their efforts to implement scientific agriculture, enslavers transformed manure into an object of statistical precision to be carefully quantified, and they then used their scientific pretensions as a means to further defend slavery as a humane endeavor.[164]

While small slaveholders in Virginia did not apply scientific agricultural practices involving dunging, large-scale Chesapeake plantations certainly relied upon enslaved men and women to prepare and cover tobacco and wheat fields with manure before the planting season.[165] Walsh and others noted that slaveholders in the Rappahannock and York River basins reserved manure for their tobacco fields.[166]

Landon Carter's diary, for instance, includes more than a hundred entries on dunging. Most of the entries involving manure record the actions of an anonymous "we" manuring the various quarters of his plantation. This rhetorical elision reflects a tendency among Carter and his peers to perceive themselves, not unlike Martin on Antigua, as the mindful center of a plantation operation and to imagine enslaved people to be the purely physical instruments of their will.[167] Entries on dunging in the diary consist of phrases such as "We are still turning the dung," "My turning of dung," "The people have only buryed the dung," "We have heaped our dung," "We have dunged all this field," or "Yesterday they began to bury the dung."[168] However, rather than an idealized collective "we," it was individual enslaved men and women who performed the dirty work of gathering, moving, turning, and preparing dung in livestock pens before piling loads of manure onto cattle carts to be spread across the fields.

A few entries mention by name the enslaved people involved in this labor. In March 1758, for instance, an enslaved man named Harry finished casting a load of dung made from sixty cattle, "very good and larger than common but not in proportion to his number of Cattle," across the Fork Quarter of Carter's estate. Other accounts record how Manuel "began this day to carry manure to" tobacco patches, or toiled at "getting the dung" via ox cart teams "to the Fork new ground." After transporting the manure to the fields, Manuel toiled at "casting dung from this years' cowyard below and when he has done that

that he is to Cast the rest into the last year's dunged ground between the two years' Cow penns which I am in hopes will make all the ground that I tend exceeding rich."[169]

Enslaved women also labored at dunging the fields around Sabine Hall and elsewhere in the upper Chesapeake region.[170] In the summer of 1778, for instance, "Grace and her three hands Yesterday finished Manuring, chopping the dung in, and sowing" rows of corn and turnips.[171] Dirty work like dunging, in the minds of enslavers, was suited for the plantation's African limbs, nerves, and sinews rather than European minds.

Like Martin, Carter's interest in dung extended into the realm of natural philosophy. Carter measured and sketched in his diary what one historian termed a "scientific manure manufactory," capable of producing a precise quantity of dung by calculating the square yardage and livestock necessary for a specific acreage of land.[172] Carter's plans suggest similarities in the interest in and implementation of "improved" dunging through quantification on Chesapeake and Caribbean plantations.

Outside of their labor, enslaved people created their own uses for animal dung in the African diaspora, as a form of medicine. Slaves used dried cow, sheep, and horse dung as materia medica for treating painful colds, and they made teas, ointments, and poultices for wounds using animal waste.[173] Using waste for healing purposes further reflects the intellectual creativity and vitality of people of African descent and their communities and indicates a refusal to submit to being treated as less than fully human.

Nonetheless, dunging and manuring on plantations further linked the enslaved to livestock in both material kinds of labor and in the minds of enslavers who already sought to compare slaves and livestock as equivalent subjects. As Andrew Kettler argues, material and sensory linkages connecting the enslaved and waste, whether on slavers or across plantation fields, furthered a European racist sensorium that contributed to dehumanization.[174] Those comparisons born out of physical, phenomenological experience then reappeared in the documentary archive of slavery, where writing transformed the material reality of plantations into neat, ideal paper representations.

The labor slaveholders extracted from enslaved people and livestock shaped the kinds of paper records, such as inventories, wills, and indentures, that fill slavery's archive.[175] In these forms of paperwork—a framework book historians use to denote the communicative and bureaucratic power of paper documents that circulate through administrative and political economic networks—enslavers possessing plantations made their material and intellectual attempts to render enslaved people and livestock interchangeable.[176] Documentary efforts therefore complemented the material practices of labor, diet, and manuring on plantations, furthering the slaveholder's desire to abstract, dehumanize, and transform the enslaved into living chattel-capital.

Slaveholders in the Chesapeake and the Caribbean listed, enumerated, and evaluated by price the enslaved and the livestock they claimed as their chattel property in probate inventories taken at the death of another slaveholder and in regular inventories kept on estates. In the 1712 probate inventory of Thomas Whitby of York County, Virginia, for instance, his executors listed among his property "2 old horses," an old gray mare and her "Yearling Coult," five cows and five calves, "3 Cows big with Calf," two steers and two bulls, thirty-one "old Sheep," and four "Sick Cows," alongside Jeffrey, Kate, Pegg, and Sarah and Moll, two enslaved girls.[177] These men, women, and children likely labored with these animals, either by feeding them, laboring with them at carting, caring for the animal in pens to collect their waste, or in manuring fields.

Lists of enslaved people and livestock appeared in plantation inventories in the eighteenth century beyond the territorial limits of Britain's Atlantic empire as settlers planted estates within the colonies of other European empires. Enslaved men, women, and children, and livestock animals, for instance, appear in the pages of an account book for Weilburg Plantation, a sugar estate situated on the Demerara River in Dutch Guiana and held by the Scottish slaveholder James Douglas.[178] In his account book, Douglas recorded purchases of sheep, horses, turkeys, "Feather'd Stock," an enslaved boy named Yorrick, and groups of anonymous African captives bought from Atlantic Africa, like the "13 Negroes" purchased by one of his managers in September 1767. Scottish planters who settled in Demerara maintained trade networks with other planters in nearby British colonies, particularly Barbados, Grenada, and Jamaica, and in Dutch Caribbean colonies such as Sint Eustatius. On a page titled "Profit & Loss" from 1769, Douglas listed valuable acquisitions made on behalf of Weilburg that year, including "a Mare named Juno," "a horse named Sampson," "a child named Nancy," two horses named Robin and Peter, two mules named Sangora and Leghorn, and a "negro Man named Moon." Douglas valued each horse at £2, twice as much as Nancy, but not as valuable as Moon, listed at £4 and 6 shillings.[179]

Valuations of enslaved people and livestock are further evident in the wills of slaveholders preserved in colonial archives across the British Atlantic world. Evidence from wills demonstrates how slaves and animals became forms of intergenerational wealth bequeathed by husbands and wives to their children. In the will of Colin Campbell of New Hope plantation in Westmoreland Parish, Jamaica, submitted before a magistrate in February 1761, the enslaver bestowed to his wife, Mary Campbell, a portion of the property he had accrued on the island. Campbell imparted to his wife on his death "twelve Negroes such as she shall chuse" and "two chaise horses, riding horses, sadle and furniture with two riding mules such as she shall chuse."[180] Among the twelve, these people likely labored as postilions, stablemen, or farriers.

In the will of Thomas Jarvis, a magistrate in Antigua whose family held the sugar plantation Popeshead in St. John Parish, the slaveholder bequeathed to his widow, Rachel, his property in cattle, horses, and eight enslaved people in his sworn will in 1786. In his will, Jarvis stipulated that the "issue" of the enslaved women given to his wife—Dinah, Fanny, and Jenny—would become the property of his daughter, Jane.[181]

In the "Valuation of Mount Tirzah Estate" held by Joseph Gardner in Westmoreland Parish, Jamaica, taken by appraisers in 1785, enslaved men and women who toiled with animals are listed, including "Nick, Head Mule Man," Cuba, who managed Gardner's "Fowl House," and Peggie, a "Doctress," who likely cared for both ill enslaved people and animals on the plantation.[182] In a "List of the Negroes on Drax Hall Plantation" in Barbados, made in 1804, there are entries for "Quashey Spencer, Groom," "Bob Horn with the Cattle," "Tullimew in stables," "Venus Horn, Stock keeper," "Margery, Raises Calves," "Providence, at the fowl house," and dozens of other men, women, and children.[183] Sixteen years later, an updated inventory added Quaco and Miah Kitty, both designated as "Cattle Keeper."

Plantation inventories and wills, much like the paperwork of the castle trade in Atlantic Africa, frustrate attempts to gain deeper insight into the interior lives of enslaved men and women as individuals possessing unique lives, minds, and perspectives on the natural world. Slavery's paperwork socially and legally reinforced the commodification of human captives by equating them with livestock and abstracting a life into a single entry in a ledger book, inventory, or will.[184]

Enslavers and their plantation enterprises in both the Caribbean and the Chesapeake transformed enslaved people and animals into vital "nerves" and "sinews" through regimes of labor, nearly identical diets of fodder, and the collection of human and animal waste for manuring. In paper documents, these arrangements can be seen in valuations of human and animal life and in descriptions of enslaved men and women like "Nick, Head Mule Man" or "Margery, Raises Calves." In material and documentary practices, planters sought to fully dispossess the enslaved of their bodily labor and autonomy, as can be seen in discussions among slaveholders of the "increase" and "decrease" of slaves or through wills legally guaranteeing the "issue" of enslaved women.

While environmental differences certainly existed between the Caribbean and the Chesapeake regions, similarities between the two must be considered as the common endeavors among slaveholders for building plantation zones and hierarchies of human and animal life. Slaveholders like Martin and Carter sought to use the enslaved as their extracorporeal limbs and conceived of themselves as minds conducting the efforts of body parts. Enslaved people themselves fully understood that these processes amounted to the complete expropriation of their bodies, as when the man at Bloxburgh encapsulated these interrelated processes by arguing "we flesh belong to buckra, and no more; we bones belong to we self." Bodily dispossession furthered a British racial imaginary and hierarchy that placed people like Hannah, Nick, Margery, and the man at Bloxburgh between fully human whites and livestock animals. And yet, as we will see in chapters 4 and 5, enslaved people in the African diaspora in the Atlantic world resisted the efforts of their enslavers to transform them into tools and commodities akin to chattel livestock by attacking, killing, and stealing animals for their own purposes.

Chapter 4

BY ONE BARBARITY OR ANOTHER

Sabotage, Slave Resistance, and Animals

Kate fled from her enslaver's household in Rock Creek near Georgetown, Maryland, in October 1755.[1] When she absconded from her enslaver is uncertain, yet it is not difficult to imagine that she chose to move out in the night, under the cover of darkness. She evaded the pursuit of Henry Threlkeld, who had purchased her in June from another slaveholder in Anne Arundel County. Kate departed from Rock Creek after being held as Threlkeld's chattel property for five months. In an advertisement published in the *Maryland Gazette,* offering a reward for her capture, Threlkeld reported, "She took with her a small Black Horse, branded on the near Buttock with a large S."

The copy described Kate as a talkative, "pert pallavering" woman, approximately thirty years old, well dressed, and attempting to pass as a free person of color. Kate's rhetorical talent served her well on the road as she spoke to other people of African descent while looking for shelter and new allies to enroll in her cause. She "is a great Rambler," the advertisement continued, and was well known in Anne Arundel and Calvert Counties "besides other Parts of the Country." Kate, it appears, was a well-traveled woman whose familiarity with the western shore of Chesapeake Bay constituted a significant advantage in her bid for self-emancipation. And she had a knack for winning friends and accomplices.

"It is supposed" the newspaper advised readers, that an enslaved man named Jemmy—perhaps her lover or kin—aided Kate in escaping, along with "the Assistance and Contrivance of some other" resourceful enslaved people "in the neighbourhood where she was bought." As Kate moved eastward toward the shoreline of Chesapeake Bay and away from her enslaver living near the Potomac River, she planned her next move.

Learning to follow the routes and decisions that Kate and other enslaved people who lived and labored with livestock animals like the black horse mentioned in the advertisement affords historians a deeper understanding of the rival geographies that enslaved communities mapped, produced, and recreated through their fugitivity. Stephanie M. H. Camp has broadened Edward Said's concept of rival geographies to articulate "alternative ways of knowing and using plantation and southern space that conflicted with planter's ideals and demands."[2] The final two chapters of this book examine two modes of slave resistance that enslaved communities in eighteenth-century British America and the early United States pursued with regard to animals and their unique knowledge of the physical environment, through the conceptual lens of rival geographies.

This chapter looks at evidence of community-wide sabotage on the plantation quarters surrounding Sabine Hall, the manorial home of Landon Carter in Richmond County, Virginia. Carter is a well-studied figure, and scholars owe a debt to Jack P. Greene and Rhys Isaac for their foundational scholarship on this settler-slaveholder and his patriarchal mentality.[3] However, my aim is to understand how enslaved people like Manuel and his wife, Sarah—as well as their neighbors Kit, Sukey, Sicely, Tom, and others—attacked and maimed plantation livestock by exploiting the physical environment, including ditches and waterlogged fields, to produce their own destructive rival geography and undermine their enslaver. Manuel saw ravines and gullies made after rains as productive spaces to assert his own autonomy by reducing his slaveholder's property. Injuring, starving, and killing animal chattels with clandestine techniques and local environmental knowledge constituted a powerful tactic of sabotage by which enslaved people critically interrupted the flow, timing, and productivity of their enslavers' plantations.[4]

Chapter 5, the second in this connected pair, follows Kate and like-minded enslaved men and women who stole horses to escape plantations in and between British American colonies from Maryland to Jamaica. Black riders in British North America unseated and emasculated their enslavers by stealing their horses and riding far beyond the boundaries of their estates to rejoin family, friends, and lovers. Scholars have plumbed runaway advertisements produced in colonial America and circulated through newspapers as an exceptionally rich archive of African American and diasporic African intellectual history.[5] Fugitive riders exploited equine mobility to produce rival geographies that linked roads, paths, waterways, plantations, and towns between enslaved and maroon communities, and as tools for reuniting families and kin and reestablishing romantic partnerships. These two chapters are interlinked by their reliance on Camp's theorization of the production of space by enslaved people for the pursuit of their own liberation against the projected power of their slaveholders.

Forms of material environmental sabotage and theft involving settler fauna joined intellectual critiques of slavery, and the through-line of this chapter and my focus on these two modes of resistance is the sheer creativity and resilience of enslaved communities in British America who resisted and unsettled their enslavers by targeting their animals. Well before the 1808 letter in which "A Slave," whom we shall meet in the book's epilogue, leveled against Thomas Jefferson the assertion that slaveholders treated and perceived people of African descent as possessing "a face somewhat resembling the human, but clearly not a human being," women and men like Sukey and Manuel challenged the fundamentally dehumanizing and animalizing logic of slavery by actively selecting animal targets to kill and steal for their own purposes.[6] Their decisions reflect their undeniable humanity and human intelligence. People of African descent in British America understood and contested the foundations and boundaries of their enslavement in the eighteenth century by selecting animals as an important arena for resistance. We can see these choices in action, for instance, on the plantations surrounding Sabine Hall in Virginia's Northern Neck peninsula.

Manuel waited patiently through several days of rain, until one morning in May 1766. When he looked out across muddy, waterlogged fields of wheat and corn, he saw opportunities to use the wet earth as a weapon against his enslaver. Manuel labored as an enslaved plowman with teams of cattle and oxen every planting and harvest season. Alongside his animal teams, Manuel plowed rows of dirt before others planted seedlings. Later in the season, he spent time manuring fields, then carting stalks and bales of tobacco and wheat to barns, and later transporting hogsheads of agricultural commodities loaded into barrels to be shipped to markets in the service of his slaveholder in Richmond County. Through his labor on the tobacco and wheat plantations of his enslaver, Manuel's everyday life became bound up with animals. His enslaver depended on Manuel's skill at training livestock animals to work. Manuel understood how regimes of human–animal labor on the plantation existed as the foundation for his enslaver's future profits and efforts to ensure the generational wealth of his descendants.

With this in mind, Manuel over time came to envision using the same productive landscape and faunal assemblages within and alongside which he labored and turn it to a different use than the extractive and violent political economy of the plantation zone. His own vision for using terrain and interfering with the animals of his enslaver successfully reimagined the topography of the estate—along with changes in weather, as the seasons turned—as a new space to undermine the slaveholder by starving, injuring, and killing his animal property. Considered this way, Manuel's thoughts and actions represent a Black subaltern environmental consciousness emerging from the Tidewater Chesapeake.

"I find," wrote the slaveholder in his diary that spring, "that it is not so much the obstinacy of my steers that won't break to drawing kindly as the Villainy of Manuel concerned." When the fields of his enslaver's estates, spread throughout the Northern Neck, became drenched from rain, Manuel "took up and turned out" one of his enslaver's steers while breaking them in to plantation labor, "because he would not work." When an ox strayed, and perhaps when Manuel sensed its hooves begin to slip or saw its legs start to buckle, he watched the creature fall hard into the muck without attempting to prevent its collapse. As the ox suffered on the ground, unable to regain its footing, the cattleman watched and did nothing. Even after he or the animal eventually climbed upright, Manuel continued to aggravate its injuries by refusing it rest, leaving it limping and "on the lift ever since." Most importantly, in later reporting the incident to the slaveholder after returning from the fields, Manuel narrated the events as an accident, and described them in a way that made it impossible for his slaveholder to prove his suspicions that the cattleman intended to use the ox's body as a target to indirectly attack his enslaver.[7]

Four years later, the slaveholder, Landon Carter, described how in March 1770 several other enslaved plowmen on his plantations—perhaps emboldened by Manuel's tactics and success—joined in the attack against these living agricultural machines.[8] "The cattle that have died this year" he listed, "are 8 in Lawson's penn, 5 in Dolmon's, and 2 steers" due to injuries caused by enslaved plowmen led by Manuel and another man, Kit.[9] In the spring the planter ordered the two men to drive the livestock to pasture at his Fork Quarter plantation "to be raised where they had plenty of food." Rather than obey their enslaver, the two men "drove them through the same marsh in the Corn field where each mired and died" after heavy rains. Manuel and Kit drew upon their knowledge of the hazards that the temporarily terraqueous landscape of marshy fields posed to mutilate the animals.

The following week, Carter observed that one of his draft oxen had broken its neck and died because of Manuel's carelessness. He "fed the Creature and then turned him out of the Cowyard," whereupon the animal fell into a ditch "and so brike his neck." Perhaps Manuel watched the animal stray, fall, and perish in the shallow ravine. "This is the third draught Steer," the slaveholder lamented, "put to a violent death by that cursed villain." After another ox died, Manuel defended himself by arguing that he simply intended to drive the animal to pasture via a "short cut," an explanation that emphasized his own attempts to be efficient in his labors. In the following weeks, Manuel continued to steer his enslaver's cattle and oxen into ditches, marshes, and other mundane yet deadly terrain to increase their chances of being critically injured or killed. In addition to his sense of the plantation's most dangerous contours, Manuel and others consciously exploited rain, sleet, and occasionally snow to "effect a great destruction amongst Creatures of all kinds."[10]

Manuel's enslaver penned his longest entry to date on the cattleman's sabotage in April 1770. "Mr. Manuel has at last compleated every scheme that he might have in hand to ruin me. Before this winter came in I was possessed of 8 oxen, 4 of them well used to the draft and 4 newly broke. In a little time he contrived that 3 of them should mire and die only because he would not see 4 of them when spelled drove to the fork to be rested along the road over the dam but suffered a rascally boy to drive them over the marsh where they mired. The other he contrived to lame." In addition, the enslaver "allowed 2 bushels of ears besides fodder" to feed his draft horses, yet "Manuel consigned two of those horses to death" by withholding their food and starving them, "and so he has continued behaving till last week when I wanted to Cart out my dung I had neither horses nor Oxen to carry a loa[d]."

As Manuel further developed his strategy, he encouraged his wife Sarah, "the Cowkeeper" who oversaw and labored with livestock in one of the plantation's cowpens, to surreptitiously let the cattle out of their pen to roam freely. Sarah weaponized this neglect, as the straying cattle mindlessly crushed tobacco hills and wheat plants under their hooves. Upon learning of the strays, the enslaver ordered Manuel and two other men to retrieve the animals. Walking slowly out into the fields, the men performed a kind of careful carelessness as they searched for the cattle, and later reported that they failed to retrieve the strays.

Repeated attacks on his livestock property rattled the slaveholder, and he decided to sell Manuel in the spring of 1770. "He was once a valuable fellow," he complained in his diary. However, Manuel's subversion became untenable. The slaveholder explained to himself how Manuel's assaults spread beyond maiming the animals. The cattleman turned "thief as before killed beef which was found upon him"—presumably intending to share the stolen meat with his wife, kin, and neighbors—and repeatedly injured and killed animals by steering them to their death in ditches, including some "20 or 30 horses and as many draught oxen." Nearly sixty livestock animals represented a significant amount of valuable living capital. "By one barbarity or another he has certainly killed these Creatures as ever he has been concerned with them and now I will part with him."[11]

Despite this pattern of sabotage, the enslaver's private complaints, and the very real and humiliating scores of dead livestock littered throughout the plantation margins, the slaveholder faltered and reconsidered his plans. Ultimately, the enslaver depended on Manuel's skilled labor and experience as a driver each season to break in new animals to labor at the plow. Carter resented his dependence on people of African descent, but after ruminating on the matter he abandoned his plans and Manuel remained on the plantation.

As spring turned to summer, Manuel and others stepped up their attacks on the livestock with which they labored in the fields. In July 1770, their enslaver wrote in his diary that several "plowmen unmercifull," led by Manuel's example, had clandestinely attacked teams of oxen on the plantations.[12] In addition, the men turned to a new set of animal targets, horses, to either expand their own mobility or use as outlets for their aggression. The enslaver noted, "If I get horses, than they are rode out in the nights by the negroes." It is possible Manuel and others used the horses at night to visit family, friends, and even lovers under the cover of darkness. Or it is possible that the men just found pleasure and a sense of power in riding horses beyond the surveillance of the enslaver and his overseers. Later that month, Manuel struck out at his enslaver again by driving another team of oxen and the cart they pulled, which was loaded with tobacco, into another ditch. "Manuel a Villain," the planter seethed, "and must be whipped."[13]

Less than a year after this episode, in 1771, Manuel managed to succeed at destroying another ox at his enslaver's Fork Quarter estate. He killed the bullock in part "for want of care" by starving it of its usual rations of corn, knowing that hunger would weaken the ox, and then forced the animal to fall, crush its legs, and perish into a muddy ditch while driving it across a landscape he knew to be dangerous. Manuel's attacks exhausted and confounded the slaveholder: "He first kills them," he wrote, "and then turns them there to be [found?]."[14] Manuel's brazenness in leaving the animals to die and later be discovered indicates his growing awareness of both the material and psychological dimensions of his attacks. Yet the slaveholder either could never definitively prove that Manuel intended to kill the animals, even as he left his bovine victims to rot in the mud, or simply could not commit to selling the cattleman because he relied on the man's otherwise normal and productive labor and skill on the estate. Each time Manuel destroyed livestock—each one being a portion of his enslaver's bovine wealth or equine sources of muscular energy, vital waste in the form of manure, and mobility—Carter punished him by ordering a whipping or beating by an overseer, and occasionally resorted to binding Manuel in irons and placing him in solitary confinement. However, Manuel survived each punishment and persisted in undermining his enslaver by maiming or killing his animals when such opportunities existed.[15]

While Manuel and other plowmen's particularly violent strategy of attacking animals was less common than other forms of resistance, their schemes to harm livestock were by no means exceptional in the environs surrounding Sabine Hall. Johnny, another enslaved man, who labored in the plantation's sheepfolds, ignored lambs and calves as they roamed beyond their pens, until they died from injuries or starvation. Like Manuel and Kit, Johnny also took advantage of environmental conditions to camouflage his attacks and blamed animal deaths on cold weather.[16]

Others starved animals by withholding or stealing their food, usually bushels of corn fodder or other grains, to slowly weaken their health, fatigue their bodies, and leave them injury prone. Jack, an enslaved man on the Fork Quarter, killed several livestock animals through starvation while enslaved on Carter's plantations. In the spring of 1766, Jack notified his enslaver that "his Corn was all gone" and requested more from the granary reserves to feed the animals under his care. The slaveholder suspected that Jack stole the forty bushels of corn he dispensed for the livestock and redistributed the corn to his kin or neighbors, as "He pretends the Cattle and sheep eat it," yet "He has but 6 calves and 15 lambs. 5 cattle have died 92 lambs and 2 oxen which was all he had."[17]

In 1770, Carter learned that one of his overseers had recently "found some shelled Corn as well as eared Corn" for feeding livestock hidden away in Manuel's quarters. Manuel's subterfuge "made good my suspicions either of not giving all the Corn he was allowed to the Oxen he drove to the horses or else has robbed me of Corn. . . . I thought it to be impossible," the enslaver wrote, "that those Creatures should look so poor when they had all along been so well fed."[18]

Enslaved people used the further pretext of ignoring roaming livestock to destroy tobacco plants and wheat stalks, and their strategies proved difficult to detect and successful at undermining their enslaver's sense of control over the landscape and his chattel property. Sicely, an enslaved woman who labored as a "cowkeeper," frequently neglected the livestock she was charged with supervising. On one occasion she "let a cow go into the mire below the Barn swamp where she perished."[19] Perhaps Manuel encouraged Sicely and others through networks of exchange, gossip, and information to try out his tactics for producing a rival geography within the plantation workscape. Another enslaved man, Jesse, whom his enslaver described in his diary as "a most vile dog," neglected the herd of pigs under his charge, with great effect. On multiple occasions Jesse was "never to be found with his hogs and they are finding out ways to get into the Corn field" and devour the crop.[20]

In an entry from 1771, Carter rode out on horseback to endeavor "if I could to find out the care of my sheep." At the time, flocks of sheep around the plantation farms had begun dying in alarming numbers. After conversing with his overseers, among whom were English and Irish servants he also seldom trusted, Carter determined that the sheep had died as a result of covert attacks carried out by the enslaved, who "may pretend they fed them, but I cannot believe them." He learned, for instance, how Rose, an enslaved woman tasked with shelling corn to feed livestock, "did not care to give it to the sheep. So it is, I dare say, every where." Another enslaved man, Tom, ignored the lambs and sheep the slaveholder tasked him with watching. After several animals died from starvation and exposure, Carter punished Tom by confining him in irons and ordering an overseer to whip him. Despite Tom's punishment, the enslaved community continued to starve other animals, and further eroded their enslaver's sense of control over the enslaved subjects he imagined ruling as their patriarch. At the Fork Quarter, George, Johnny, and a "stout Girl" starved lambs, ewes, and yearling calves and used the pretext of "excessive wetness" to injure animals as they pastured.[21]

Sukey, an elderly woman who labored in a cowpen, exacted retribution against their enslaver for denying her time to visit with her granddaughter, and in protest for him not providing her grandchildren with enough food, by ignoring animals on the plantation. Like Manuel, Sicely, and Jesse, Sukey used neglect and her own knowledge of the cattle's tendency to roam to alter the plantation landscape and damage crops. She "turned out all my Cattle" one night, wrote the enslaver, "on my Cowpen ground which have done me a prodigeous mischief" by crushing several fields of wheat, tobacco, and corn and by straying away. Sukey's actions inspired others to attempt similar forms of resistance camouflaged as carelessness, which resulted in either dead animals or trampled plants. Attacks on animals by the enslaved through neglect were frequently timed with seasonal changes in weather. During the winter of 1770, enslaved people ignored calves and cattle during a snowstorm, and later used the hazardous terrain created by snowfall to kill stray animals as they roamed beyond their pens.[22]

The enslaved community surrounding Sabine Hall further exploited ambiguous incidents involving animal deaths that appeared coincidental to further their own aims as a community. Upon hearing that a "young bull killed one steer and lamed another yesterday," their enslaver learned how the enslaved later ate one of the dead steers.[23] Suspicious that the animal's death resulted from a clandestine plot, the slaveholder worried that the episode was actually a coordinated "contrivance" staged by the enslaved for their own nutritional benefit. If so, their plan had the double effect of denying their enslaver a laboring draft animal and providing the enslaved community with portions of protein-rich meat, allowing the slaves an opportunity to narrow the caloric gap between white and Black people that slaveholders actively created in southeastern America.[24]

Enslaved people in the eighteenth-century British Caribbean also attacked plantation livestock as a method of subverting their enslavers as well as defying the legal regimes of island colonies. Since 1749, Jamaican law had criminalized "the clandestine killing and marking of cattle" on the island by either free Black hunters or enslaved Africans.[25] In 1760, the House of Assembly passed stricter legislation to severely limit enslaved people's ability to possess or exchange livestock or own horses. On Antigua, one planter complained of having "lost several working Cattle last Crop, some of them owing to the Devilish disposition" of the enslaved, who used overwork and exhaustion to injure and kill the animals.[26]

Through extensive research involving the legal records for St. Andrew and other parishes on the island, Diana Paton has illuminated how, in addition to overworking animals, enslaved people illicitly stole sheep, goats, cattle, hogs, and fowl to sell in underground markets throughout Jamaica.[27] Overseer diaries, too, afford further insight into enslaved sabotage involving animals in Jamaica. In 1765, enslaved people on Egypt, a sugar estate in Westmoreland Parish, killed cattle, raided the fowl house, and let cattle roam in cane fields to destroy sugar plants as targeted acts of resistance.[28] These attacks combined the tactics of killing, stealing, and neglecting livestock and reflect the shared knowledge of plantation saboteurs who held secret conversations—perhaps spoken in whispers, hinted at through gesture, or camouflaged in coded language—beyond earshot of overseers. Moreover, the accumulated knowledge of sabotage spread as people learned from each other via observation.

Slave tactics for targeting livestock to abuse and kill in the Caribbean existed in ways that were quite like those in Virginia. In a 1786 letter to an absentee planter in England, John Fowler, an estate manager residing on the Martha Brae River in Trelawny Parish, Jamaica, reported that an "Overseer, who seems a well Informed Experienced man has represented, that a Spell of Mules are wanted" on the plantation under his care. The manager suspected that the overseer's request resulted from "the Negroes of Working Old Mules overmuch," leading to their subsequent injury and death.[29] While the letter is silent on the nature of this overwork, it's likely that men and women on this estate used uneven and hazardous terrain, starvation, and aggressive driving techniques to push these mules over the brink.

Enslaved people's attacks on livestock also could be marshaled to reverse slaveholders' decisions to sell them away from their communities. In 1791, Thomas Jarvis in St. George Parish, Antigua, sold an elderly enslaved man, Fusso, to another enslaver, William Gunthorpe. In a letter to Gunthorpe, Jarvis described Fusso as "a civil, quiet fellow, and has ever been constant and attentive to business." After speaking with a plantation doctor employed by Gunthorpe, however, Jarvis learned, to his surprise, that the doctor "thought your Cattle had been injured for want of Fusso." Again, the letter does not explicitly state the nature of Fusso's tactics, but it is possible he either overworked or ignored the cattle as they became injured. Jarvis wrote to Gunthorpe that he could not fathom "the Idea suggested of your Cattle being injured" by Fusso.[30]

It may be that Fusso intentionally mistreated the animals, either in the hope of being returned to Jarvis or to intimidate his new enslaver and his overseer. Whether by directly attacking animals or by using countercolonial environmental knowledge to abuse their bodies, enslaved people like Fusso consciously decided to target livestock as a means of undermining their own exploitation and dehumanization at the hands of their enslavers. Such conscious decisions further highlight how enslaved people thought about animals, including stealing animals, to articulate their own humanity.

Enslaved men on the plantations surrounding Sabine Hall stole horses for their own purposes as well, especially for increasing their personal mobility and autonomy. Several of the men Landon Carter held as his chattel property and relied upon as agricultural laborers used their enslaver's horses during the night as their own living machines to ride and move among plantation spaces. In an entry from 1771, the planter wrote, "Peter the plowman, a night Walker, really sick. I have discovered he rides my plow horses in the night."[31] Whether Peter rode the horses he labored alongside during the day at night to meet with other enslaved men and women under the moonlight or for his own enjoyment and pleasure is unclear. However, his defiance encouraged others living around Sabine Hall to follow suit.

Around the same time as Peter's night rides, Carter discovered that another man, Pater, appeared during a day's work in 1771 drowsy and lethargic due to night riding. "I must suppose," the planter suspected, "that he was out all night upon one of my cart horses."[32] Other references to night riding appear in similarly opaque entries. Peter, along with another man, Tom, stole their enslaver's horses for night riding on multiple occasions. Late one evening in 1775, Carter's son-in-law, Reuben Beale, "catched Mulatto Peter on the gray Colt Parker rides and Johny's son on the Rippon Hall horse."[33] Carter ordered Tom to be whipped and Peter to be "curiously handled." Peter's precise punishment is unclear, given the absense of description in the diary; however, it is possible that it involved some form of torture. The following year, Carter's grandson caught another man, Johnny, "night riding a horse," and despite being earlier "locked up and tied neck and heels with his hands behind him, was broke out and has not been seen or heard since."[34]

Night riding, like other forms of resistance with animals in the Tidewater Chesapeake, involved enslaved people's use of countercolonial environmental knowledge and rival geographies. The actions taken by fugitive Black riders, however, were not exceptional or limited to the men held by Landon Carter in Richmond County. Between 1730 and 1791, slaveholders in Britain's American colonies and the early republic of the United States paid for approximately one hundred advertisements in newspapers from Maryland to Jamaica offering rewards for the arrest of enslaved men and women who, like Kate, whose escape on a black horse began this chapter, stole horses and rode away.

After finding Jemmy, who "secreted" her, Kate hid out near a plantation in West River. Kate "bragg'd" to so many people about her flight that her enslaver, Threlkeld, was confident her friends and kin in Anne Arundel County "promised to conceal her whenever she would run away from me." We cannot know whether she kept the black horse branded with an S with her, sold or traded the animal, or simply abandoned it on the way to West River. However, in chapter 5, I will interpret her decision to steal the animal as a strategic and intellectual one that reflected her own rival geography and critique of slavery.

Chapter 5

SHE HAS BRAGG'D

Fugitives, Animals, and the Limits of Slavery

When fugitive diasporic African and African American men and women took the reins from their enslavers, they mounted a real challenge to the cultural, political, and envirotechnical foundations of slavery in British America, and later the United States, on three fronts. First, Black equestrians struck out at the intellectual justifications of slavery, including racist arguments defending the enslavement of Africans on the grounds of being intellectually inferior and naturally suited for plantation labor. For instance, Reverend Hugh Jones, who served as chaplain for the House of Burgesses in Virginia and later as a parish minister in Maryland's Charles and Cecil Counties, elaborated in print the racist argument that Africans were "of a more servile Carriage, and slavish Temper" and "by Nature cut out for hard Labour and Fatigue."[1] Unruly women like Kate upended the belief that they were either "servile" or "cut out" for slavery when they climbed into the saddle of their enslavers' horses.

Black riders additionally undermined an aristocratic human–animal ideology that made up a significant aspect of Britain's imperial identity in the early modern world. Britons throughout the empire saw themselves as assimilating, improving, and disciplining foreign subjects, including people and animals, through their colonial and imperial ventures. Donna Landry explains that beginning in the late sixteenth century, English elites articulated a set of cultural values around mastering Arabian horses to demonstrate their ability to tame the natural world and distant cultures. Disciplining and overpowering "bloody shouldered" Arabians demonstrated the capacity of English elites to bend non-human nature to their will.[2] Women and men like Kate physically enacted a counterpoint to this human–animal imperial ideology.

Perhaps the most important lens for understanding the meaning of Kate's decisions lies in seeing how Africans and African Americans threatened a form of English masculinity that was bound up with equestrianism. Horsemanship bound together in a rider and their horse the ideals of bodily autonomy, kinesthetic mastery, and manly stature, and an imagined sovereignty over the natural world. Monica Mattfeld places this male "centauric" identity squarely at the center of English conceptions of liberty and empire in the early modern world.[3] The analysis presented here, of newspaper advertisements as evidence of human–animal relationships, adds to a growing scholarly conversation at the intersection of histories of slavery and equine history, developed by historians and geographers such as Katherine C. Mooney, Charlotte Carrington-Farmer, and David Lambert.[4] Kate and her peers, who labored on the ground as their enslavers rode high, recognized this gendered human–animal relationship for what it was and decided to reverse it while traveling on horses.

Slaveholders in British America put horse–human values into action when they rode out on horseback across their estates and used the animal's speed, bulk, and verticality to intimidate and surveil enslaved people laboring on the ground. In the Caribbean, planters and overseers further used horses to hunt and recapture people engaged in *marronage* (escaping from slavery) or living in remote mountain or forest hideouts. Richard Ligon's 1657 map of Barbados, for instance, depicts a white man on horseback pursuing two enslaved people on foot, firing his gun directly toward them.[5] Slaveholders further linked their dominance over horses and enslaved people through the physical practice of branding.[6] Moreover, as slave patrols on horseback began to proliferate, overseers and other white servants policed the boundaries of the plantation South in the service of slavery as a social and economic institution.[7]

In addition to the cultural valences of equestrianism, people of African descent took advantage of their temporary equine transportation to renew and restore bonds of family and extended kinship. Enslaved men stole horses to reunite with their wives, fathers and mothers, and other family members throughout British America. In the spring of 1732, Owen, a man enslaved on a plantation near Goose Creek, South Carolina, rode away from his enslaver on a "bay colour'd Horse, which had a white Ring about his Neck." In an advertisement printed in the *South-Carolina Gazette*, the slaveholder explained that Owen would likely travel to his wife, who was enslaved on another estate in the colony.[8] Cuffee similarly escaped a plantation in Annapolis in 1749 with the assistance of "a small Bay Mare." Cuffee stole away with "a broad cloth Coat with broad metal Buttons, dark colour'd German Serge Breeches with metal buttons, an Irish Linnen Shirt, a white Cap, and an old Beaver Hat." Robert Swan, his enslaver, added in the *Maryland Gazette* that Cuffee likely traveled south-west toward Piscataway in Prince George's County, "where he has a Wife."[9]

Many enslaved people used horses to significantly increase the range of their own bodily mobility. Peter, described as being "between a mulato and mustee [of Afro-Indigenous descent]," escaped from his enslaver in South Carolina in 1749 by taking a "young red roan gelding of great spirit, about 13 hands high, 5 years old next spring, with a blaze in his face, a roman nose, a short tail, and 3 white feet, and branded on the mounting buttock K."[10] Peter used the animal's speed to substantially increase his ability to flee, in partic-ular because he lived with a disability, probably the result of dangerous labor or a violent punishment. Peter's enslaver described him as being "remarkable for limping, his right thigh having been broke near two years since." Slavery, as Stefanie Hunt-Kennedy has shown, produced both physical disfigurement and the social category of disability itself, as advertisements like this one rep-resented people of African descent as deformed bodies to be policed and de-tected by identifiable impairments.[11]

After escaping the plantation, Peter was betrayed by another enslaved man, who informed their enslaver that Peter "supposed he will proceed alone, ei-ther to some of the Indian nations, Georgia, St. Augustine, or the Northward." The slaveholder suspected that Peter might seek refuge near Santee, where his wife lived; Pedee, where he might find friends and allies; or further, to the western edge of the Lowcountry, at Four Holes, Saluda, or New Windsor.[12] The spirited gelding afforded Peter significant locomotive range to move across the towns, creeks, and plantation landscapes of the colony. It is also possible, as the advertisement speculated, that Peter fled to St. Augustine, knowing his chances for freedom would be greater in free Black settlements in the northern borderlands of New Spain, such as Gracia Real de Santa Teresa de Mosé.[13] Peter would have approached Indigenous towns cautiously, as the co-lonial government frequently hired fighters and trackers among the Catawba Nation to recapture maroons.[14]

In the spring of 1755, Cain, a man formerly held as chattel property and serving as a coachman for his slaveholder, fled the town of Brandon in Prince George County, Virginia. His enslaver, Colonel Nathaniel Harrison, described Cain as a tall, elderly, "smooth-tongued Fellow," known for his guile. Cain traveled south in pursuit of a woman "belonging to Major Thomas Hall" whom he "used to visit as a Wife." An advertisement submitted in the *Virginia Ga-zette* said, "He took with him a dark-grey Mare, low in Flesh, paces well, and branded on the Buttock and Shoulder, but can't remember the Brand." In addition, Cain had pilfered a fine "Country-made Saddle with Leather Housing," a pair of boots, a dark riding coat, a new white jacket, "Breeches, Oznabrig Shirts, and Plenty of other Apparel."[15] Perhaps Cain had worked with this mare through his labors as a coachman and his theft reflected plans he had conceived of well before he stole the horse.

Cain's sartorial choices and literal self-fashioning raise the question about the extent to which fugitives on horseback used clothing to elude their captors. An advertisement from 1738 mentioned that Bellfast, standing "pretty tall, . . . had on a blue Coat, the Sleeves turned up with Black" and rode "a young grey Horse, branded upon the buttock" as he traveled along the Wassamassaw Road. Along with the horse, Bellfast stole a "Trunk with Women's Apparel" from his enslaver at Silk Hope in Berkeley County.[16] It's possible that Bellfast intended to use the clothes as a disguise, rendering them one more tactic for evading pursuers in his journey away from his enslaver on the Cooper River.

Advertisements involving fugitive women stealing horses appeared with less frequency in colonial newspapers in the British Atlantic. However, several records document how women disrupted horse–human relations under slavery to increase their own mobility. An Igbo woman in St. Andrew Parish, Jamaica, for instance, stole a "young bay horse" while running away in the spring of 1730. A penkeeper in Liguanea caught the woman and the horse and advertised her arrest in the *Weekly Jamaica Courant* in June. The advertisement stated that whoever could "prove their just right, and describe her marks" could claim the woman and the animal from their captor.[17]

In October 1734, Flora, an enslaved woman on James Island, South Carolina—one of the Sea Islands between the Santee and St. Johns Rivers—fled from her enslaver's estate with a horse. The slaveholder described Flora's body in his advertisement in the *South-Carolina Gazette*, including the scar on her forehead, and reported that she had been seen recently around Charleston. He added that as she escaped she stole from a neighbor's stable "a Horse marked EP on the mounting shoulder." The horse could be recognized by its "lost one eye, a star in his face, with some white running from it toward his nose," and its black-and-chestnut-colored coat. Flora's enslaver offered a reward of £3 for whoever captured her, and thirty shillings for the horse.[18]

Hagar fled from her enslaver, a house and ship painter in Charleston, who advised readers in 1735 that she might travel south on horseback to Johns Island or further west to the Edisto River. Dressed in a "blue negro cloth gown,"

Hagar escaped mounted on "a black horse about 13 hands high, branded on the mounting shoulder DB, and on the off buttock EI." Hagar's enslaver offered the same reward for whoever apprehended her or the horse: £4.[19]

The decisions of the Igbo woman, Flora, and Hagar to steal horses amounted to a significant gendered critique of an ideology that situated horsemanship as the exclusive province of free, white European men. Astride their horses, these women visibly challenged white beliefs about the proper place of Black women in white settler society by using their bodies and by instantiating their own subversive relationships with animals.

Accounts of men and women escaping together using equines also appear in the archives of runaway advertisements. Andrew and Moll, who may have been romantic partners, friends, or siblings, stole a horse together as they departed from their enslaver's plantation on the Ashley River in South Carolina in 1751. In his advertisement alerting his neighbors of their flight, the slaveholder described Andrew, age forty, as speaking "indifferent English," and Moll, age thirty, as a dissembling, persuasive woman possessing "a most artful knack of framing and delivering a story" and adept in deception. Perhaps it was Moll who convinced Andrew to steal the slaveholder's horse. Their enslaver valued Moll the most, and he posted a reward of £3 for whoever returned her to his plantation, while only forty shillings each for whoever recaptured Andrew or the horse.[20]

Numerous runaway advertisements hint at the existence of far-reaching networks of support among enslaved people in the southeastern colonies of British America. In October 1739, three enslaved men—England, Prosper, and Prince—ran away together from their enslaver's plantation in Goose Creek. The advertisement described England as an older man and a bricklayer and added that his sons, Prosper and Prince, were both "young Mustee" men. Prince escaped with an "Iron round one Leg" and "took with him out of the Stable, a large Bay natural pacing Stallion" branded *IW* on the mounting shoulder. "It is supposed" that the men hid out near Dorchester.[21] Of the three, Prince most likely exploited the mobility of the horse, since he was weighed down by the restraints placed on his leg. Moreover, given that England's sons were African-Indigenous, perhaps the three found sanctuary among multiethnic maroon settlements or camps throughout the colony.[22] Another advertisement from 1755 mentions Toby, "a likely mustee fellow" and a carpenter and cooper by training, who escaped from his enslaver on the Ponpon or Edisto River, on horseback.[23]

In 1757, a slaveholder in Charleston placed an advertisement for two men,

Will and Harry, who escaped his plantation and took "with them an old saddle and 2 bridles, also 2 horses, one a pretty large dark gelding, with a switch tail, paces slow, and branded on the buttock BLP in one; the other a small likely bay mare, with a switch tail, paces slow."[24] Perhaps due to exposure to the harsh winters of the late Little Ice Age, or some brutal form of torture or punishment, Will had "lost all his toes on one foot."[25] Will's disability might indicate why he persuaded Harry to join him and assist him in stealing the horses and fleeing South Carolina.

Horsepower, particularly the speed the animal's bodies provided, could potentially counter some of the surveillance of enslavers who detailed in print disabilities like Will's disfigured foot or other disfigurements that did not directly impede an individual's mobility, such as facial scars. Jesse, for instance, used a "full-blooded, dark sorrel stud, with a large blaze down his face" to quickly escape from his enslaver at Stony Creek in Orange County, North Carolina. The enslaver broadcast that Jesse could be identified by "his face much scarified by a burn" and by burn scars on his hand.[26]

Another slaveholder, living near Rock Creek, Maryland, announced in the *Maryland Gazette* in September 1760 that "a likely well-made Mulatto Fellow" named Tom had fled his enslaver's estate with the aid of his own human–animal network. In his flight, Tom purloined a "Check Shirt, and Cotton Jacket and Breeches" and a "black horse about 14 Hands high, branded very plain on the off Thigh CF." Like Kate, perhaps Tom envisioned that the animal's coloring would provide a valuable camouflage at night. Anthony Holmead, the slaveholder, mentioned that Tom "has some Accomplices, and may possibly change his Name, and endeavour to pass for a Freeman."[27] Two brothers, Peter and Joe, fled their enslaver's plantation in Amelia Township, South Carolina, on the southern banks of the Congaree River, in November 1762. An advertisement in the *South Carolina Gazette* described the men as skilled tradesmen—valuable for their craft as "shoe-makers, tanners, sawyers and jobing carpenters"—and for being "remarkably sensible." In addition to the clothes they carried, Peter and Joe "took with them two black horses" as they departed.[28]

Comparatively few people characterized as mulatto appear in advertisements mentioning horse theft, other than those labeled as either diasporic or creole Africans or as mustee. Rente, a twenty-year-old man described as a "young likely mulatto fellow," fled from his enslaver on the Stono River while wearing a "red pea jacket" and breeches, and took with him "a horse." Rente's enslaver included a standard warning against those "masters of vessels" who may harbor Rente as he navigated the Lowcountry's aquatic waterscape of creeks, rivers, and islands.[29]

Branding and the ubiquity of brands on enslaved people's bodies and the bodies of horses limited the use of camouflage tactics among fugitive riders. Whenever possible, slaves chose horses without brands, specifically for their relative anonymity; however, the animals could still be identified by their color, breed, height, and other features. Caesar picked out "a brown bay Horse, unbranded, with a Glass Eye and a Blaze" mark on its face as he stole himself away from his enslaver's estate on the Stono River.[30] Caesar's own body was unbranded, but he would have witnessed enslaved people and horses in the Carolina Lowcountry being sold with brands, often bearing the initials of their enslaver or a slave trader, and likely would have considered the advantages of the animal's unmarked body as he escaped.

Multiethnic collaborations between people of African descent and white servants to undermine slaveholders and landed elites rarely occurred in British America. However, at least one advertisement involving horse theft points toward the oftentimes fleeting alliances made between enslaved people and indentured servants. In 1768, a planter from Loudoun County, Virginia, posted an advertisement in the *Maryland Gazette* for the capture of an "English Convict Servant" and an enslaved man named Jack. The slaveholder mentioned that Jack "lost the greatest Part of his Toes with the Frost" and was a "brisk lively Fellow." Jack and the anonymous English servant "stole out of my Stable, Two Horses, one a bay, about 14 Hands high, shod before, has a Star in his Forehead, hanging Mane and Switch Tail, Brand not known; the other a large sorrel Horse, shod all round, has a Star in his Forehead, and goes well" and a "small grey Horse." The planter concluded that the servant might have "black'd themselves, as there was some Coal and Tallow found in a Kettle of theirs."[31]

Advertisements mentioning groups of enslaved people stealing a single horse raise the question of how fugitives used equine mobility in tandem with walking or perhaps running while escaping their enslavers. Sam, Charles, and Paul fled from their enslaver's estate on the Ogeechee River, Georgia, in 1774. Sam, age fifty-two, thought to lead away "a "black mare, about 14 hands high, with a star on her forehead."[32] Whether the three men scattered in different directions is impossible to know, but it is not unreasonable to imagine Sam on horseback scouting ahead of Charles and Paul, looking out for patrollers or any white traveler who might attempt to arrest them. Or perhaps they sold or traded the animal or used it as a beast of burden to carry supplies as they fled.

Stealing multiple horses while escaping plantations offered fugitive riders a threefold advantage: mobility, mobile goods for trading, and the means to assist others in riding away. In the fall of 1741, an enslaved man named Cudgoe stole away from his enslaver's plantation in Goose Creek. In the *South-Carolina Gazette*, Cudgoe's slaveholder advised his fellow planters and slave patrols that he took with him "a large strawberry rhone Mare and her Colt with one Eye." One year later, Cudgoe and his horses continued to elude capture. The Goose Creek planter who submitted the advertisement describing Cudgoe and offering a reward for his arrest added that since his escape, someone, possibly the fugitive rider, had further carried away "two white trotting horses" from his neighbor's stables.[33]

In the winter of 1756, an enslaved man named Ketch used the opportunity of an errand involving horses to undertake marronage. Ketch's enslaver, a reverend in Augusta, Georgia, tasked him with taking "2 horses, the one a bright sorrel, the other a grey (both trotters)" from Charleston to the estate of Peter Taylor in Goose Creek. The nature of his errand at Taylor's is unclear, but Reverend Copp expected Ketch to return to Charleston "with the said horses." Ketch, who certainly must have devoted time and thought to gaining Copp's trust, stole the two trotters while leaving Charleston. Copp warned in the advertisement he submitted to the *South-Carolina Gazette* that Ketch was a "cunning fellow" who he suspected would drive the horses south to James Island to find his father, or ride westward to St. George in Dorchester County, where his grandmother lived.[34]

Slave riders exploited their enslavers' trust after serving faithfully as messengers. Sampson, age forty-five and "an African by birth," escaped from his enslaver in Nixonton on the Albemarle Sound in 1792 with a "black horse with small ears and a large head, about 14 hands high. . . . It is presumed," continued the advertisement, "that a further description would be unnecessary, as the above named fellow is well known in the district, having frequently rode express through the country, and often as a servant to his former owner."[35]

Winter weather and the heightened surveillance that accompanied Christmas celebrations on plantations posed significant challenges for people hoping to escape the bonds of their enslavers. Using horsepower to move across icy or frosted roads and dodge patrols would have increased a fugitive's chances for success during the holiday. Jefferey stole a "dark Bay Horse" from his enslaver's estate on the Ashley River in 1740 at Christmastime.[36] Even though many slaveholders allowed enslaved people several days away from their normal plantation labors, Christmas was not an especially liberatory time, as overseers and enslavers typically stepped up their scrutiny of enslaved communities, fearing that they might use the holiday to rebel.[37]

People who stole multiple horses likely used the animals to move between overland routes and waterways and to provide other fugitives with vehicles for their escape. In 1762, a slaveholder in Calvert County, Maryland, disclosed that an enslaved man, Sam, had fled his estate with two horses. Thomas Reynolds, his enslaver, described Sam as forty years old, a skilled carpenter and cooper, and as having "more Sense than Honesty." In addition, Sam traveled with "a Mare and Horse which he calls his own." Reynolds supposed that Sam fled south toward Virginia and added that he "understands going by Water," which suggests Sam's familiarity with riverine or maritime transport, perhaps from his labor as a waterman on the Patuxent River.[38]

In February 1764, an enslaved young man named Ben, held at the Baltimore Iron Works on the Patapsco River, fled his bondage under unusual circumstances. In addition to his clothes, Ben took with him "A black Stallion . . . a natural Pacer, hanging Mane, and short Tail. A dark brown Gelding, about 14 Hands high, shod round, hanging Mane, and short bob Tail . . . A grey Gelding, of the English running Breed, near 15 Hands high, gallops and trots well." While the gelding appears to have been a racehorse, it is likely Ben worked with the other two, who were described as wagon horses at the ironworks. The advertisement for Ben and the three horses offered a reward of a £5 for the capture of Ben and fifty shillings each for the horses.[39]

People of African descent continued to partner in stealing horses to flee from enslavers through the American Revolutionary War.[40] Two men, Abraham and Lewis, escaped on horseback from their enslaver in New Bern, North Carolina, in 1778, the midst of the war. The slaveholder in New Bern speculated that the men would "keep together," change their names, and attempt to pass as free men as they traveled on the horse toward South Carolina "to enter on board some vessel, in order to make their escape to the West Indies."[41] Abraham reportedly planned to seek his family in the Dutch Caribbean colony of Sint Eustatius, and his tactics reveal how enslaved people imagined connecting terrestrial and maritime space with animals.

Enslaved people in the British Caribbean rarely stole multiple horses while escaping their enslavers, but it was sometimes reported. The *Cornwall Chronicle*, in July 1783, advertised that a "mulatto man slave" named Dan had escaped the prison in St. Ann Parish, Jamaica, that spring. The slaveholder who held

Dan in bondage at Drax Hall suggested he may have been in hiding at another one of the slaveholder's smaller estates. "He is a dangerous fellow," the advertisement read, "goes armed, and is supposed to have stolen two horses since he made his escape." Dan used his enslaver's equine mobility to significantly increase his own, because he lived with a disability that was the result of a brutal punishment. The advertisement described how Dan had withstood having "his leg cut off for robbing the late Mr. John McDonald, then overseer of Drax Hall; information has been received, that since his escape, he uses a neat cork leg and wears trowsers."[42]

Advertisements offer several examples of slaveholders' recognition of fugitive Black riders' intelligence and ability to outwit their pursuers. One advertisement from 1746 described how a young man named Stephen stole a gray horse from his enslaver in King William County, Virginia. The advertisement noted that Stephen "is very artful and cunning." Ben, an enslaved man in Gloucester County, Virginia, was described as possessing "a smooth Tongue, and a very good Knack at telling a Story," which, along with a horse and his own assertiveness, assisted him in his escape.[43] Thomas Boman's slaveholder mentioned in an advertisement that Boman could "read, write and cypher" and that as he fled from enslavement on the Roanoke River he took with him a bridled and saddled "grey Roan Horse" laden with a pair of "Money-Scales and Weights."[44] Thomas, a blacksmith by trade, rode south and was reported crossing the Tar River in the spring of 1752.

In an advertisement submitted by Isaac Webster, regarding a man named Peter who fled the Bush River Furnace in Baltimore, an operator at the furnace complex noted that Peter rode "a small Grey Gelding" south toward Yorktown. The slaveholder added that Peter "talks good English, and will almost deceive any one by his crafty Lies."[45] In 1777, a subscriber to the *Maryland Journal and Baltimore Advertiser* in Alexandria submitted an advertisement regarding an enslaved man, Jack, who stole a four-year-old "bright bay Horse" as he fled. The advertisement also warned that Jack "is a smooth plausible fellow" who would present himself as a free man.[46]

These advertisements give some sense of how fugitive riders and other escapees forced slaveholders to reckon with Black intellect despite commonplace racist ideas of Black intellectual inferiority. However, many advertisements did not include any mention of Black intelligence and simply depicted the physical characteristics of runaways and their horses. One advertisement printed in Charleston in 1748, for instance, depicted Daniel as a "tall lusty Negro Man" who "is very black." Daniel took with him "a large dark Roan Horse" as he escaped.[47]

Despite the archival lacunae of enslaved riders' thoughts about the horses they stole, select advertisements contain traces of their own understanding of the human–animal relationships they produced and sustained through the act of riding away. In the winter of 1792, for instance, Chance stole away from his enslaver in Halifax, North Carolina, situated on the southern banks of the Roanoke River, with a horse, clothing, and four silver dollars. The copy included that Chance "has a set of remarkable fine teeth which he shows very much when he speaks, of a smiling countenance" and that he carried on his back numerous scars from being "very much whipped." Like Sam of Calvert County, mentioned earlier, Chance took a "horse which he called his own."[48] Chance, Sam, and others made their own claims to possessing these horses, and their rival claims add up to an important intellectual counterpoint to the claims to mastery that British and, later, American aristocrats intended to embody as equestrians.

Women and men like Sarah, Hagar, Jack, Flora, Ben, and Moll keenly understood how cattle, oxen, sheep, and horses were "creatures of empire" that slaveholders relied upon to build up and sustain agricultural labor regimes on plantations across Britain's North American and Caribbean colonies in the eighteenth century.[49] Furthermore, enslavers on horseback used equine verticality and bulk to intimidate enslaved people toiling on the ground. Animal bodies, then, were a crucial site of the contested foundations of slavery and settler colonialism within North America, and people of African descent rightly targeted them through acts of sabotage and theft to unsettle their slaveholder's sense of power. Enslaved people transformed ditches, marshes, stables, rivers, and backcountry roads into connected spaces within rival geographies of power. Places like the ditch Manuel used to injure livestock or the paths that Kate navigated as she rode her black horse away from Rock Creek and toward her friends and family fit within Black social networks of communication and added to a growing materialist environmental awareness among enslaved people of the ways in which physical landscapes and settler fauna could be instruments for resistance.

Enslaved people's decisions to kill or steal animals further represents the active production of rival geographies such as the nearly unreachable *mocambos*, or fugitive settlements, sited in mountain zones throughout the African diaspora, as in the Blue Mountains of Jamaica, or the mangrove swamps along the

Brazilian coastline, where fugitive enslaved people settled, knowing that their captors intensely feared such places.[50] Taken together, these diverse spaces and contexts reflect linkages in the African diaspora between enslaved people, maroons, and free people of color who fashioned their own human–animal relationships within particular landscapes to produce rival geographies of power.

Two artworks in particular stage these rival geographies and alternative ways of interacting with animals. *The Hunted Slaves,* by Richard Ansdell (1861), evokes the terror endured by fugitive enslaved people being hunted by dogs. On the left side of the image, two snarling dogs approach a pair of escapees, a man and a woman, who occupy the right of the image. The man wields an ax in defense of his partner, and he has already struck and killed a third dog, which lies below their feet. In *The Hunted Slaves,* the pair engaged in marronage are forced to protect their refuge, fight back against the dogs, and defend themselves from the animals that slaveholders used to recover their departed property. *A Ride for Liberty—The Fugitive Slaves,* by Eastman Johnson (1862), presents an altogether different scene, in which a family of enslaved fugitives has expropriated a horse in their bid for freedom. Unlike the people mentioned in advertisements, this painting represents a family—a man and a woman, their small child, and the infant the woman holds to her breast—together riding a horse at either dawn or dusk.

Studying these rival geographies affords comparisons between diasporic African environmental knowledge and Native American approaches to geography, mobility, and power. Consider that Manuel and his compatriots often used wintry weather as one more weapon in their armamentarium to injure and kill livestock. This approach is not unlike the tactics of Wabanaki raiders who weaponized snowdrifts and fresh snowfalls to attack, terrorize, and unsettle New Englanders in the seventeenth century.[51]

The attacks and thefts detailed here are intended as a return to the Campian framework of reconstructing rival geographies of power that bear witness to just how contested the physical terrain of slavery was in British America. Learning to think like Manuel and travel with women like Kate opens space for imagining histories of slavery, the environment, and fugitivity that existed alongside the envirotechnical expertise carried to the Americas by people of African descent.[52]

Epilogue

Enslavers leveraged dehumanizing animal comparisons and rhetoric against captives everywhere slavery existed, from the slave castles of the Gambia River, Gold Coast, and Bight of Benin to the plantation landscapes of the Caribbean and Chesapeake Bay. Indentured servants, including Irish and English women and men, complained in letters about being treated like animals.[1] In 1756, Elizabeth Sprigs, an English indentured servant in Maryland, reported to her father that she and other servants were "tied up and whipp'd to that Degree that you'd not serve an Animal," and that whites faced harsh treatments from their employers.[2] However, English and, later, American law and culture never questioned the legal, social, and political status of indentured servants as fully human beings who freely contracted their labor and retained their rights as legal individuals. Atlantic Africans, on the other hand, did not retain their personhood but rather existed as the legal chattel property of their slaveholders.

Enslaved people of African descent understood slavery to be a fundamentally dehumanizing, animalizing experience that their captors and purchasers strove to achieve through material conditions that later produced intellectual arguments justifying slavery as natural, moral, or economically necessary. New England petitions for freedom are a rich archive for grappling with African American challenges to these ideas. One petition, authored by a "Great Number" of enslaved people in 1777, put forth that slavery violated natural and civil law and that the institution existed "in defiance of all the tender feelings of humanity" as captives were "Brough hear Either to Be sold Like Beast of Burthen & Like them Condemnd to Slavery for Life."[3] Prince Hall addressed the Massachusetts General Court a decade later, in 1788, in a petition representing a collective of freeman, including three men seized, enslaved, and sold to Caribbean plantations. Hall described the experience of captives at slave markets, where slavers "Seal them there Like Sheep for the Slarter."[4]

In the late eighteenth century and into the early decades of the nineteenth century, writers of African descent who survived capture, the Middle Passage, and enslavement in the British Atlantic centered animalization as a core component of slavery as a philosophical and material system. In their writing, speech, and public presence they forced white readers and listeners to reckon with how slavery compromised the humanity of both the enslaved and the enslavers. Slavery, in their arguments, jeopardized the category of the human itself. Three intellectuals who succinctly brought this critique to the fore are Quobna Ottobah Cugoano, "A Slave," and Mary Prince.

Atlantic African intellectuals writing in the milieu of late eighteenth-century abolitionist campaigns centered rhetorical arguments around animalization in printed narratives recounting their captivity and enslavement. Quobna Ottobah Cugoano articulated the centrality of slave animalization and dehumanization at the center of Atlantic slaving and plantation slavery in his treatise *Thoughts and Sentiments on the Evil and Wicked Traffic of the Slavery and Commerce of the Human Species*, published in 1787. Unlike previously published personal narratives, such as Ukasaw Gronniosaw's *Narrative* (1772), Oladuah Equiano's *The Interesting Narrative* (1789), or Venture Smith's *A Narrative of the Life and Adventures of Venture* (1798), Cugoano's text combined aspects of the individual slave narrative with discussions within contemporary moral philosophy.

Cugoano survived slavery, from his capture in Assinee to his first passage to Cape Coast Castle in 1770. Born in Agimaque—present-day Ajumako, Ghana— a predominantly Fante-speaking town on the Gold Coast, around 1757, Cugoano's first captors transported him southward to a coastal fort, where slaving vessels moved captives to the dungeons below the massive slave castle. At the first castle, Cugoano "asked my guide what I was brought there for, he told me to learn the ways of the *browfow*, that is the white faced people." After being sold and transported aboard a vessel at Cape Coast, Cugoano survived the "brutish, base, but fashionable way of traffic" of the Middle Passage to the island of Grenada in the Caribbean. Cugoano labored alongside other captives on a sugar plantation for a comparatively brief period. In the Caribbean he witnessed women and men "hardened and stupid with many cruel beatings and lashings, or perhaps faint and pressed with hunger and hard labour."[5]

After less than a year of brutal slavery, Cugoano again traveled across the Atlantic, this time as a "servant" of an English gentleman. In 1772, Cugoano obtained his freedom in the wake of the Court of King's Bench judgment in *Somerset v. Stewart*, decided by Lord Mansfield. Around 1786, Cugoano found intellectual allies and enthusiastic companions among a circle of other formerly enslaved writers, including Olaudah Equiano and numerous other "Sons of Africa" in London.[6] Despite his relatively short time as an enslaved person in Grenada, the brutality of plantation slavery stayed with Cugoano as he developed as a philosopher in England.

Entering the discourse and debates of the Enlightenment in his *Thoughts and Sentiments,* Cugoano wrote candidly of "very discouraging" feelings and reflections as he studied the ideas of European intellectuals who argued that Africans could not obtain any significant degree of knowledge but rather were by "nature designed him for some inferior link in the chain, fitted only to be a slave."[7] David Hume, Immanuel Kant, Edward Long, and Thomas Jefferson, to name a few, argued in print that people of African descent were "naturally inferior" to white people.[8] Kant, perhaps the most recognizable figure of the Enlightenment, argued that people of African descent occupied "the lowest of all the other levels which we have mentioned as racial differences."[9]

These writers' ideas harked back to an intellectual tradition of "natural slavery," originating in Aristotle's *Politics,* that in late medieval Europe was elaborated by scholars such as Thomas Aquinas. Unlike other moral philosophers, who considered ethical subjects in a more abstracted realm, Cugoano personally met with slavers "who make no scruple to deal with the human species, as with the beasts of the earth." From the outset, Cugoano and others consciously articulated and affirmed to their readers their own humanity while also laying out their dehumanization under slavery. Animal comparisons and descriptors abound in Cugoano's writing, including his account of the "brutish" Middle Passage and "brutal" slavery in Grenada. However, *Thoughts and Sentiments* is not only a narrative of being reduced to an animal-like status under slavery but also an analytical account of slavery in total as a fundamentally animalizing system throughout the Atlantic world. Throughout the treatise, Cugoano links material regimes of labor and trade, which mingled slaves and animals, with intellectual apologies for natural slavery.

Cugoano's opponents who defended slavery, he argued, understood slavery in terms of a hierarchical world consisting of free whites, enslaved Black people, and animals. James Tobin, a slaveholder on Nevis, who likened the possibility of future Black emancipation in the British Atlantic to a "world turn'd up side down," in which horses saddle men and the normal roles of humans and animals become reversed. Rather than dispute this characterization, Cugoano mocked his opponent, writing that the prospect of seeing slavers "saddled and bridled" would be "no unpleasant sight."

Cugoano affirmed that the dehumanizing attitudes of Tobin and others engendered the animalization of enslaved people throughout the African diaspora in the Caribbean and North America. Impoverished white servants and beggars in English society remained fully human men and women, whereas slavery fundamentally transformed people of African descent from people to "the situation of a horse or a dog." Captives on plantations and in domestic spaces became "like animals" that "are bought and sold," tortured, worn out by exhausting labor, hunger, and psychological abuse.[10]

In his text, Cugoano draws only once upon the metaphor of slaves being like mechanical tools. By contrast, he repeatedly defines slavery, more than a dozen times, as a process by which slaveholders turned people into animals, in particular into domesticated animals like dogs, cattle, and horses. Animalization began from the moment slavers preyed on people in Atlantic Africa. Atlantic Africans "are hunted after as the prey in the desart, and doomed to destruction as the beasts that perish."[11]

Thoughts and Sentiments is an especially momentous text, given Cugoano's articulation of Blackness as a new social category in the Atlantic world, reflecting the deep history and ongoing animalization of people of African descent by slaveholders. Cugoano's critique of slavery appealed to his readers' sense of a common humanity, arguing that treating "our fellow-creatures, as with the beasts of the earth" undermined the Christian moral foundations of Britain and all other nations invested in slavery.[12] In addition, the violence at the core of slavery transformed slavers and slaveholders into animals as well. Over and again, Cugoano describes slavers as "ravenous beasts," "tygers and wild beasts," and other predatory animals.[13]

Establishing a common humanity was a crucial, if unrealized, aim of Cugoano's philosophical writing. Turning to Biblical justifications, Cugoano rejected the polygenist arguments of Long and Jefferson that advanced the idea of essentially separate biological races of humankind. Simply put, said Cugoano, "there are no inferior species." The book's title itself conveys Cugoano's argument of a singular "human species."

Many of the ideas within *Thoughts and Sentiments* resemble those of earlier abolitionist texts, including Thomas Clarkson's *An Essay on the Slavery and Commerce of the Human Species*, written in 1785 and first published the following year. In his book, Clarkson made similar allusions to slaveholders treating enslaved people as cattle or dogs.[14]

Cugoano's thesis has not gone unnoticed by scholars.[15] Colin Dayan has demonstrated that British and American slave law reduced enslaved people to the legal status of dogs, cattle, and other forms of animate property.[16] Bénédicte Boisseron discusses slaveholders' use of dogs as tools to surveil and intimidate enslaved people.[17] Likewise, postcolonial scholars and theorists associated with Afropessimism, namely Achille Mbembe and Frank B. Wilderson III, locate Blackness as a historical subjectivity produced by animalization.[18] Mbembe articulates this process as "being placed forcefully in the zone of undifferentiation between human and animal."[19] For Wilderson, Blackness itself is the antithesis of human, and therefore is the ultimate Other that all conceptions of humanity are defined against.

However, rather than focus on laws or the use of animals as rhetorical weapons that slaveholders wielded against the enslaved, Cugoano's text principally addresses enslaved people as prey at the moment of their captivity in Atlantic Africa, becoming livestock through public sales, and existing as "beasts of burden" in plantation fields and other exhausting, extractive workscapes.[20] *Thoughts and Sentiments* is a principal text within the Black Atlantic insofar as Cugoano joins these material sites of animalization throughout the African diaspora to a growing intellectual discourse surrounding slavery and animality among slavers, Black writers, and abolitionists.

Historians do not know with certainty whether "A Slave" who wrote a letter to Thomas Jefferson on November 30, 1808, was in fact an enslaved person of African descent or a white abolitionist posing as a slave.[21] A Slave might be a woman, a man, or a group of women and/or men writing together in collaboration. The National Archives record for this letter to the third president of the United States appears to subtly point toward A Slave being a white author, listing the letter as written by Pseudonym "A Slave." Neoclassical pseudonymous letters appeared in print and in manuscript as common forms of public writing in Revolutionary and early republican American discourse.[22] When men wrote letters under the guise of Cato or Catullus, they aimed to affix to their arguments and ideas the prestige of classical republican rhetoric and the cachet of antiquity.

It is certainly possible that a white abolitionist wrote under the persona of A Slave. However, A Slave's intellectual critique of slavery joined Cugoano's fundamental thesis that slavery dehumanized and animalized the enslaved. Moreover, given the precedent of Benjamin Banneker's public letter to Jefferson in 1791, and the public letters of enslaved and formerly enslaved people such as a free man in Philadelphia named Cato, published in *Philadelphia Freedom's Journal* in 1781, it is as likely that A Slave was in fact a slave who joined in with the public written attacks on slavery in the new nation.[23]

A Slave's letter is filled with repeated uses of the word *inhuman* as a keyword for understanding slavery. *Inhuman* appears twenty-one times in the text. Eighteenth- and nineteenth-century readers in the English-speaking Atlantic world understood *inhuman* to refer to a perversion of a person's original innate humanity.[24] Reducing someone to an inhuman status meant that others denied their original humanity and instead chose to act as if formerly human beings were now objects or animal-like chattel. *Inhumanity* also included an unnatural pleasure in the suffering and abjection of others. Like Cugoano's description of slavers as animal-like predators, A Slave characterized slaveholders as less than fully human. They turned their reader's attention to the "inhuman conduct" of slaveholders and overseers, the "inhuman tyrants" who lay claim to rule over the bodies and minds of the enslaved. Slavery reduced slavers to the status of mindless drones, akin to bees that "were never more busy about a hive than these inhuman monsters are with the people of colour."

Inhumanity also referred to the transformation of people into less than fully human objects under slavery. As Jennifer L. Morgan and others have argued, slavers knew that the enslaved were human but acted as if they were animal-like to exploit their real human emotions and psychologically assault Black communities. Two million women, men, and children, wrote A Slave, lived "almost naked, starved and abused in a most inhuman and bruital manner." Inhuman slavery, they argued, existed in direct contradiction to the new nation's ideals of being either a "free republick" or a godly nation. Again, A Slave's rhetoric joined critiques of the American Revolution and the new United States made by Cato, the formerly enslaved man in Philadelphia, and other enslaved people like Felix, as part of an unfinished movement to achieve the natural liberty of all people.[25]

A Slave pointed out that slavery in the early republic relied on a continuous phenomenological denial of African humanity. "Its quite good enough for Negroes," A Slave wrote, "who the sainted pilgrims say, are only a black beast of the Manilla class, with a flat nose, thick lips, woolly head, ivory teeth; and with a face somewhat resembling the human, but clearly not a human being." Ideas about enslaved people as animal-like began on slaving voyages to Atlantic Africa, where slavers frequently wrote about Atlantic Africans' "woolly" hair. A Slave's reference to "ivory" teeth further evoked combined expeditions for slaving and purchasing ivory in West Africa.

Enslaved people's animal-like existence forced them to "prove our human-nature" time and again, and A Slave pointed to the unambiguity of the Declaration of Independence, which proclaimed "that all men, (not all white men) are created equal." Addressing Jefferson, the document's principal author, A Slave pointedly questioned him: "Are we men, or are we beasts?" A Slave's letter includes other familiar arguments against slavery made by abolitionists, slaves, and free people of color: that it is comparable to naval impressment, that it engenders sexual violence against women, and that it "destroys all the physical & commercial distinctions of labour & property. It is a mere monopoly of men, and all their abilities and services."

Though their identity is unknowable, A Slave's letter joins a Black intellectual tradition forged in the Atlantic crucible of slavery and revolution in the late eighteenth century. Slavery, these thinkers argued, perverted the true nature of humanity—both white and Black humanity. This argument appeared over and again in Black writing and speech in the early republic. Lemuel Haynes, a veteran of the American Revolutionary War and Congregational minister in Connecticut, preached in several of his sermons that slavery transformed people into "Beasts of the field."[26]

In her memoir of her enslavement, Mary Prince described being sold as an enslaved girl at the age of twelve on Bermuda, in 1800. Indelible in her memory, Prince recalled how in the dawn of the morning of her sale, her mother dressed her and her sisters, Hannah and Dinah, in new osnaburg clothes and led them to the market where they would be sold. Her mother cried out, "I am going to carry my little chickens to market." Writing later, as a forty-three-year-old woman reflecting on this experience, Prince made sure to emphasize to her readers that her mother's words that morning continued to haunt her.[27]

Lined up with her sisters, awaiting their sale, Prince's heart pounded "with grief and terror so violently" that she trembled. When the vendue master who would be arranging their sale arrived, Prince remembered that she knew she and her sisters would be offered up to a new enslaver, "for sale like sheep or cattle."[28] As the oldest of her sisters, the vendue master selected Prince to be sold first. This man did not speak to Prince as he conducted the sale.

She remembered that the auctioneer "took me by the hand, and led me out into the middle of the street, and, turning me slowly round, exposed me to the view of those who attended the vendue." Prospective buyers encircled Prince and "examined and handled me in the same manner that a butcher would a calf or a lamb he was about to purchase, and who talked about my shape and size in like words—as if I could no more understand their meaning than the dumb beasts." As she stood there, sensing the penetrating gaze of her would-be butchers, an enslaver bought Mary Prince for £38. Prince watched in horror as Hannah and Dinah endured the same humiliating experience. When the sale ended, Prince's mother embraced and kissed her daughters, "mourned" for them, and begged them to survive, persist, and endure.

After severing her from her mother and family, Prince's new enslaver carried her away to Spanish Point, a rocky headland in Pembroke Parish, on the western side of the archipelago. Enslaved women in the home of Prince's slaveholder, after seeing this new arrival enter in tears, stressed to her that she had "come here to work" and not to cry. Prince learned from an enslaved woman named Hetty, whom she described as "French Black," what kind of toil would be expected of her. Through conversation with Hetty, and observing Hetty's labor in the field, Prince came to understand that her life would become deeply entangled with the lives of nonhuman animals.[29]

In her memoir, Prince introduced Hetty to her readers as the "most active woman I ever saw, and she was tasked to her utmost." Immediately after her arrival, Hetty escorted Prince to assist her in milking their enslaver's cows. "She then fetched home the sheep, and penned them in the fold; drove home the cattle, and staked them about the pond site; fed and rubbed down my masters' horse, and gave the hog and fed the cow their suppers."[30] In addition, Prince and Hetty made dinner for their enslaver, prepared beds in the house, cared for his children and put them to sleep. Prince remembered how comforting it could be to simply look into Hetty's eyes and face, and she "felt glad that she [Hetty] was there." That night, however, after Hetty was berated by the wife of their enslaver for failing to finish her work in a timely manner, the enslaver reached for his "long cow-skin" whip to attack Hetty, whose screams startled Prince as she lay awake in bed.

This single day in Prince's life encapsulates two important aspects of enslavement in the British Atlantic world during the long eighteenth century. First, Prince herself understood both her enslavement and her sale as an enslaved child as being compared to and evaluated as if she were an animal. Historians should recognize and respect this understanding of slavery. Second, in studying Hetty's grueling labors with animals—milking cows, herding, penning sheep, staking cattle, feeding and caring for horses, and feeding pigs—Prince and others, enslaved both on Caribbean islands and on plantations in the southern colonies of North America, lived and labored in close proximity to livestock, and their lives were inextricably connected with the nonhuman world.

Throughout her narrative, Prince returned time and again to the theme of slaveholders comparing her to a nonhuman animal. Six years after she was enslaved on Spanish Point, Prince's enslaver sold her again to another slaveholder, on Grand Turk Island. This time, Prince did not have an opportunity to say good-bye to her mother or family. On the sloop from Bermuda to the Turks Islands, Prince turned over in her thoughts how English men and women "think that black people are like cattle, without natural affection. But my heart tells me it is far otherwise."[31]

Upon their arrival on Grand Turk, Prince encountered her new enslaver, who possessed several salt ponds on the island. On his estate, she ate "Indian corn boiled with water," worked thigh-deep in the salt pans from four in the morning until late in the evening, well after sunset, and then returned to the house of the enslaver, where she and the other slaves "slept in a long shed, divided up into narrow slips, like the stalls used for cattle." Prince dwelled on how slavery appeared to produce and rely upon a kind of mundane violence to maintain disciplinary structures of hierarchy on plantations. She remembered her enslaver assaulting an elderly enslaved man, Daniel, who after being beaten and exposed to stinging saltwater would writhe "on the ground like a worm."[32] Prince labored in the salt pans for a decade before her enslaver transported her with him as he retired to Bermuda.

On her return to Bermuda, Prince took up the work familiar to Hetty and others, as she "attended upon a horse and cow besides—also going upon errands. I had to curry the horse—to clean and feed him—and sometimes to ride him a little." In 1815, Prince endured being sold again, this time to an enslaver in Antigua, Adam Wood. On Antigua, Prince watched other enslaved people cut grass to feed cattle as she labored inside the enslaver's domicile. Long days and nights of labor as a domestic slave on a sugar plantation exhausted Prince. She wrote that she worked for hours without rest, "like a horse."[33] Over and again she returned to this theme, that her life had become reduced to an animal-like state of abjection. However, Prince affirmed her own humanity in 1826, when she chose to marry a free Black man in Antigua, Daniel James.

When Wood traveled to England in 1828 with his family, he brought Prince along as a domestic slave. The journey separated Mary and Daniel, who had been married for two years. In England, Prince, who suffered from painful rheumatism in her hands, pleaded that her enslavers not make her launder the family's clothes, as the hot and cold water aggravated her pain. After repeated arguments and threats to push her to homelessness and ruin, Prince left their household. Later she recalled the decision and how she had "thought it very hard, after I had lived with them for thirteen years, and worked for them like a horse, to be driven out in this way, like a beggar."[34] She survived in England by seeking the charity of the Moravian Church and later abolitionists from the London Anti-Slavery Society.

In the conclusion to her memoir, written and published in 1831, Prince posed several important questions to her readers in Britain and its colonies throughout the Atlantic world. "I am often much vexed," she began, "and I feel great sorrow when I hear some people in this country say, that the slaves do not need better usage, and do not want to be free." How, she wondered, did slaveholders arrive at the conclusion that the enslaved were "disgraced and thought no more of than beasts?" How could enslavers, and those men like the vendue master who orchestrated the slave market, dare to forcibly separate families—mothers and their children, husbands and wives, sisters and brothers—"just as cattle are sold and separated"? And how did English people themselves, whose society within Europe forbade chattel slavery at home, "go out into the West Indies," as if the Caribbean islands could be considered separate from Britain, to "act in such a beastly manner"?[35]

Prince repeatedly drew her readers' attention to the fact that enslavers in the colonies "tie up slaves like hogs—moor them up like cattle, and they lick them, so as hogs, or cattle, or horses, never were flogged." She also foregrounded her own lived experience as an enslaved woman, writing "I have been a slave myself—I know what slaves feel—I can tell by myself what other slaves feel, and by what they have told me." Every family separation, every flogging, every day of exhausting labor and near-starvation, and every comparison between enslaved people and animals added up to a complete worldview produced by a material system of human–animal relations. "And then when we are quite done up, who cares for us, more than for a lame horse? This is slavery."[36]

Returning to the words of the women and men in Virginia in their 1723 letter to Edmund Gibson, the bishop of London, sheds light on the intellectual continuities between the millions of enslaved people in British America and later Enlightenment thinkers like Cugoano, A Slave, and Prince. Unlike indentured servants, the enslaved knew that in "verJennia" and elsewhere, the laws "keeps and makes them and there seed Slaves forever."[37] Enslavement rested on a legal regime that equated people of African descent with animal chattel, as living capital whose lives were often compared to those of the cattle that slaves labored alongside.

Seeing the history of race and racialization under slavery in the British Atlantic world through the lens of human–animal relationships makes clearer the uniqueness of the letter writers' ideas and lives as Black people who knew full well that their slaveholders intended to weaken their confidence, community, and hopes and confine their lives to a doglike state. Yet they nevertheless refused. Instead, they dared to imagine a world that recognized and reckoned with Black humanity in its fullness. Their refusal reverberates into the present, and we are tasked with listening carefully and learning from their rejection of dehumanization.

NOTES

Prologue

1. Anonymous letter [to the bishop of London], August 4, 1723, Fulham Papers at Lambeth Palace Library, 42 vols. (Swem Library, College of William and Mary, microfilm) 17:167–16. The letter is transcribed and reproduced in full in Antonio T. Bly, "'Reed through the Bybell': Slave Education in Early Virginia," *Book History* 16, no. 1 (2013): 1–33. See also Thomas N. Ingersoll, "'Releese Us out of This Cruell Bondegg': An Appeal from Virginia in 1723," *William and Mary Quarterly* 51, no. 4 (1994): 777–82. On terminology, I use the term *enslaved people* first and foremost in the text to emphasize the humanity of those enslaved. However, to vary the flow of the text and avoid repetitious diction, I also use the term *slave* to refer to an enslaved person.

2. Kirsten Fischer, Suspect Relations: Sex, Race, and Resistance in Colonial North Carolina (Ithaca, NY: Cornell University Press, 2002), 181; Jennifer L. Morgan, Laboring Women: Reproduction and Gender in New World Slavery (Philadelphia: University of Pennsylvania Press, 2004), 18, 33, 48, 105.

3. Sarah Hand Meacham, "Pets, Status, and Slavery in the Late-Eighteenth-Century Chesapeake," *Journal of Southern History* 77, no. 3 (2011): 521–554.

4. Joshua Bennett, *Being Property Once Myself: Blackness and the End of Man* (Cambridge, MA: Harvard University Press, 2020).

5. Unlike the women and men examined by Bennett, these writers did not lay claim to alternative forms of the human, in contrast to the hegemonic Man of Western colonialism, through blackness and animality, but rather laid claims to being as human as those legally recognized as persons in Europe.

6. David Livingstone Smith, *On Inhumanity: Dehumanization and How to Resist It* (Oxford: Oxford University Press, 2020). A similar point is made by Edward B. Rugemer, "The Development of Mastery and Race in the Comprehensive Slave Codes of the Greater Caribbean during the Seventeenth Century," *William & Mary Quarterly* 70, no. 3 (2013): 429–458, esp. 439, 457. See also Nicholas T. Rinehart, "The Man That Was a Thing: Reconsidering Human Commodification in Slavery," *Journal of Social History* 50, no. 1 (2016): 28–50.

7. Kenneth Stow, *Jewish Dogs: An Image and Its Interpreters* (Stanford, CA: Stanford University Press, 2006).

8. Stanley Elkins, *Slavery: A Problem in American Institutional and Intellectual Life* (Chicago: University of Chicago Press, 1959), 82.

9. This point itself is not mine but is an argument already made in Walter Johnson, *River of Dark Dreams: Slavery and Empire in the Cotton Kingdom* (Cambridge, MA: Harvard University Press, 2013), 222–228. Here, too, I am drawing on the terminology of first, middle, and final passages as developed by Johnson and others, in which the first passage extends from the moment of capture to the point of being forcibly marched to a trading fort or slave castle, the middle passage

is the transatlantic voyage, and the final passage is the journey from the slave market to the slave-holder's domicile. See Walter Johnson, "Time and Revolution in African America: Temporality and the History of Atlantic Slavery," in *Rethinking American History in a Global Age*, ed. Thomas Bender (Oakland: University of California Press, 2002), 148–67.

10. Aimé Césaire, *Discourse on Colonialism* (New York: Monthly Review Press, 1972); Frantz Fanon, *The Wretched of the Earth* (New York: Grove Press, 1963); Sylvia Wynter, "Unsettling the Coloniality of Being/Power/Truth/Freedom: Towards the Human, After Man, Its Overrepresentation—An Argument," *CR: The New Centennial Review* 3, no. 3 (2003): 257–337. See also newer scholarship building on this tradition such as Kyle Keeler, "Becoming More Than an Englishman: Igbo Cosmologies, Nonhuman Animals, and Olaudah Equiano's Refusal of Anthropocentrism," *Early American Literature* 56, no. 2 (2021): 395–413; David Baumeister, "Black Animality from Kant to Fanon," *Theory & Event* 24, no. 4 (2021): 951–976; Samantha Pergadia, "Like an Animal: Genres of the Nonhuman in the Neo-Slave Novel," *African American Review* 51, no. 4 (2018): 289–304.

11. Achille Mbembe, *Critique of Black Reason* (Durham, NC: Duke University Press, 2017); Zakiyyah Iman Jackson, *Becoming Human: Matter and Meaning in an Antiblack World* (New York: New York University Press, 2020); Lewis R. Gordon, *Existentia Africana: Understanding Africana Existential Thought* (New York: Routledge, 2000); Frank B. Wilderson III, *Afropessimism* (New York: Liveright, 2020). See also James E. Ford III, "The Difficult Miracle: Reading Phillis Wheatley against the Master's Discourse," *CR: The New Centennial Review* 18, no. 3 (2018): 181–224.

12. David Brion Davis, *The Problem of Slavery in the Age of Emancipation* (New York: Vintage, 2014), 38.

Introduction

SLAVERY AND HUMAN–ANIMAL RELATIONSHIPS

1. Winthrop D. Jordan, *White Over Black: American Attitudes Toward the Negro, 1550–1812* (Chapel Hill: University of North Carolina Press, 1968), 28.

2. John William Blake, *Europeans in West Africa, 1540–1560*, vol. 2 (Farnham: Hakluyt Society, 2010), 326–46.

3. It should be noted at the start that John Lok's comments were not unique, nor was there was anything exceptional among Europeans about this early English view. For example, the Portuguese chronicler Gomes Eanes de Zurara wrote, circa 1453, that sub-Saharan Africans were "brutish" and "beasts," and later, circa 1509, Duarte Pacheco Pereira claimed that Wangara people had faces, teeth, and tails like dogs. See Alvin O. Thompson, "Race and Colour Prejudices and the Origin of the Trans-Atlantic Slave Trade," *Caribbean Studies* 16, no. 3/4 (1976): 29–59.

4. Kim F. Hall, *Things of Darkness: Economies of Race and Gender in Early Modern England* (Ithaca, NY: Cornell University Press, 1995), 51. See also Sujata Iyengar, *Shades of Difference: Mythologies of Skin Color in Early Modern England* (Philadelphia: University of Pennsylvania Press, 2005).

5. Urvashi Chakravarty, "'Fitt for Faire Habitacion': Kinship and Race in *A Vewe of the Present State of Irelande*," *Spenser Studies* 35, no. 1 (2021): 21–46.

6. Alden T. Vaughan and Virginia Mason Vaughan, "Before Othello: Elizabethan Representa-

tions of Sub-Saharan Africans," *William and Mary Quarterly* 54, no. 1 (1997): 19–44; Emily Weissbourd, "'Those in Their Possession': Race, Slavery, and Queen Elizabeth's 'Edicts of Expulsion,'" *Huntington Library Quarterly* 78, no. 1 (2015): 1–19.

7. Erica Fudge, *Perceiving Animals: Humans and Beasts in Early Modern English Culture* (Urbana: University of Illinois Press, 2002); Fudge, *Brutal Reasoning: Animals, Rationality, and Humanity in Early Modern England* (Ithaca, NY: Cornell University Press, 2006).

8. Fudge, *Brutal Reasoning*, 55.

9. Ronald Pollitt, "John Hawkins's Troublesome Voyages: Merchants, Bureaucrats, and the Origin of the Slave Trade," *Journal of British Studies* 12, no. 2 (1973): 26–40.

10. Guinea Company, letter to James Pope, 17 September 1651, in Elizabeth Donnan, ed., *Documents Illustrative of the History of the Slave Trade to America* (New York: Octagon Books, 1965), 1:126–28.

11. Guinea Company, letter to Bartholomew Haward, 9 December 1651, in Donnan, *Documents Illustrative of the History of the Slave Trade*, 1:129.

12. George Downing, letter to John Winthrop Jr., 26 August 1645, in Donnan, *Documents Illustrative of the History of the Slave Trade*, 1:125–26.

13. Richard Ligon, A True & Exact History of the Island of Barbados Illustrated with a Mapp of the Island, as also the Principall Trees and Plants there, set forth in their due proportions and shapes, drawne out by their severall and respective scales (London: Printed for Humphrey Moseley, 1657), 137.

14. Jean Barbot, "A Description of the Coasts of North and South Guinea," 1732, cited in Donnan, *Documents Illustrative of the History of the Slave Trade*, 1:289, 294.

15. Ivana Elbl, "Cross-Cultural Trade and Diplomacy: Portuguese Relations with West Africa, 1441–1521," *Journal of World History* (1992): 165–204.

16. John K. Thornton, *Warfare in Atlantic Africa, 1500–1800* (London: University College London Press, 1999).

17. James L. A. Webb Jr., "The Horse and Slave Trade between the Western Sahara and Senegambia," *Journal of African History* 34, no. 2 (1993): 221–46.

18. Thomas Herbert, *Some Years Travels into Divers Parts of Africa, and Asia the Great* (London: Printed by R. Everingham, 1677), 3, 9.

19. David G. Sweet, "Black Robes and 'Black Destiny': Jesuit Views of African Slavery in 17th-Century Latin America," *Revista De Historia De América*, no. 86 (1978): 87–133.

20. Morgan Godwyn, *The Negro's and Indians Advocate* (London, 1680), 3, 80.

21. Philippe Rosenberg, "Thomas Tryon and the Seventeenth-Century Dimensions of Antislavery," *William and Mary Quarterly*, 3rd series, 61, no. 4 (2004): 609–42.

22. Cotton Mather, *Small Offers towards the Tabernacle in the Wilderness* (Boston, 1689), 58.

23. Stephen J. Stein, "George Whitefield on Slavery: Some New Evidence," *Church History* 42, no. 2 (1973): 244.

24. Roger A. Ekirch, "'A New Government of Liberty': Hermon Husband's Vision of Backcountry North Carolina, 1755," *William and Mary Quarterly* 34, no. 4 (1977): 632–46, at 641–42.

25. Marcy Norton, "Going to the Birds: Animals as Things and Beings in Early Modernity," in *Early Modern Things: Objects and Their Histories, 1500–1800*, ed. Paula Findlen (London: Routledge, 2013), 53–83.

26. Sara D. Schotland, "Africans as Objects: Hogarth's Complex Portrayal of Exploitation," *Journal of African American Studies* 13, no. 2 (2009): 147–63.

27. Caroline Bressey, "Cultural Archaeology and Historical Geographies of the Black Presence in Rural England," *Journal of Rural Studies* 25, no. 4 (2009): 386–95. Knapton's portrait of the Spencers and Shaw can be found in the collections at Althorp House in West Northamptonshire, United Kingdom.

28. Mia L. Bagneris, *Colouring the Caribbean: Race and the Art of Agostino Brunias* (Manchester: Manchester University Press, 2017).

29. Samuel Charles Wilks, *Memoirs of The Life, Writings and Correspondence of Sir William Jones*, vol. 2 (London: John W. Parker, 1835), 284–86.

30. The story of South Asian slavery in the British Empire is beyond my scope. For more on this topic, see Andrea Major, *Slavery, Abolitionism and Empire in India, 1772–1843* (Liverpool: Liverpool University Press, 2012).

31. Gregory E. O'Malley, *Final Passages: The Intercolonial Slave Trade of British America, 1619–1807* (Chapel Hill: University of North Carolina Press, 2014).

32. Walter Johnson, "To Remake the World: Slavery, Racial Capitalism, and Justice," *Boston Review*, February 20, 2018, https://bostonreview.net/forum/walter-johnson-to-remake-the-world.

33. Morgan, *Laboring Women*, 87, 105.

34. Cedric J. Robinson, *Black Marxism: The Making of the Black Radical Tradition* (London: Zed Press, 1983), 125.

35. Jennifer L. Morgan, *Reckoning with Slavery: Gender, Kinship, and Capitalism in the Early Black Atlantic* (Durham, NC: Duke University Press, 2021).

36. Stephanie E. Smallwood, "Reflections on Settler Colonialism, the Hemispheric Americas, and Chattel Slavery," *William and Mary Quarterly* 76, no. 3 (2019): 407–16; Susan Staves, "Chattel Property Rules and the Construction of Englishness, 1660–1800," *Law and History Review* 12, no. 1 (1994): 123–53. See also Catherine Hall, "Gendering Property, Racing Capital," *History Workshop Journal*, no. 78 (2014): 22–38.

37. William Moraley, *Infortunate: The Voyage and Adventures of William Moraley, an Indentured Servant*, ed. Susan E. Klepp and Billy G. Smith (University Park: Pennsylvania State University Press, 2010), 96.

38. Jeffrey Brace, *The Blind African Slave: Memoirs of Boyrereau Brinch, Nicknamed Jeffrey Brace*, ed. Kari Winter (Madison: University of Wisconsin Press, 2005), 137.

39. Jordan, *White Over Black*, 28.

40. David Livingstone Smith, "Paradoxes of Dehumanization," *Social Theory and Practice* (2016): 416–43.

41. Jordan, *White Over Black*, 30–32.

42. Vahé Baladouni, "Etymological Observations on Some Accounting Terms," *Accounting Historians Journal* 11, no. 2 (1984): 101–9.

43. Jordan, *White Over Black*, 233.

44. Malcolm Heath, "Aristotle on Natural Slavery," *Phronesis* 53, no. 3 (2008): 243–70.

45. David Brion Davis, *The Problem of Slavery in Western Culture* (Ithaca, NY: Cornell University Press, 1966); Karl Jacoby, "Slaves by Nature? Domestic Animals and Human Slaves," *Slavery and Abolition* 15, no. 1 (1994): 89–99. Keith Bradley, a scholar of ancient Rome, writes that Ro-

man slaveholders saw enslaved people as an "animal—an ox, a cow or mule that had to be put through its paces before a deal could be made; indeed the aedilician edict that regulated the sale of slaves also regulated the sale of cattle and beasts of burden and required similar disclosure of diseases and defects." Bradley, *Slavery and Society at Rome* (Cambridge: Cambridge University Press, 1994), 53. See also Bradley, "Animalizing the Slave: The Truth of Fiction," *Journal of Roman Studies* 90 (2000): 110–25.

46. David Brion Davis, *Inhuman Bondage: The Rise and Fall of Slavery in the New World* (Oxford: Oxford University Press, 2006), 2–3.

47. Virginia DeJohn Anderson, *Creatures of Empire: How Domestic Animals Transformed Early America* (Oxford: Oxford University Press, 2004), 24, 44.

48. Joshua Abram Kercsmar, "Wolves at Heart: How Dog Evolution Shaped Whites' Perceptions of Indians in North America," *Environmental History* 21, no. 3 (2016): 516–40.

49. Jon T. Coleman, *Vicious: Wolves and Men in America* (New Haven, CT: Yale University Press, 2008), 36, 43–44.

50. Brett Rushforth, *Bonds of Alliance: Indigenous and Atlantic Slaveries in New France* (Chapel Hill: University of North Carolina Press, 2012), 35–51.

51. Davis, *Inhuman Bondage*, 29.

52. John Lawson, *A New Voyage to Carolina* (London, 1709), 201.

53. Claudio Saunt, "'The English Has Now a Mind to Make Slaves of Them All': Creeks, Seminoles, and the Problem of Slavery," *American Indian Quarterly* 22, no. 1/2 (1998): 157–80; Christina Snyder, *Slavery in Indian Country: The Changing Face of Captivity in Early America* (Cambridge, MA: Harvard University Press, 2010), 102, 128.

54. Colin Dayan, *The Law Is a White Dog* (Princeton, NJ: Princeton University Press, 2011), 124. See also Veronica Hendrick, "Codifying Humanity: The Legal Line between Slave and Servant," *Texas Wesleyan Law Review* 13 (2006): 685–97.

55. Chernoh M. Sesay, "The Revolutionary Black Roots of Slavery's Abolition in Massachusetts," *New England Quarterly* 87, no. 1 (2014): 99–131.

56. Adrienne Davis, "'Don't Let Nobody Bother Your Principle': The Sexual Economy of Slavery," in *Sister Circle: Black Women and Work*, ed. Sharon Harley and the Black Women and Work Collective (New Brunswick, NJ: Rutgers University Press, 2002), 103–27; Angela Y. Davis, *Women, Race, & Class* (New York: Random House, 1981); Gregory D. Smithers, *Slave Breeding: Sex, Violence, and Memory in African American History* (Gainesville: University Press of Florida, 2012); Deborah Gray White, *Ar'n't I a Woman? Female Slaves in the Plantation South* (New York: W. W. Norton and Co., 1985). See also Stephanie E. Jones-Rogers, *They Were Her Property: White Women as Slave Owners in the American South* (New Haven, CT: Yale University Press, 2019); Wendy Anne Warren, "'The Cause of Her Grief': The Rape of a Slave in Early New England," *Journal of American History* 93, no. 4 (2007): 1031–49.

57. Morgan, *Laboring* Women, 105.

58. Most recently, critical theorists building on these analyses are pushing historians to consider how the categories of human and animal themselves are products of early modern slavery and colonialism and how people of African descent have challenged this binary through alternative forms of being with nonhuman life. See especially Bennett, *Being Property Once Myself*; Jackson, *Becoming Human*.

59. This is quite different from the use of *entanglement* by environmental humanists, who use the term to stress nonhuman agency. See Deborah Bird Rose et al., "Thinking through the Environment, Unsettling the Humanities," *Environmental Humanities* 1, no. 1 (2012): 1–5.

60. Philip D. Morgan, "Slaves and Livestock in Eighteenth-Century Jamaica: Vineyard Pen, 1750–1751," *William and Mary Quarterly* 52, no. 1 (1995): 47–76.

61. Douglas Hall, *In Miserable Slavery: Thomas Thistlewood in Jamaica, 1750–86* (Mona: University of West Indies Press, 1999), 79–80, 82, 94.

62. Judith Carney, *Black Rice: The African Origins of Rice Cultivation in the Americas* (Cambridge, MA: Harvard University Press, 2001); Andrew Sluyter, *Black Ranching Frontiers: African Cattle Herders of the Atlantic World, 1500–1900* (New Haven, CT: Yale University Press, 2012).

63. David Lambert, "Master–Horse–Slave: Mobility, Race and Power in the British West Indies, c. 1780–1838," *Slavery & Abolition* 36, no. 4 (2015): 618–41.

64. David Silkenat, *Scars on the Land: An Environmental History of Slavery in the American South* (Oxford: Oxford University Press, 2022).

65. Norton, "Going to the Birds."

Chapter 1

NOE BOOGES, NOE SLAVES

Animals in the Castle Trade of West Africa

1. "John Carter, Whidah, 1 March 1686," in *The English in West Africa,1685–1688*, ed. Robin Law (Oxford: Published for the British Academy by Oxford University Press, 2001), 327–31.

2. Hugh Thomas, *The Slave Trade: The Story of the Atlantic Slave Trade: 1440–1870* (New York: Simon and Schuster, 1997), 324.

3. Joan M. Fayer, "African Interpreters in the Atlantic Slave Trade," *Anthropological Linguistics* 45, no. 3 (2003): 281–95; Robin Law, *Ouidah: The Social History of a West African Slaving "Port," 1727–1892* (Columbus: Ohio State University Press, 2004), 43, 127. Law describes how in Ouidah, in particular, *agou*, or interpreters/translators, were valuable Hueda officials in the slave trade.

4. Jan Hogendorn and Marion Johnson, *The Shell Money of the Slave Trade* (Cambridge: Cambridge University Press, 1986), 5, 9.

5. "John Carter, Whidah, 11 November 1686," in Law, *The English in West Africa, 1685–1688*, 332.

6. "John Carter, Whidah, 6 January 1686/7," in Law, *The English in West Africa, 1685–1688*, 337. The dates in these transcriptions, completed by Robin Law, are recorded according to the Julian, or Old Style, calendar that continued to be used in official records in England until 1751, and any letters dated between 1 January and 24 March are dated for both conventions.

7. "George Nanter, Whidah, 5 January 1687," in Law, *The English in West Africa, 1685–1688*, 389–90. Law suggests that "pranes [=proves?]" in his transcription.

8. Stephanie E. Smallwood, *Saltwater Slavery: A Middle Passage from Africa to American Diaspora* (Cambridge, MA: Harvard University Press, 2009), 35.

9. Smallwood, *Saltwater Slavery*, 71; Trevor Burnard, "Collecting and Accounting: Representing Slaves as Commodities in Jamaica, 1674–1784," in *Collecting across Cultures: Material Exchanges*

in the Early Modern Atlantic World, ed. Daniela Bleichmar and Peter Mancall (Philadelphia: University of Pennsylvania Press, 2011), 177–91.

10. Herbert Klein, *The Atlantic Slave Trade,* 2nd ed. (Cambridge: Cambridge University Press, 2010), 115; Hogendorn and Johnson, *Shell Money of the Slave Trade,* 114–24. Marion Johnson provides an outstanding account of local enumerations of cowries, including their change over time, in her two-part article series "The Cowrie Currencies of West Africa," cited here and published in the *Journal of African History.*

11. Smallwood, *Saltwater Slavery,* 35.

12. Michael McCormick, "Rats, Communications, and Plague: Toward an Ecological History," *Journal of Interdisciplinary History* 34, no. 1 (2003): 1–25.

13. The letters cited in this chapter originate from MSS Rawlinson, C. 745, 746, and 747, held at the Bodleian Library, Oxford University. I am extremely grateful for the dedicated scholarly generosity and excellent scholarship of Robin Law, who painstakingly transcribed and published these collections in three volumes cited here.

14. P. E. H. Hair, "Attitudes to Africans in English Primary Sources on Guinea up to 1650," *History in Africa* 26 (1999): 43–68.

15. William A. Pettigrew, "Free to Enslave: Politics and the Escalation of Britain's Transatlantic Slave Trade, 1688–1714," *William and Mary Quarterly* (2007): 3–38.

16. William Pettigrew, *Freedom's Debt: The Royal African Company and the Politics of the Atlantic Slave Trade, 1672–1752* (Chapel Hill: University of North Carolina Press, 2013), 198. On bioprospecting and extraction projects of the Royal African Company in the early eighteenth century, see Matthew David Mitchell, "'Legitimate Commerce' in the Eighteenth Century: The Royal African Company of England under the Duke of Chandos, 1720–1726," *Enterprise & Society* 14, no. 3 (2013): 544–78.

17. The African Company Act of 1750 passed by Parliament dissolved the Royal African Company.

18. Marisa J. Fuentes, *Dispossessed Lives: Enslaved Women, Violence, and the Archive* (Philadelphia: University of Pennsylvania Press, 2016). I do not want to suggest that the victims of slave raids or captives did not engage the nonhuman environment through forms of resistance to slavery, though the records are scarce and my focus here has undoubtedly overlooked other possibilities. Louis Nelson, however, has noted that inland villagers targeted by raiders often used horns made from cow bones to warn of incursions. This does present an intriguing connection to the similar use of cow horns by enslaved people in the West Indies, and cow horns in Jonkonnu celebrations. See Louis P. Nelson, "Architectures of West African Enslavement," *Buildings & Landscapes: Journal of the Vernacular Architecture Forum* 21, no. 1 (2014): 88–125, at 92.

19. Marcus Rediker, "History from Below the Water Line: Sharks and the Atlantic Slave Trade," *Atlantic Studies* 5, no. 2 (2008): 285–97.

20. William Beinart and Lotte Hughes, *Environment and Empire* (Oxford: Oxford University Press, 2007), 24. For important discussions of animals in British imperial environmental history, see Alfred Crosby, *Ecological Imperialism: The Biological Expansion of Europe, 900–1900* (Cambridge: Cambridge University Press, 1986); Anderson, *Creatures of Empire*; George Colpitts, *Pemmican Empire: Food, Trade, and the Last Bison Hunts in the North American Plains, 1780–1882* (Cambridge: Cambridge University Press, 2014); Andrea Smalley, *Wild By Nature: North American Animals Confront Colonization* (Baltimore: Johns Hopkins University Press, 2017).

21. James Beattie, Edward Melillo, and Emily O'Gorman, eds., *Eco-Cultural Networks and the British Empire: New Views on Environmental History* (London: Bloomsbury Publishing, 2014), 3–20; Kenneth Morgan, *Slavery and the British Empire: From Africa to America* (Oxford: Oxford University Press, 2007), 12.

22. Alexander Falconbridge, *An Account of the Slave Trade on the Coast of Africa* (London: James Phillips, 1788), 37. On the memorialization of the slave trade and the Door of No Return, see Brempong Osei-Tutu, "Cape Coast Castle and Rituals of Memory," in *Materialities of Ritual in the Black Atlantic,* ed. Akinwumi Ogundiran and Paula Saunders (Bloomington: Indiana University Press, 2014), 317–38.

23. Akinwumi Ogundiran, "Of Small Things Remembered: Beads, Cowries, and Cultural Translations of the Atlantic Experience in Yorubaland," *International Journal of African Historical Studies* 35, no. 2/3 (2002): 427–57; Paul E. Lovejoy, *Transformations in Slavery: A History of Slavery in Africa* (Cambridge: Cambridge University Press, 2011), 103–5; Marion Johnson, "The Cowrie Currencies of West Africa, Part I," *Journal of African History* 11, no. 1 (1970): 17–49; Jan S. Hogendorn and H. A. Gemery, "Continuity in West African Monetary History? An Outline of Monetary Development," *African Economic History,* no. 17 (1988): 127–46; J. D. Fage, "African Societies and the Atlantic Slave Trade," *Past & Present,* no. 125 (1989): 97–115.

24. Hogendorn and Johnson, *Shell Money of the Slave Trade,* 166.

25. Hogendorn and Johnson, *Shell Money of the Slave Trade,* 19, 106; Eugenia W. Herbert, "Portuguese Adaptation to Trade Patterns Guinea to Angola (1443–1640)," *African Studies Review* 17, no. 2 (1974): 411–23.

26. Ogundiran, "Of Small Things Remembered," 432, 442, 447.

27. Hogendorn and Johnson, *Shell Money of the Slave Trade,* 16; James Walvin, *Slavery in Small Things: Slavery and Modern Cultural Habits* (Chichester: Wiley and Sons, 2017), 40.

28. Fage, "African Societies and the Atlantic Slave Trade," 105.

29. Hogendorn and Johnson, *Shell Money of the Slave Trade,* 22.

30. Hogendorn and Johnson, *Shell Money of the Slave Trade,* 7, 13, 15. For a history of cowries around the world, see Bin Yang, *Cowrie Shells and Cowrie Money: A Global History* (New York: Routledge, 2019).

31. Hogendorn and Johnson, *Shell Money of the Slave Trade,* 5, 23, 29, 81–83, 157.

32. Hogendorn and Johnson, *Shell Money of the Slave Trade,* 6

33. Ogundiran, "Of Small Things Remembered," 432, 442; Hogendorn and Johnson, *Shell Money of the Slave Trade,* 101.

34. Robert Smith, "Peace and Palaver: International Relations in Pre-Colonial West Africa," *Journal of African History* 14, no. 4 (1973): 599–621, at 609.

35. Neil L. Norman, "Hueda (Whydah) Country and Town: Archaeological Perspectives on the Rise and Collapse of an African Atlantic Kingdom," *International Journal of African Historical Studies* 42, no. 3 (2009): 387–410, esp. 408–9.

36. Ogundiran, "Of Small Things Remembered," 439, 447.

37. Robin Law, "West Africa's Discovery of the Atlantic," *International Journal of African Historical Studies* 44, no. 1 (2011): 1–25, esp. 20–24.

38. Hogendorn and Johnson, *Shell Money of the Slave Trade,* 37–47, 81, 157. For an example of an advertisement from the EIC in London, see East India Company, Court of Managers, *London:*

The Court of Managers for the United-Trade to the East Indies will put up to sale at the East-India-House in Leaden-Hall Street, on the 19th of March, 1705/06, the following goods, broadsheet (London, 1706), available from Gale Primary Sources, "Eighteenth Century Collections Online," https://www.gale.com/primary-sources/eighteenth-century-collections-online.

39. Johnson, "Cowrie Currencies of West Africa, Part I," 18; John Thornton, *Africa and Africans in the Making of the Atlantic World, 1400–1800* (Cambridge: Cambridge University Press, 1998), 45.

40. Ogundiran, "Of Small Things Remembered," 429. Writing from his post on the Gambia River, Francis Moore noted that "Cowries are Shells which go as Money" in Upper Guinea. See Moore, *Travels into the Inland Parts of Africa* (London: D. Henry and R. Cave, 1738), 7. On cowries in Senegambia, see M. Hiskett, "Materials Relating to the Cowry Currency of the Western Sudan—II: Reflections on the Provenance and Diffusion of the Cowry in the Sahara and the Sudan," *Bulletin of the School of Oriental and African Studies, University of London* 29, no. 2 (1966): 339–66; Liza Gijanto, "Personal Adornment and Expressions of Status: Beads and the Gambia River's Atlantic Trade," *International Journal of Historical Archaeology* 15, no. 4 (2011): 637–68. To date, I have been unable to find any marine ecology research on the ecological impact of the removal of cowries from Maldives.

41. Lovejoy, *Transformations in Slavery*, 79. Lovejoy observes, for example, that Oyo traders at coastal ports exchanged cowries for slaves and later used the cowries at northern markets to purchase horses from North African traders crossing the Sahara. See also Ghislaine Lydon, *On Trans-Saharan Trails: Islamic Law, Trade Networks, and Cross-Cultural Exchange in Nineteenth-Century Western Africa* (Cambridge: Cambridge University Press, 2009), 74–76, 252–54.

42. Johnson, "Cowrie Currencies of West Africa, Part I."

43. "Andrew Crosbie, Guydah, 1 September 1682," in *The English in West Africa, 1681–1683*, ed. Robin Law (Oxford: Published for the British Academy by Oxford University Press, 1997), 237–39.

44. "Arthur Wendover, James Fort, Accra, 10 February 1680," in Law, *The English in West Africa, 1681–1683*, 154.

45. "John Carter, Whidah, 22 November 1686," in Law, *The English in West Africa, 1685–1688*, 333–34.

46. "Arthur Wendover, James Fort, Accra, 20 February 1680," in Law, *The English in West Africa, 1681–1683*, 154–55.

47. "William Cross, Ophra in Arda, 18 August 1681," in Law, *The English in West Africa, 1681–1683*, 219–21.

48. "Charles Towgood, Aboard the Cape Coast Briganteen, Allampo Road, 5 March 1682," in Law, *The English in West Africa, 1681–1683*, 270–71.

49. "James Thorne, Ophra in Arda, 19 August 1681," in Law, *The English in West Africa, 1681–1683*, 221–23.

50. "John Carter, Whidah, 22 November 1686," in Law, *The English in West Africa, 1685–1688*, 334.

51. Robin Law, "'The Common People Were Divided': Monarchy, Aristocracy and Political Factionalism in the Kingdom of Whydah, 1671–1727," *International Journal of African Historical Studies* 23, no. 2 (1990): 211–12, 216. Law notes that it is unclear whether Captain Carter took

his name from his partnership with John Carter or the name simply reflected a title common around Ouidah.

52. "Josiah Pearson, Widah Factory, 24 November 1694," in *The English in West Africa, 1691–1699*, ed. Robin Law (Oxford: Published for the British Academy by Oxford University Press, 2006), 581.

53. "James Thorne, Ophra in Arda, 18 December 1681," in Law, *The English in West Africa, 1681–1683*, 221–23; see also "John Winder, Ophra in Arda, 23 March, 1681/82," 229–232.

54. "James Thorne, Ophra in Arda, 19 August 1681," in Law, *The English in West Africa, 1681–1683*, 221–23.

55. "Arthur Wendover, Appa, 17 July 1682," in Law, *The English in West Africa, 1681–1683*, 232–37.

56. "Mark Bedford Whiting, James Forte, Accra, 27 May 1686," in Law, *The English in West Africa, 1685–1688*, 273–74.

57. "Mark Bedford Whiting, James Forte, Accra, 29 June 1686," in Law, *The English in West Africa, 1685–1688*, 274.

58. "Daniell Gates, Allampo, 6 March 1681/82," in Law, *The English in West Africa, 1681–1683*, 315–16.

59. "James Bayly, from on board the Adventure, at Mingo [Ningo], 26 September 1687," in Law, *The English in West Africa, 1685–1688*, 364.

60. Thomas Phillips, *A Journal of a Voyage Made in the* Hannibal *of London, Ann. 1693, 1694* (London: Walthoe, 1732), 216.

61. "Josiah Pearson, Whidah," in Law, *The English in West Africa, 1691–1699*, 584.

62. "William Piles, Tersee, 22 June 1697," in Law, *The English in West Africa, 1691–1699*, 600–601.

63. "William Piles, Pono, 30 June 1697," in Law, *The English in West Africa, 1691–1699*, 601.

64. James Houstoun, *Some New and Accurate Observations Geographical, Natural and Historical. Containing a True and Impartial Account of the Situation, Product, and Natural History of the Coast of Guinea, so far As Relates to the Improvement of that Trade, for the Advantage of Great Britain in General, and the Royal African Company in Particular* (London: Printed for J. Peele, 1725), 2.

65. James Houstoun, *Memoirs of the life and travels of James Houstoun, M. D. (formerly Physician and Surgeon-General to the Royal African Company's Settlements in Africa, and late Surgeon to the Royal Assiento Company's Factories in America* (London: Printed for the author, 1747), 127.

66. Mitchell, "Legitimate Commerce." Mitchell points out that among the projects James Brydges commissioned in this period were the missions led by Captain Trengove, Robert Plunkett, Samuel Heartsease, and a "mineralist," accompanied by Nicholas Baynton, who sought to locate gold mines, identify new commodities for acclimatization and cultivation, and establish a company garden at Cape Coast Castle.

67. Houstoun, *Some New and Accurate Observations*, 4, 32–33.

68. Johnson, "Cowrie Currencies of West Africa, Part I." The creatures Houstoun found most likely did not resemble the species of cowries taken from the Indian Ocean, *Monetaria moneta*.

69. Saidiya V. Hartman, *Lose Your Mother: A Journey along the Atlantic Slave Route* (New York: Farrar, Straus and Giroux, 2007), 209–10. On vampire cowries in oral history, see Elizabeth

Isichei, *Voices of the Poor in Africa: Moral Economy and the Popular Imagination* (Rochester, NY: University of Rochester Press, 2002), 67–69; Rosalind Shaw, *Memories of the Slave Trade: Ritual and the Historical Imagination in Sierra Leone* (Chicago: University of Chicago Press, 2002), 9.

70. Isichei, *Voices of the Poor in Africa,* 67–69.

71. Kenneth Davies, *The Royal African Company* (London: Longmans, Green and Company, 1957), 40–41.

72. In several Fante-, Twi-, and Akan-speaking cultures, rituals involving animal sacrifice purified communities and sanctified the social bonds of individuals within their communities. On animal sacrifice, see Kwasi Konadu, *The Akan Diaspora in the Americas* (Oxford: Oxford University Press, 2010) 36, 104; Anthony Ephirim-Donkor, *African Religion Defined: A Systematic Study of Ancestor Worship among the Akan* (London: Rowman & Littlefield, 2016), 229, 234; Walter Rucker, *Gold Coast Diasporas: Identity, Culture, Power* (Bloomington: Indiana University Press, 2015), 196; Rebecca Shumway, *The Fante and the Transatlantic Slave Trade* (Rochester, NY: University of Rochester Press, 2011), 131, 135, 199; T. C. McCaskie, "Denkyira in the Making of Asante C. 1660–1720," *Journal of African History* 48, no. 1 (2007): 1–25, at 21. Nineteenth-century authors also reported the use of sheep as sacrificial animals on the Gold Coast. See William Hutton, *A Voyage to Africa: Including a Narrative of an Embassy to One of the Interior Kingdoms in the Year 1820* (London: Longman, 1821), 225. Hutton writes that in the Ashanti Empire "the Moors indeed set them the example of sacrificing sheep." In his book on the Gold Coast, Henry Meredith also relates that the Ashanti emperor used sheep as diplomatic gifts to the African Company of Merchants at Winneba. See Meredith, *An Account of the Gold Coast of Africa* (London: Longman, 1812), 1:148. Thomas Edward Bowdich made similar observations in his work. Bowdich, *Mission from Cape Coast Castle to Ashantee, with a Statistical Account of that Kingdom* (London: John Murray, 1819), 74, 116.

73. Law, *The English in West Africa, 1691–1699,* 1–2.

74. "Christopher Clarkson, Dickies Cove, 15 August 1692," in Law, *The English in West Africa, 1691–1699,* 3; Patricia Seed, *Ceremonies of Possession in Europe's Conquest of the New World, 1492–1640* (Cambridge: Cambridge University Press, 1995).

75. "Christopher Clarkson, Dickies Cove, 15 August 1692."

76. Robin Law, "Human Sacrifice in Pre-Colonial West Africa," *African Affairs* 84, no. 334 (1985): 53–87. Law cites the Dutch physician Olfert Dapper's *Description of Africa,* 1668, which cites primary sources from Dutch merchants employed by the West India Company.

77. Konadu, *Akan Diaspora in the Americas,* 36, 104; Ephirim-Donkor, *African Religion Defined,* 229, 234; Rucker, *Gold Coast Diasporas,* 196; Shumway, *The Fante and the Transatlantic Slave Trade,* 135, 199. Sheep also figured in religious rituals involving sacrifice in Ouidah in this period; see Law, *Ouidah.*

78. In his letter to George I, Agaja, the king of Dahomey who reigned from 1718 to 1740, wrote that he would sacrifice "oxen, hoggs, sheep, and goats" for the safe return of the go-between Bulfinch Lambe and his companion, Captain Tom. For an excellent analysis of Agaja's letter, dated 1724, and a transcription of the letter, see Robin Law, "Further Light on Bulfinch Lambe and the 'Emperor of Pawpaw': King Agaja of Dahomey's Letter to King George I of England, 1726," *History in Africa* 17 (1990): 211–26.

79. Kwamina B. Dickson, *An Historical Geography of Ghana* (Cambridge: Cambridge University Press, 1969), 36, 47, 209.

80. Allan Kulikoff, *From British Peasants to Colonial American Farmers* (Chapel Hill: University of North Carolina Press, 2000), 236; Barbara Jean Harris, *English Aristocratic Women, 1450–1550: Marriage and Family, Property and Careers* (Oxford: Oxford University Press, 2002), 120, 133.

81. Bruce Thomas Boehrer, *Animal Characters: Nonhuman Beings in Early Modern Literature* (Philadelphia: University of Pennsylvania Press, 2011), 164, 167.

82. Davies, *Royal African Company*, 247–49, 268–69.

83. Harvey M. Feinberg, "Africans and Europeans in West Africa: Elminans and Dutchmen on the Gold Coast during the Eighteenth Century," *Transactions of the American Philosophical Society* 79, no. 7 (1989): 1–186.

84. Davies, *Royal African Company*, 12–42; Nelson, "Architectures of West African Enslavement," 97. Nelson notes that the English began slave trading along the Gambia River in 1618, though these efforts were not as systematic or planned as the slaving efforts of the Royal African Company. For discussions of English slave trading in the late sixteenth century and early seventeenth century, see Eric Williams, "The Golden Age of the Slave System in Britain," *Journal of Negro History* 25, no. 1 (1940): 60–106; L. P. Jackson, "Elizabethan Seamen and the African Slave Trade," *Journal of Negro History* 9, no. 1 (1924): 1–17; Pollitt, "John Hawkins's Troublesome Voyages."

85. At Dixcove, the Royal African Company established a successful trade alliance with the nearby kingdom of Denkyira. Though trading comparatively little in slaves, the fort became valuable as a provisioning station for ships coasting among the African Company's forts, carrying enslaved people and other cargo from the forts to Cape Coast. On Dixcove, see Law, *The English in West Africa, 1691–1699*, 1–2.

86. On European perceptions of West African fetishism as irrational, see William Pietz, "The Problem of the Fetish: Bosman's Guinea and the Enlightenment Theory of Fetishism," *Res: Anthropology and Aesthetics*, no. 16 (1988): 105–24, esp. 105–7. Pietz demonstrates that Europeans developed the concept of fetishism in the eighteenth century to contrast African irrationality with European Enlightenment rationality, an intellectual development that further justified participation in the Atlantic slave trade until the nineteenth century.

87. Law, *The English in West Africa, 1691–1699*, 90–91.

88. John Thornton, *Warfare in Atlantic Africa, 1500–1800* (London: University College London Press, 1999), 127–48; Robin Law, "The Komenda Wars, 1694–1700: A Revised Narrative," *History in Africa* 34, no. 1 (2007): 133–68.

89. Law, *The English in West Africa, 1691–1699*, 1–2, 90–91.

90. "William Gabb, Succondee, 27 April 1698," in Law, *The English in West Africa, 1691–1699*, 127.

91. "William Gabb, Succondee, 10 May 1698," in Law, *The English in West Africa, 1691–1699*, 130.

92. "James Nightingale at Commenda, 15 February 1681/82," in Law, *The English in West Africa, 1681–1683*, 36–37. Law notes that a *prendee* was a fine.

93. "William Cross, Commenda, 8 September 1686," in Law, *The English in West Africa, 1685–1688*, 88.

94. "Gerrard Gore, Commenda, 1 July 1698," in Law, *The English in West Africa, 1691–1699*, 229–230.

95. "Captain Nedd, Dickes Cove, 28 June 1698," in Law, *The English in West Africa, 1691–1699*, 81.

96. Entries from 22 March 1703 and 10 May 1703, in memorandum book kept at Cape Coast Castle from 13 January 1703 to 2 January 1704, Royal African Company, Records, series T70, 11, National Archives, London.

97. "Thomas Willson, Commenda, 10 December 1694," in Law, *The English in West Africa, 1691–1699*, 142. On Cabess, see David Henige, "John Kabes of Komenda: An Early African Entrepreneur and State Builder," *Journal of African History* 18, no. 1 (1977): 1–19.

98. "Thomas Willson, Commenda, 16 December 1694," in Law, *The English in West Africa, 1691–1699*, 142.

99. "Edward Searle at James Fort, Accra, 3 March 1695/96, to William Cooper, chief factor at Winneba," in Law, *The English in West Africa, 1691–1699*, 547–48.

100. Entry from 19 June 1704, memorandum book, Cape Coast Castle.

101. Entries dated 20 November 1714 and 23 February 1714/15, in the Commenda Fort diary, Royal African Company, Records, T70.1464, National Archives, London.

102. "Richard Thelwall, Annamaboe, 23 January 1682/83," in Law, *The English in West Africa, 1681–1683*, 125.

103. "James Walker, Succondee, 27 October 1687," in Law, *The English in West Africa, 1685–1688*, 59–60.

104. On *asafo* companies on the Gold Coast, see Shumway, *The Fante and the Transatlantic Slave Trade*, 16, 22, 82.

105. Vincent Carretta and Ty M. Reese, eds., *The Life and Letters of Philip Quaque, the First African Anglican Missionary* (Athens: University of Georgia Press, 2012), 52, 54, 126.

106. Caroline Grigson, *Menagerie: The History of Exotic Animals in England* (Oxford: Oxford University Press, 2016), 47, 53, 72; Louise E. Robbins, *Elephant Slaves and Pampered Parrots: Exotic Animals in Eighteenth-Century Paris* (Baltimore: Johns Hopkins University Press, 2002), 22. Factors for the Royal African Company also sought animal curiosities for their patrons in England. A letter dated 7 January 1682 from Richard Thelwall at Anomabu, for instance, mentions how the factor had scoured the land surrounding the factory looking for "green birds."

107. Entries for 28 June and 5 July 1715, Royal African Company, Records, T70.89, as quoted in Helen Julia Paul, "The South Sea Company and the Royal African Company's Combined Slaving Activities," paper presented at the Economic History Society Conference, Reading, 2006.

108. Moore, *Travels into the Inland Parts of Africa*, 40, 45, 62.

109. Francis Spilsbury, *Account of a Voyage to the Western Coast of Africa: Performed by His Majesty's Sloop Favourite, In the Year 1805* (London: Printed for Richard Phillips, 1807), 26.

110. Nelson, "Architectures of West African Enslavement," 107.

111. Mary Fissell, "Imagining Vermin in Early Modern England," *History Workshop Journal*, no. 47 (1999): 1–29.

112. "Arthur Richard, Anishan, 13 September 1681," in Law, *The English in West Africa, 1681–1683*, 76.

113. Nelson, "Architectures of West African Enslavement," 88, 98–99, 101, 110, 112.

114. Kenneth Kiple, *The Caribbean Slave: A Biological History* (Cambridge: Cambridge University Press, 2002), 71–74.

115. "Richard Thelwall, Anamaboe, 1 February 1681," in Law, *The English in West Africa, 1681–1683*, 107–8.

116. "Thomas Price, James Fort, Accra, 30 June 1687," in Law, *The English in West Africa, 1685–1688*, 295.

117. Smallwood, *Saltwater Slavery*, 141, 144, 194.

118. "Francis Smith, Dickis Cove Fort, 20 January 1692," in Law, *The English in West Africa, 1691–1699*, 12.

119. "Edward Searle, Charles Fort, Annimaboe, 11 December 1693," in Law, *The English in West Africa, 1691–1699*, 311.

120. "Edward Searle, Charles Fort, Annimaboe, 21 February 1694," in Law, *The English in West Africa, 1691–1699*, 313.

121. "Ralph Hassell, James Fort, Accra, 11 October 1681," in Law, *The English in West Africa, 1681–1683*, 175.

122. "Ralph Hassell, James Fort, Accra, 18 October 1681," in Law, *The English in West Africa, 1681–1683*, 177.

123. "Richard Thelwall, Annamaboe, 28 September 1682," in Law, *The English in West Africa, 1681–1683*, 119–20.

124. "Hugh Hilling Mumford, 20 March 1686/87," in Law, *The English in West Africa, 1685–1688*, 373–374.

125. "Henry Wood, off Axim, 3 June 1686," in Law, *The English in West Africa, 1685–1688*, 353–54. Law notes that *rott* here refers to rats.

126. "William Piles, St. Thomas, 30 December 1697," in Law, *The English in West Africa, 1691–1699*, 623–24.

127. "Ralph Hassell, James Fort, Accra, 11 October 1681," in Law, *The English in West Africa, 1681–1683*, 414.

128. "Hugh Hilling, Mumford, 28 October 1686," in Law, *The English in West Africa, 1685–1688*, 370–71.

129. "William Cross, Charles Fort, Annimaboe, 3 July 1692," in Law, *The English in West Africa, 1691–1699*, 294.

130. "John Rootsey, Annimaboe, 27 May 1695," in Law, *The English in West Africa, 1691–1699*, 338.

131. "Thomas Bucknell, Succondee, 23 August 1686," in Law, *The English in West Africa, 1685–1688*, 28–29.

132. "Thomas Bucknell, Succondee, 21 September 1686," in Law, *The English in West Africa, 1685–1688*, 29–30.

133. "Ralph Hassell, Annamabo, 1 April 1687," in Law, *The English in West Africa, 1685–1688*, 201.

134. "Thomas Willson, Commenda, 7 February 1695/96," in Law, *The English in West Africa, 1691–1699*, 188.

135. "Thomas Willson, Commenda, 3 March 1695/96," in Law, *The English in West Africa, 1691–1699*, 190–91.

136. Houstoun, *Some New and Accurate Observations*, 30.

137. John Newton, *The Journal of a Slave Trader (John Newton), 1750–1754*, ed. Bernard Martin and Mark Spurrell (London: Epworth Press, 1962), 32.

138. Crosby, Ecological Imperialism, 270.

139. Stephanie E. Smallwood, "The Politics of the Archive and History's Accountability to the Enslaved," *History of the Present* 6, no. 2 (2016): 117–32, at 127.

140. Annette Gordon-Reed, *The Hemingses of Monticello: An American Family* (New York: W. W. Norton & Co., 2008), 23.

141. Daniel Kumler Flickinger, *Ethiopia, Or, Twenty Years of Missionary Life in Western Africa* (Dayton, OH: United Brethren Printing House, 1873), 112.

Chapter 2

SHOWING THEIR SLAVES HOW TO COLLECT

Enslaved People and the Origins of Early Modern Science

1. Joseph Ewan and Nesta Ewan, *John Banister and His Natural History of Virginia, 1678–1692* (Urbana: University of Illinois Press, 1970), 74–75.

2. Helen C. Rountree, *The Powhatan Indians of Virginia: Their Traditional Culture* (Norman: University of Oklahoma Press, 1989), 6, 39–44. Banister's letter was likely written to either the physician Martin Lister or the botanist Leonard Plukenet.

3. Ewan and Ewan, *John Banister and His Natural History of Virginia*, 75.

4. James Delbourgo, "Divers Things: Collecting the World under Water," *History of Science* 49, no. 2 (2011): 149–85; Delbourgo, *Collecting the World: Hans Sloane and the Origins of the British Museum* (Cambridge, MA: Harvard University Press, 2017); Kathleen S. Murphy, "Collecting Slave Traders: James Petiver, Natural History, and the British Slave Trade," *William & Mary Quarterly* 70, no. 4 (2013): 637–70; Susan Scott Parrish, *American Curiosity: Cultures of Natural History in the Colonial British Atlantic World* (Chapel Hill: University of North Carolina Press, 2012), 259–306.

5. Thomas Sprat, *The History of the Royal Society of London, for the Improving of Natural Knowledge* (London: T. R. and J. Allestry, 1667), 407–8. On the tangled histories of the Royal Society and the Royal African Company, see Mark Govier, "The Royal Society, Slavery and the Island of Jamaica, 1660–1700," *Notes and Records of the Royal Society* 53, no. 2 (1999): 203–17.

6. Lyon G. Tyler, "Pedigree of a Representative Virginia Planter, Edward Digges, Esq.," *William and Mary Quarterly* 1, no. 4 (1893): 208–13.

7. Ewan and Ewan, *John Banister and His Natural History of Virginia*, 87.

8. John Banister, "The Extracts of Four Letters from Mr. John Banister to Dr. Lister, Communicated by Him to the Publisher," *Philosophical Transactions (1683–1775)* 17 (1693): 667–92.

9. On Banister's plantation, which his son John inherited, see Thomas Jefferson Wertenbaker, *The Planters of Colonial Virginia* (Princeton, NJ: Princeton University Press, 1922), 158.

10. Ewan and Ewan, *John Banister and His Natural History of Virginia*, 91.

11. Edmund Berkeley and Dorothy S. Berkeley, "Another 'Account of Virginia': By the Reverend John Clayton," *Virginia Magazine of History and Biography* (1968): 415–36, at 421.

12. Gordon-Reed, *Hemingses of Monticello*, 23; Smallwood, "Politics of the Archive."

13. Steven Shapin, *A Social History of Truth: Civility and Science in Seventeenth-Century England* (Chicago: University of Chicago Press, 2011), 355–408.

14. Elizabeth Yale, *Sociable Knowledge: Natural History and the Nation in Early Modern Britain* (Philadelphia: University of Pennsylvania Press, 2016).

15. J. C. De Graft Johnson, "The Fanti Asafu," *Africa: Journal of the International African Institute* 5, no. 3 (1932): 307–22; Kwame Yeboah Daaku, *Trade and Politics on the Gold Coast, 1600–1720: A Study of the African Reaction to European Trade* (Oxford: Clarendon Press, 1970), 98–99; Bayo Holsey, *Routes of Remembrance: Refashioning the Slave Trade in Ghana* (Chicago: University of Chicago Press, 2008), 31; Judith Spicksley, "Pawns on the Gold Coast: The Rise of Asante and Shifts in Security for Debt, 1680–1750," *Journal of African History* 54, no. 2 (2013): 147–75. As was the fate of many go-betweens in the Atlantic world, Barter's grip on the slave trade led the company, led by Agent-General Dalby Thomas, to oust him from Cape Coast in 1703.

16. Willem Bosman, *Nauwkeurige Beschryving van de Guinese Goud- Tand- en Slave-Kust* (Utrecht: Anthony Schouten, 1704), 51–52. Barter lived in what one scholar describes as a "miniature castle" sited next to Cape Coast. See I. Chukwukere, "Akan Theory of Conception: Are the Fante Really Aberrant?," *Africa: Journal of the International African Institute* 48, no. 2 (1978): 135–48.

17. Doran H. Ross, "'Come and Try': Towards a History of Fante Military Shrines," *African Arts* 40, no. 3 (2007): 12–35; Ansu K. Datta and R. Porter, "The Asafo System in Historical Perspective," *Journal of African History* 12, no. 2 (1971): 279–97.

18. James Delbourgo, "Listing People," *Isis* 103, no. 4 (2012): 735–42, at 737.

19. James Petiver, *Musei Petiveriani centuria prima, rariora naturae continens: viz. animalia, fossilia, plantas, ex variis mundi plagis advecta, ordine digesta, et nominibus propriis signata*, ([London], 1695–1703), 87–89; Petiver, *Catalogus Classicus & topicus, omnium rerum figuratarum in V. decadibus, seu primo volumine Gazophylacii naturæ & artis; singulis ad proprias tabulas & numeros relatis. A Jacobo Petiver, . . .* ([London, 1709]); Petiver, *Gazophylacii naturae & artis decas septima & octava. In qud Animalia, Quadrupeda, Aves, Pisces, Reptilia, Infecta, Vegetabilia, Fossilia & Lapides Figura insignes, Corpora Marina, Stirpes Minerales e Terra eruta, &c. Item Antiquaria, Numismata, Gemmae excisae, Lucernae, Urnae, Instrumenta varia, Machinae, Busta, Effigies clarorum Virorum, omniaque Arte producta. Descriptionibus brevibus & iconibus illustrantur. Patronis suis & moecenatibus d.d.d. Jacobus Petiver. S.R.S.* ([London, 1711?]). All available from Gale Primary Sources, "Eighteenth Century Collections Online."

20. Sarah Irving, *Natural Science and the Origins of the British Empire* (New York: Routledge, 2015.)

21. On Kirckwood, see Murphy, "Collecting Slave Traders," 653; Maria M. Romeiras et al., "Botanical Exploration of the Cape Verde Islands: From the Pre-Linnaean Records and Collections to Late 18th Century Floristic Accounts and Expeditions," *Taxon* 63, no. 3 (2014): 625–40; Winifred J. Harley, "The Ferns of Liberia," *Contributions from the Gray Herbarium of Harvard University*, no. 177 (1955): 58–101.

22. Raymond P. Stearns, "James Petiver, Seventeenth-Century Promoter of Natural Science," in *Proceedings of the American Antiquarian Society* 62, no. 2 (1952), 243–365, at 280–81.

23. Edmund Berkeley and Dorothy Smith Berkeley, "The Most Common Rush or Vilest

Weed: Some Unpublished Letters of James Petiver to William Byrd II," *Virginia Magazine of History and Biography* 95, no. 4 (1987): 481–95.

24. Given his power and status, it is very unlikely that Barter collected for Petiver to increase his political authority on the Gold Coast. It may be that he either collected to include himself within Petiver's network, hoping to learn of new products or innovations in medical or economic botany, or perhaps simply to indulge his own interest for collecting animals. Dominik Nagl has written a fascinating history of Barter's son, also named Thomas, who likely became enslaved in Boston in 1712 after traveling from the Gold Coast to London, Weymouth, New York, Cadiz, Virginia, and Boston. Nagl's article adds to the literature on the crystallization of Blackness and slavery in the early Black Atlantic world. See Nagl, "The Governmentality of Slavery in Colonial Boston, 1690–1760," *Amerikastudien / American Studies* 58, no. 1 (2013): 5–26.

25. Raymond Phineas Stearns notes that it is likely Petiver learned of the Griggs through a shipowner, George Searle, who traded in the West Indies. Stearns, *Science in the British Colonies of America* (Urbana: University of Illinois Press, 1970), 345.

26. "Petiver to Thomas Grigg, 11 December 1700," in Stearns, *Science in the British Colonies*, 345.

27. David Barry Gaspar, *Bondmen and Rebels: A Study of Master–Slave Relations in Antigua* (Durham, NC: Duke University Press, 1993), 36, 94, 103, 105, 110, 113. The Griggs also rented land and enslaved people from Clement Tudway. See Sarah Barber, "Not worth one Groat": The Status, Gentility and Credit of Lawrence and Sarah Crabb of Antigua," *Journal of Early American History* 1, no. 1 (2011): 26–61.

28. Stearns, *Science in the British Colonies*, 334, 345–46; Delbourgo, "Listing People," 738; Parrish, *American Curiosity*, 271. Among Petiver's other collectors on Antigua were Daniel Mackenning and Mr. Rickets, "gardener to Mr. Gale at Falmouth."

29. Among Petiver's other women contacts in America were Hannah English Williams of Charleston, South Carolina, and Mary Danson, daughter of John Archdale, colonial governor of Carolina. On Williams, see Beatrice Scheer Smith, "Hannah English Williams: America's First Woman Natural History Collector," *South Carolina Historical Magazine* 87, no. 2 (1986): 83–92; "Early Letters from South Carolina upon Natural History," *South Carolina Historical and Genealogical Magazine* 21, no. 1 (1920): 3–9; Charlotte Porter, "Natural History Discourse and Collections: The Roles of Collectors in the Southeastern Colonies of North America," *Museum History Journal* 1, no. 1 (2008): 129–46; Stearns, *Science in the British Colonies*, 346; James Petiver, "An Account of Animals and Shells Sent from Carolina to Mr. James Petiver, FRS," *Philosophical Transactions* 24, no. 1704–05: 1952–60, at 1953–54.

30. Emily Mann, "To Build and Fortify: Defensive Architecture in the Early Atlantic Colonies," in *Building the British Atlantic World: Spaces, Places, and Material Culture, 1600–1850*, ed. Daniel Maudlin and Bernard L. Herman (Chapel Hill: University of North Carolina Press, 2016), 31–52.

31. Stearns, *Science in the British Colonies*, 351. Stearns notes that John Searle's brother, George Searle, was a ship captain in the Caribbean.

32. "Thomas Walduck's Letters from Barbados, 1710," *Journal of the Barbados Museum and Historical Society*, 15, no. 1 (1947): 27–51; Stearns, "James Petiver," 243–365, 316.

33. "Thomas Walduck's Letters from Barbados, 1710–1711," *Journal of the Barbados Museum and Historical Society*, 15, no. 3 (1948): 137–49, at 144, 148.

34. "Thomas Walduck's Letters from Barbados, 1710–1711," 137–49.

35. Hilary McDonald Beckles, *Natural Rebels: A Social History of Enslaved Black Women in Barbados* (New Brunswick, NJ: Rutgers University Press, 1989), 43, 133–35, 143.

36. See James Brodie and Dr. Preston, "An Account of a Faetus, Voided by the Ulcered Navil of a Negro in Nevis, by Mr. James Brodie; Communicated by Dr. Preston," *Philosophical Transactions (1683–1775)* 19 (1695): 580–81; James Parsons, "An Account of the White Negro Shewn before the Royal Society: In a Letter to the Right Honourable the Earl of Morton, President of the Royal Society, from James Parsons, M. D. F. R. S.," *Philosophical Transactions (1683–1775)* 55 (1765): 45–53; James Bate and Alexander Russel, "An Account of the Remarkable Alteration of Colour in a Negro Woman: In a Letter to the Reverend Mr. Alexander Williamson of Maryland, from Mr. James Bate, Surgeon in That Province. Communicated by Alexander Russel, M. D. F. R. S," *Philosophical Transactions (1683–1775)* 51 (1759): 175–78; William Byrd. "An Account of a Negro-Boy That Is Dappel'd in Several Places of His Body with White Spots. By William Byrd, Esq, F. R. S," *Philosophical Transactions (1683–1775)* 19 (1695): 781–82; John H. Appleby, "Human Curiosities and the Royal Society, 1699–1751," *Notes and Records of the Royal Society of London* 50, no. 1 (1996): 13–27; James Delbourgo, "The Newtonian Slave Body: Racial Enlightenment in the Atlantic World," *Atlantic Studies* 9, no. 2 (2012): 185–207.

37. St. Julien R. Childs, "A Letter Written in 1711 by Mary Stafford to Her Kinswoman in England," *South Carolina Historical Magazine* 81, no. 1 (1980): 1–7.

38. Pettigrew, "Free to Enslave," 28–29; Adrian Finucane, *The Temptations of Trade: Britain, Spain, and the Struggle for Empire* (Philadelphia: University of Pennsylvania Press, 2016), 53–83.

39. Arne Bialuschewski, "A True Account of the Design, and Advantages of the South-Sea Trade: Profits, Propaganda, and the Peace Preliminaries of 1711," *Huntington Library Quarterly* 73, no. 2 (2010): 273–85; Abigail Leslie Swingen, *Competing Visions of Empire: Labor, Slavery, and the Origins of the British Atlantic Empire* (New Haven, CT: Yale University Press, 2015), 172–95.

40. Carl Wennerlind, *Casualties of Credit: The English Financial Revolution, 1620–1720* (Cambridge, MA: Harvard University Press, 2011), 197–234.

41. Philip D. Curtin, *The Atlantic Slave Trade: A Census* (Madison: University of Wisconsin Press, 1972), 131; Morgan, *Slavery and the British Empire*, 59–61; John G. Sperling, *The South Sea Company: An Historical Essay and Bibliographical Finding List* (Cambridge, MA: Harvard University Press, 1962), 13–15.

42. A *pieza de India*, defined by the *asiento*, was a captive "with no defects at least 58 inches tall." Sperling, *South Sea Company*, 14. The company did sell some captives at inland cities, including Bogotá. On the Royal Navy and the South Sea Company, see Helen J. Paul, *The South Sea Bubble: An Economic History of its Origins and Consequences* (London: Routledge, 2010), 6–7, 27, 38, 42, 54–55, 58, 72–73, 109.

43. Finucane, *Temptations of Trade*, 41.

44. Sperling, *South Sea Company*, 20–25; George H. Nelson, "Contraband Trade under the Asiento, 1730–1739," *American Historical Review* 51, no. 1 (1945): 55–67; Christian Cwik, "The End of the British Atlantic Slave Trade or the Beginning of the Big Slave Robbery, 1808–1850," in *The Second Slavery: Mass Slaveries and Modernity in the Americas and in the Atlantic Basin*, ed.

Javier Lavina and Michael Zeuske (Berlin: LIT Verlag, 2014), 19–38, at 26. Beyond the legally permitted traffic in enslaved captives under the asiento, company officials also engaged in smuggling and illicit trade throughout New Spain.

45. Sperling, *South Sea Company,* 21; Murphy, "Collecting Slave Traders," 666; Arthur S. Aiton, "The Asiento Treaty as Reflected in the Papers of Lord Shelburne," *Hispanic American Historical Review* 8, no. 2 (1928): 167–77.

46. Murphy, "Collecting Slave Traders," 666; Edith Duncan Johnston, "Dr. William Houstoun, Botanist," *Georgia Historical Quarterly* 25, no. 4 (1941): 325–39.

47. "Quadrupeds," Sir Hans Sloane Collection, Manuscript Catalogs, Natural History Museum, London.

48. William Toller, "Reproducción facsimilar de la 'Historia de un Viaje al Río de la Plata y Buenos Aires desde inglaterra.' Ano MDCCXV por William Toller," *Revista Histórica: Publicación del Museo Histórico Nacional* 23, no. 67-6 (May 1955): 1–33. Murphy, "Collecting Slave Traders," 645, 662–63. Petiver's South Sea Company collectors included David Patton, surgeon aboard the slave ship *Elizabeth;* Mr. Cooke, a surgeon at Panama; Thomas Dover, the company's chief factor at Buenos Aires; John Burnett, surgeon at Porto Bello and Cartagena; and George Jesson, captain of the slave ship *William and Sarah.* During his career as a factor for the South Sea Company at Buenos Aires, Dover forwarded samples of the valuable cinchona plant back to Petiver in London. On Petiver's South Sea Company contacts, see Stearns, *Science in the British Colonies,* 384–85; Kenneth Dewhurst and Rex Doublet, "Thomas Dover and the South Sea Company," *Medical History* 18, no. 2 (1974): 107–21.

49. Dewhurst and Doublet, "Thomas Dover and the South Sea Company," 112; Daniel Schavelzon, "On Slaves and Beer: The First Images of the South Sea Company Slave Market in Buenos Aires," *African and Black Diaspora: An International Journal* 7, no. 2 (2014): 119–28.

50. Finucane, *Temptations of Trade,* 38.

51. Dewhurst and Doublet, "Thomas Dover and the South Sea Company," 111.

52. Virginia Bever Platt, "The East India Company and the Madagascar Slave Trade," *William and Mary Quarterly* (1969): 548–77, at 563, note 30; Nelson, "Contraband Trade under the Asiento," 60.

53. James Ferguson King, "Descriptive Data on Negro Slaves in Spanish Importation Records and Bills of Sale," *Journal of Negro History* 28, no. 2 (1943): 204–19.

54. Schavelzon, "On Slaves and Beer," 126.

55. Aiton, "Asiento Treaty as Reflected in the Papers of Lord Shelburne," 171.

56. General account of the Portobelo and Panama factory and of the Balance of the Books of Debtors and Creditors of the Factoría, Archivo General de Indias, Seville, Seccíon Contaduría, 226, cited in Rafael Donoso Anes, "Accounting and Slavery: The Accounts of the English South Sea Company, 1713–22," *European Accounting Review* 11, no. 2 (2002): 441–52. On "indultado" slaves, see Alex Borucki, *From Shipmates to Soldiers: Emerging Black Identities in the Río de la Plata* (Albuquerque: University of New Mexico Press, 2015), 6.

57. Colin A. Palmer, "The Company Trade and the Numerical Distribution of Slaves to Spanish America, 1703–1739," in *Africans in Bondage: Studies in Slavery and the Slave Trade,* ed. Philip D. Curtin and Paul Lovejoy (Madison: African Studies Program, University of Wisconsin–Madison, 1986), 27–43. Ringworm, or dermatophytosis, is not an animal but rather a fungal infection.

58. Stearns, *Science in the British Colonies*, 384–85.

59. In 1708, Dover joined a privateering voyage led by Woodes Rogers and William Dampier that for four years raided Spanish treasure ships in the Caribbean and along the Spanish Main. Dover's medical and commercial expertise as a surgeon in the slave trade likely played a role in selecting Toller for the position. On Dover, see Dewhurst and Doublet, "Thomas Dover and the South Sea Company," 107–121; Finucane, *Temptations of Trade*, 21.

60. Richard B. Sheridan, "The Guinea Surgeons on the Middle Passage: The Provision of Medical Services in the British Slave Trade," *International Journal of African Historical Studies* 14, no. 4 (1981): 601–25; King, "Descriptive Data on Negro Slaves."

61. Finucane, *Temptations of Trade*, 34.

62. Gustavo Verdesio, *Forgotten Conquests: Rereading New World History from the Margins* (Philadelphia: Temple University Press, 2001), 114–15.

63. Dewhurst and Doublet, "Thomas Dover and the South Sea Company," 112.

64. Thomas Falkner, another South Sea Company surgeon, also practiced and wrote a natural history of New Spain after joining the Society of Jesus in 1732. On Falkner, see Álvaro Fernández Bravo, "Catálogo, Colección y Colonialismo Interno: Una lectura de la 'Descripción de la Patagonia' de Thomas Falkner (1774)," *Revista de Crítica Literaria Latinoamericana* (2004): 229–49; Miguel de Asúa, *Science in the Vanished Arcadia: Knowledge of Nature in the Jesuit Missions of Paraguay and Río de la Plata* (Leiden: Brill, 2014).

65. Toller, "Reproducción facsimilar," 16.

66. Toller, "Reproducción facsimilar," 18.

67. Kathleen S. Murphy, "A Slaving Surgeon's Collection: The Pursuit of Natural History through the British Slave Trade to Spanish America," in *Curious Encounters: Voyaging, Collecting, and Making Knowledge in the Long Eighteenth Century*, ed. Adriana Craciun and Mary Terrall (Toronto: University of Toronto Press, 2019), 138–58.

68. Murphy, "Collecting Slave Traders," 662; Stearns, *Science in the British Colonies*, 385.

69. Murphy, "A Slaving Surgeon's Collection," 145.

70. Finucane, *Temptations of Trade*, 63, 66–67.

71. Luis Eduardo Fajardo, "Dos Comerciantes Británicos en Cartagena a Principios del siglo XVIII," *Boletín Cultural y Bibliográfico* 43, no. 71–72 (2006): 2–19.

72. Murphy, "A Slaving Surgeon's Collection," 143.

73. Finucane, *Temptations of Trade*, 65; Sloane MS 4046, British Library, London.

74. Portions of Sloane's "Vertebrate" catalog are reproduced in Arthur MacGregor and Alistair McAlpine, *Sir Hans Sloane: Collector, Scientist, Antiquary, Founding Father of the British Museum* (London: British Museum Press, 1994), 84–85. In Sloane's manuscript catalogs, further evidence of South Sea Company collectors is available, including entries listing woodpeckers and magpies collected at Rio de la Hacha, and "the under mandibles of this Toucan from Cartagena in America by Mr. Houstoun," presumably William Houstoun, a surgeon and protégé of Sloane who served the South Sea Company at Cartagena, Veracruz, and Jamaica.

75. "Birds," Sir Hans Sloane Collection, Manuscript Catalogs, Natural History Museum, London.

76. Sloane MS 4045, folio 37, British Library, London; James A. Rawley, "Richard Harris,

Slave Trader Spokesman," *Albion: A Quarterly Journal Concerned with British Studies* 23, no. 3 (1991): 439–58.

77. "Insects," and "Quadupeds," Sir Hans Sloane Collection, Manuscript Catalogs, Natural History Museum, London.

78. Rawley, "Richard Harris," 441–42.

79. William Smith, *A Natural History of Nevis, and the Rest of the English Leeward Charibee Islands in America* (London: J. Bentham, 1745), 10.

80. John Nichols, *Illustrations of the Literary History of the Eighteenth Century* ([London]: Nichols, Son, and Bentley, 1817), 1:790.

81. Smith, *Natural History of Nevis,* 2–3.

82. Smith describes these events as equal parts scientific curiosity and sociable leisure, noting that the slaveholders watch "standing by on high Rocks to see the Pastime."

83. Smith, *Natural History of Nevis,* 7–10, 17.

84. Elizabeth Tonkin, "Autonomous Judges: African Ordeals as Dramas of Power," *Ethnos* 65, no. 3 (2000): 366–86; T. Lauder Brunton and Walter Pye, "On the Physiological Action of the Bark of Erythrophleum Guinense, Generally Called Casca, Cassa, or Sassy Bark," *Philosophical Transactions of the Royal Society of London* 167 (1877): 627–58; Thomas S. Githens, *Drug Plants of Africa* (Philadelphia: University of Pennsylvania Press, 1949); Katrina Keefer, "Poro, Witchcraft and Red Water in Early Colonial Sierra Leone: GR Nylander's Ethnography and Systems of Authority on the Bullom Shore," *Canadian Journal of African Studies/Revue canadienne des études africaines* 55, no. 1 (2021): 39–55.

85. F. N. Howes, "Fish-Poison Plants," *Bulletin of Miscellaneous Information (Royal Botanic Gardens, Kew),* no. 4 (1930): 129–53.

86. Smith, *Natural History of Nevis,* 50–51.

87. Smith, *Natural History of Nevis,* 20, 92; Stuart Peterfreund, "From the Forbidden to the Familiar: The Way of Natural Theology Leading Up to and beyond the Long Eighteenth Century," *Studies in Eighteenth-Century Culture* 37, no. 1 (2008): 23–39.

88. Smith, *Natural History of Nevis,* 231.

89. Amy R. W. Meyers and Margaret Beck Pritchard, eds., "Introduction," in *Empire's Nature: Mark Catesby's New World Vision* (Chapel Hill: University of North Carolina Press, 1998), 1–33.

90. Mark Catesby, *The Natural History of Carolina, Florida, and the Bahama Islands* (London, 1731), 1:18. Copy held at the Library Company of Philadelphia, Pennsylvania.

91. David Brigham, "Mark Catesby and the Patronage of Natural History in the First Half of the Eighteenth Century," in Meyers and Pritchard, *Empire's Nature,* 91–146.

92. W. Raymond Wood, "An Archaeological Appraisal of Early European Settlements in the Senegambia," *Journal of African History* 8, no. 1 (1967): 39–64; Donald R. Wright, "Darbo Jula: The Role of a Mandinka Jula Clan in the Long-Distance Trade of the Gambia River and Its Hinterland," *African Economic History,* no. 3 (1977): 33–45; Liza Gijanto and Sarah Walshaw, "Ceramic Production and Dietary Changes at Juffure, Gambia," *African Archaeological Review* 31, no. 2 (2014): 265–97.

93. Wood, "Archaeological Appraisal," 42.

94. Francis Moore, *Travels into the Inland Parts of Africa,* v–vi.

95. Matthew H. Hill, "Towards a Chronology of the Publications of Francis Moore's *Travels into the Inland Parts of Africa, History in Africa* 19 (1992): 353–68.

96. Moore, *Travels into the Inland Parts of Africa*, xxii.

97. John Atkins, *A Voyage to Guinea, Brasil, and the West-Indies; in His Majesty's Ships, the* Swallow *and* Weymouth (London: Printed for Caesar Ward and Richard Chandler, 1735), 39.

98. Moore, *Travels into the Inland Parts of Africa*, 63. On Barsally, see Martin A. Klein, "Servitude among the Wolof and Sereer of Senegambia," in *Slavery in Africa: Historical and Anthropological Perspectives*, ed. Suzanne Miers and Igor Kopytoff (Madison: University of Wisconsin Press, 1977), 335–63. To date, I have found no sources on Demel, presumably another Wolof-speaking state.

99. Moore, *Travels into the Inland Parts of Africa*, 20.

100. Moore, *Travels into the Inland Parts of Africa*, 75–76.

101. On Yamyamacunda, see Christopher DeCorse, "Tools of Empire: Trade, Slaves, and the British Forts of West Africa," in *Building the British Atlantic World: Spaces, Places, and Material Culture, 1600–1850*, ed. Daniel Maudlin and Bernard L. Herman (Chapel Hill: University of North Carolina Press, 2016), 169–75.

102. Moore, *Travels into the Inland Parts of Africa*, 124–25.

103. Francis J. Dallett Jr., "Griffith Hughes Dissected," *Journal of the Barbados Museum and Historical Society* 23, no. 1 (1955): 3–29; Griffith Hughes, "A Letter from the Reverend Mr. Griffith Hughes, Minister of St. Lucy's Parish in Barbadoes, to Martin Folkes, Esq; President of the Royal Society, concerning a Zoophyton, Somewhat Resembling the Flower of the Marigold," *Philosophical Transactions (1683–1775)* 42 (1742): 590–93.

104. Griffith Hughes, *The Natural History of Barbados* (London: Printed for the author, 1750), 272.

105. Annalisa Marzano, *Harvesting the Sea: The Exploitation of Marine Resources in the Roman Mediterranean* (Oxford: Oxford University Press, 2013), 143.

106. Thomas Thompson, *An Account of Two Missionary Voyages* (London: Printed for Benj. Dod., 1758), 23; Sylvia R. Frey and Betty Wood, *Come Shouting to Zion: African American Protestantism in the American South and British Caribbean to 1830* (Chapel Hill: University of North Carolina Press, 2000), 28–29; Ty M. Reese, "'Sheep in the Jaws of So Many Ravenous Wolves': The Slave Trade and Anglican Missionary Activity at Cape Coast Castle, 1752–1816," *Journal of Religion in Africa* 34, no. 3 (2004): 348–72. Thompson, given his education in theology and the stated positions of the Society, preached the harmonious compatibility of slavery with Christianity. After his residency as chaplain at Cape Coast, the reverend returned to England and published *The African Trade for Negro Slaves, Shewn to be Consistent with the Principles of Humanity*, dedicated to his patrons, the African Company of Merchants, in 1772. On the Society for the Propagation of the Gospel and slavery, see Travis Glasson, *Mastering Christianity: Missionary Anglicanism and Slavery in the Atlantic World* (Oxford: Oxford University Press, 2011), 75–110; Glasson, "Missionaries, Methodists, and a Ghost: Philip Quaque in London and Cape Coast, 1756–1816," *Journal of British Studies* 48, no. 1 (2009): 29–50.

107. Glasson, *Mastering Christianity*.

108. Thompson, *An Account of Two Missionary Voyages*, 27–29.

109. Michael A. Salmon, *The Aurelian Legacy: British Butterflies and Their Collectors* (Oakland: University of California Press, 2000), 114–15.

110. Drury to Pallas, 12 November 1767, cited in T. D. A. Cockerell, "Dru Drury, an Eighteenth Century Entomologist," *Scientific Monthly* 14, no. 1 (1922): 67–82, at 70.

111. Dru Drury, *Illustrations of Natural History* (London: Printed for the author, 1782), 3:xvii.

112. On Kuckhan as a slaveholder, see *The Laws of Jamaica: 1792–1799* (Kingston: Alexander Aikman and Son, 1811). Kuckhan forwarded a collection of insects to the Royal Society before his death in 1775 and contributed a paper to the *Philosophical Transactions* in 1770: "Four Letters from Mr. T. S. Kuckhan, to the President and Members of the Royal Society, on the Preservation of Dead Birds," *Philosophical Transactions (1683–1775)* 60 (1770): 302–20. Kuckhan's letter indicates his own interest in collecting and preserving specimens, an interest supported by his wealth as a slaveholder at his plantation, Charlottenburgh, in St. Andrew Parish. Abbot collected insects and birds for Drury and other English naturalists in Virginia and Georgia from 1773 until approximately 1797. On Abbot, see Joseph Ewan, "The Natural History of John Abbot: Influences and Some Questions," *Bartonia* no. 51 (1985): 37–45.

113. On Jarratt, see Douglass Adair and Devereux Jarratt, "The Autobiography of the Reverend Devereux Jarratt, 1732–1763," *William and Mary Quarterly* (1952): 346–93. On Greenway, see Edward Wyatt, "Dr. James Greenway, Eighteenth Century Botanist, of Dinwiddie County, with an Account of Two Generations of His Descendants," in *Genealogies of Virginia Families: From Tyler's Quarterly Historical and Genealogical Magazine* (Baltimore: Genealogical Publishing Company, 2007), 1:130–40.

114. Drury to Mr. Hugh, going to Africa with Capt. Johnson, 22 March 1762, in Cockerell, "Dru Drury," 70.

115. A. Starr Douglas and E. Geoffrey Hancock, "Insect Collecting in Africa during the Eighteenth Century and William Hunter's Collection," *Archives of Natural History* 34, no. 2 (2007): 293–306, at 298.

116. Douglas and Hancock. "Insect Collecting in Africa," 299. British travelers and slavers referred to Príncipe, in the Gulf of Guinea, as "Princess Island."

117. Douglas and Hancock, "Insect Collecting in Africa," 299. In addition to the crewmen of the *Hound* and the *Tartar,* Drury enlisted the assistance of a captain of another ship, the *Vernon,* in 1770, and another slave trader based in Liverpool, Captain Larkes, in 1771.

118. Douglas and Hancock, "Insect Collecting in Africa," 298.

119. E. Geoffrey Hancock and A. Starr Douglas, "William Hunter's Goliath Beetle, *Goliathus goliatus* (Linnaeus, 1771), re-visited," *Archives of Natural History* 36, no. 2 (2009): 218–30.

120. Starr Douglas, "The Making of Scientific Knowledge in an Age of Slavery: Henry Smeathman, Sierra Leone and Natural History," *Journal of Colonialism and Colonial History* 9, no. 3 (2008); Deirdre Coleman, *Romantic Colonization and British Anti-Slavery* (Cambridge: Cambridge University Press, 2005), 35; John Coakley Lettsom, *The Works of John Fothergill* (London: Printed for Charles Dilly, 1784), 3:183–96.

121. Douglas, "Making of Scientific Knowledge."

122. Kristina Kindmark and György Nováky, "Imperiets Budbärare: Henry Smeathman å resa i Sierra Leone 1771–1774," in *Från Karakorum till Silijan: Resor Under Sju Sekler,* ed. Hanna

Hodacs and Åsa Karlsson (Lund: Historiska Media, 2000), 163–96, at 187. Smeathman did not ultimately create a slave trading firm; however, he did sail aboard a slave ship to the West Indies and held several enslaved people in bondage. The definitive biography of Smeathman is Deirdre Coleman, *Henry Smeathman, the Flycatcher: Natural History, Slavery, and Empire in the Late Eighteenth Century* (Liverpool: Liverpool University Press, 2018).

123. Henry Smeathman's letters to Dru Drury, MS D.26, 23 February 1775, Henry Smeathman Collection, University Library, Uppsala University, Sweden.

124. Henry Smeathman, "Some Account of the Termites, Which Are Found in Africa and Other Hot Climates. In a Letter from Mr. Henry Smeathman, of Clement's Inn, to Sir Joseph Banks, Bart. P. R. S," *Philosophical Transactions of the Royal Society of London* (1781), 139–92, at 140–41, 165, 167.

125. Kindmark and Nováky, "Imperiets Budbärare," 184.

126. Smeathman to Drury, 8 August 1772, Mr. Smeathman's letters to Mr. Drury, MS D.26, 1–3, quoted in Douglas, "Making of Scientific Knowledge."

127. Parrish, *American Curiosity*, 272.

128. Karl Offen, "Puritan Bioprospecting in Central America and the West Indies," *Itinerario* 35, no. 1 (2011): 15–48; Karen Ordahl Kupperman, "Errand to the Indies: Puritan Colonization from Providence Island through the Western Design," *William and Mary Quarterly* 45, no. 1 (1988): 70–99.

129. "Alexander Garden to Carolus Linnaeus, Charlestown, 20 June 1771," in James Edward Smith, ed., *A Selection of the Correspondence of Linnaeus, and Other Naturalists, from the Original Manuscripts* (London: Printed for Longman, Hurst, Rees, Orme, and Brown, 1821), 2:330–37. This man is also, most likely, the "servant" mentioned in a paper written by John Ellis discussing an animal sent by Garden to London. Ellis, "An Account of an Amphibious Bipes; By John Ellis, Esq; F. R. S. To the Royal Society," *Philosophical Transactions (1683–1775)* 56 (1766): 189–92. Chigoe fleas are known to entomologists as *Tunga penetrans*.

130. "Alexander Garden to Carolus Linnaeus, Charlestown, 20 June 1771," 2:330–31.

131. For an excellent analysis of this man's labor and skill in natural history, see Whitney Barlow Robles, "Flatness," in *The Philosophy Chamber: Art and Science in Harvard's Teaching Cabinet, 1766–1820*, ed. Ethan W. Lasser (New Haven, CT: Yale University Press, 2017), 190–209.

132. "Alexander Garden to Carolus Linnaeus, Charlestown, 20 June 1771," 2:331–35.

133. Christopher M. Parsons and Kathleen S. Murphy, "Ecosystems under Sail: Specimen Transport in the Eighteenth-Century French and British Atlantics," *Early American Studies* 10, no. 3 (2012): 503–29.

134. The literature on Linnaeus is vast. For a relevant selection on his ideas about improvement and empire, see Lisbet Koerner, *Linnaeus: Nature and Nation* (Cambridge, MA: Harvard University Press, 2000); Staffan Müller-Wille, "Nature as a Marketplace: The Political Economy of Linnaean Botany," *History of Political Economy* 35, no. 5 (2003): 154–72.

135. Margaret Denny, "Linnaeus and His Disciple in Carolina: Alexander Garden," *Isis* 38, no. 3/4 (1948): 161–74.

136. George C. Rogers Jr., David R. Chesnutt, and Peggy J. Clark, eds., *The Papers of Henry Laurens*, vol. 6, *August 1, 1768–July 31, 1769* (Columbia: University of South Carolina Press, 1978), 181; Stearns, *Science in the British Colonies*, 599–619.

137. Edmund Berkeley and Dorothy Smith Berkeley, *Dr. Alexander Garden of Charles Town* (Chapel Hill: University of North Carolina Press, 1969), 275, 280.

138. Simon Schaffer et al., eds., *The Brokered World: Go-Betweens and Global Intelligence* (Sagamore Beach, MA: Science History Publications, 2009).

139. Shaw, *Memories of the Slave Trade*, 215.

140. John Matthews, *A Voyage to the River Sierra-Leone: On the Coast of Africa; Containing an Account of the Trade and Productions of the Country, and of the Civil and Religious Customs and Manners of the People* (London: Printed for B. White and Son, 1788); Shaw, *Memories of the Slave Trade,* 215.

141. Coleman, *Henry Smeathman, the Flycatcher,* 91–92.

142. Matthews, *Voyage to the River Sierra-Leone,* 181.

143. Matthews, *Voyage to the River Sierra-Leone,* 41.

144. Matthews, *Voyage to the River Sierra-Leone,* 42.

145. Indeed, Royal African Company surveyor William Smith recalled a mandrill that, in his estimate, resembled an African. See Smith, *A New Voyage to Guinea* (London: Printed for John Nourse, 1744), 52–53.

146. Steven Shapin and Simon Schaffer, *Leviathan and the Air-Pump: Hobbes, Boyle, and the Experimental Life* (Princeton, NJ: Princeton University Press, 1985), 22–25.

147. Matthews, *Voyage to the River Sierra-Leone,* 158–59.

148. In 1788, the Committee of the Liverpool African Merchants, a group of slave traders, commissioned Matthews, along with Robert Norris and Archibald Dalzel, to testify before Parliament in support of the slave trade. See Gomer Williams, *History of the Liverpool Privateers and Letters of Marque: With an Account of the Liverpool Slave Trade* (London: William Heinemann, 1897), 611.

149. Deirdre Coleman, "'Aetherial Journies, Submarine Exploits': The Debatable Worlds of Natural History in the Eighteenth Century," in *Romanticism's Debatable Lands,* ed. Claire Lamont and Michael Rossington (New York: Palgrave Macmillan, 2007), 223–36, at 227; Roy A. Rauschenberg, "John Ellis, Royal Agent for West Florida," *Florida Historical Quarterly* 62, no. 1 (1983), 1–24; Marc J. Ratcliff, "Temporality, Sequential Iconography and Linearity in Figures: The Impact of the Discovery of Division in Infusoria," *History and Philosophy of the Life Sciences* 21, no. 3 (1999): 255–92.

150. Ellis to Linnaeus, 31 January 1766 and 21 October 1766, in Smith, *A Selection of the Correspondence of Linnaeus,* 1:185–91.

151. John Ellis, *The Natural History of Many Curious and Uncommon Zoophytes* (London: Printed for Benjamin White and Son, 1786), 96, 185.

152. Nini Rodgers, *Ireland, Slavery and Anti-Slavery: 1612–1865* (New York: Palgrave Macmillan, 2007), 147–48, 192, 212; Polly Pattullo, *Your Time Is Done Now: Slavery, Resistance, and Defeat: The Maroon Trials of Dominica (1813–1814)* (New York: New York University Press, 2015), 43, 74; Richard K. MacMaster, "From Ulster to the Carolinas: John Torrans, John Greg, John Poaug, and Bounty Immigration, 1761–1768," in *The Irish in the Atlantic World,* ed. David T. Gleeson (Columbia: University of South Carolina Press, 2010).

153. Ellis, *Natural History of Many Curious and Uncommon Zoophytes,* 5–7, 17, 65, 81–83, 91–95, 109, 114, 180.

154. John Ellis, "An Account of the Sea Pen, or *Pennatula Phosphorea* of Linnaeus; Likewise a Description of a New Species of Sea Pen, Found on the Coast of South-Carolina, with Observations on Sea-Pens in General. In a Letter to the Honourable Coote Molesworth, Esq; MD and FRS from John Ellis, Esq; FRS and Member of the Royal Academy at Upsal," *Philosophical Transactions (1683–1775)* 53 (1763): 419–35.

155. Susannah Gibson, "On Being an Animal, or, the Eighteenth-Century Zoophyte Controversy in Britain," *History of Science* 50, no. 4 (2012): 453–76.

Chapter 3

WE FLESH BELONG TO BUCKRA

Human–Animal Labor on American Plantations

1. Samuel Martin to Samuel Martin Jr., 16 June 1758, British Museum, Additional Manuscripts, 41346, folder 210, quoted in Richard Sheridan, "Samuel Martin, Innovating Sugar Planter of Antigua," *Agricultural History* 34, no. 3 (1960): 126–139, at 128. Green Castle is sometimes referred to in documents as Greencastle.

2. Mrs. Lanaghan, *Antigua and the Antiguans* (London: Saunders and Otley, 1844), 2:79, 353.

3. Samantha Rebovich Bardoe, "Resistance and Reform: Landscapes at Green Castle, Antigua," in *The Limits of Tyranny*, ed. James A. Delle (Knoxville: University of Tennessee Press, 2015), 65–92.

4. Sheridan, "Samuel Martin, Innovating Sugar Planter of Antigua," 129; Samantha Anne Rebovich, "Landscape, Labor, and Practice: Slavery and Freedom at Green Castle Estate, Antigua," PhD dissertation, Syracuse University, 2011.

5. Samuel Martin to Samuel Martin Jr., 14 June 1758, British Museum, Additional Manuscripts, 41346, folder 208, quoted in Sheridan, "Samuel Martin, Innovating Sugar Planter of Antigua," 129.

6. Samuel Martin to Samuel Martin Jr., 14 June 1758.

7. Book historians disagree when the first edition of *An Essay Upon Plantership* was published; however, there is agreement that the earliest date may have been 1750.

8. Samuel Martin, *An Essay Upon Plantership*, humbly inscrib'd to all the planters of the British sugar-colonies in America. The Second Edition, Corrected and Enlarged (Antigua: T. Smith, 1750), 1–2.

9. Quoted in Patrick Richardson, *Empire & Slavery* (New York: Harper and Row, 1968), 118; Morgan, "Slaves and Livestock"; Kenneth Morgan, "Bristol West India Merchants in the Eighteenth Century," *Transactions of the Royal Historical Society* 3 (1993): 185–208.

10. Janet Schaw, *Journal of a Lady of Quality: Being the Narrative of a Journey from Scotland to the West Indies, North Carolina, and Portugal, in the Years 1774 to 1776* (New Haven, CT: Yale University Press, 1921), 78.

11. James F. Dator, "'Choicest of the Cargoe': Antigua, the Codringtons, and the Slave Trade, ca. 1672–1808," in *An Archaeology and History of a Caribbean Sugar Plantation on Antigua*, ed. Georgia L. Fox (Gainesville: University Press of Florida, 2020), 145–57, at 149.

12. Ulrich B. Phillips, "An Antigua Plantation, 1769–1818," *North Carolina Historical Review* 3, no. 3 (1926): 439–45.

13. Samuel Martin to Christopher Baldwin, 23 May 1776, British Museum, Additional Manuscripts, 41346, folder 208, quoted in Sheridan, "Samuel Martin, Innovating Sugar Planter of Antigua," 137.

14. Mary Lindemann, *Medicine and Society in Early Modern Europe* (Cambridge: Cambridge University Press, 1999), 107.

15. Carla Mazzio, "Acting with Tact: Touch and Theater in the Renaissance," in *Sensible Flesh: On Touch in Early Modern Culture,* ed. Elizabeth D. Harvey (Philadelphia: University of Pennsylvania Press, 2003), 159–86, at 174.

16. Monique Allewaert, *Ariel's Ecology: Plantations, Personhood, and Colonialism in the American Tropics* (Minneapolis: University of Minnesota Press, 2013), 1–28.

17. Lorena S. Walsh, "Slave Life, Slave Society, and Tobacco Production in the Tidewater Chesapeake, 1620–1820," in *Cultivation and Culture: Labor and the Shaping of Slave Life in the Americas,* ed. Ira Berlin and Philip D. Morgan (Charlottesville: University Press of Virginia, 1993), 184. Walsh has shown that by the late eighteenth century, about half of Chesapeake slaveholders had adopted plow culture.

18. John Archdale, *A New Description of that Fertile and Pleasant Province of Carolina* (London, 1707).

19. Ben Marsh, "Silk Hopes in Colonial South Carolina," *Journal of Southern History* 78, no. 4 (2012): 807–54.

20. Russell R. Menard, "Plantation Empire: How Sugar and Tobacco Planters Built Their Industries and Raised an Empire," *Agricultural History* 81, no. 3 (2007): 309–32; Trevor Burnard, *Planters, Merchants, and Slaves: Plantation Societies in British America, 1650–1820* (Chicago: University of Chicago Press, 2015); Trevor Burnard and John Garrigus, *The Plantation Machine: Atlantic Capitalism in French Saint-Domingue and British Jamaica* (Philadelphia: University of Pennsylvania Press, 2016.)

21. Menard, "Plantation Empire," 323.

22. Martin, *An Essay Upon Plantership,* 7.

23. Sheridan, "Samuel Martin," 129; Martin, *An Essay Upon Plantership,* 2, 10.

24. On entanglement as a historical concept, see Ralph Bauer and Marcy Norton, "Introduction: Entangled Trajectories: Indigenous and European Histories," *Colonial Latin American Review* 26, no. 1 (2017): 1–17.

25. Norton, "Going to the Birds."

26. Edward B. Rugemer, *Slave Law and the Politics of Resistance in the Early Atlantic World* (Cambridge, MA: Harvard University Press, 2018), 13.

27. Ligon, *True & Exact History,* 3, 108.

28. Judith Carney, "Landscapes and Places of Memory: African Diaspora Research and Geography," in *The African Diaspora and the Disciplines,* ed. Tejumola Olaniyan and James Sweet (Bloomington: Indiana University Press, 2010), 101–18.

29. Ligon, *True & Exact History,* 58; Charlotte Carrington-Farmer, "Trading Horses in the Eighteenth Century: Rhode Island and the Atlantic World," in *Equestrian Cultures: Horses, Human Society, and the Discourse of Modernity,* ed. Kristen Guest and Monica Mattfeld (Chicago: Univer-

sity of Chicago Press), 92–109; Mac Griswold, *The Manor: Three Centuries at a Slave Plantation on Long Island* (New York: Farrar, Straus and Giroux, 2013).

30. Ligon, *True & Exact History*, 22–23.

31. Ligon, *True & Exact History*, 46.

32. David W. Galenson, "The Atlantic Slave Trade and the Barbados Market, 1673–1723," *Journal of Economic History* 42, no. 3 (1982): 491–511.

33. Ligon, *True & Exact History*, 89.

34. Judith Carney, "Seeds of Memory: Botanical Legacies of the African Diaspora," in *African Ethnobotany in the Americas,* ed. Robert Voeks and John Rashford (New York: Springer Science and Business Media, 2013), 13–34, at 20–22.

35. Ligon, *True & Exact History*, 88–89.

36. Richard S. Dunn, *Sugar and Slaves: The Rise of the Planter Class in the English West Indies, 1624–1713* (Chapel Hill: University of North Carolina Press, 1972), 192; Ligon, *True & Exact History*, 90.

37. Samuel Clarke, *A True and Faithful Account of the Four Chiefest Plantations of the English in America* (London, 1670), 73.

38. Bonham Richardson, *The Caribbean in the Wider World, 1492–1992: A Regional Geography* (Cambridge: Cambridge University Press, 1992), 48.

39. Ligon, *True & Exact History*, 113.

40. Ligon, *True & Exact History*, 58; David Watts, *The West Indies: Patterns of Development, Culture and Environmental Change Since 1492* (Cambridge: Cambridge University Press, 1987), 198–99, 229, 391. Judith Carney observes that Spanish settlers transported North African camels as draft animals to Peru beginning in the sixteenth century. See Carney "Seeds of Memory," 21.

41. Clarke, *A True and Faithful Account*, 73.

42. Vere Langford Oliver, *The History of the Island of Antigua: One of the Leeward Caribbees in the West Indies, from the First Settlement in 1635 to the Present Time* (London: Mitchell and Hughes, 1896), 2:1, 30–31, 44, 85, 147, 179, 193, 225, 256, 297, 303, 306, 327–328, 373.

43. James R. Bryant, "The Office of Master in Chancery: Colonial Development," *American Bar Association Journal* 40, no. 7 (1954): 595–98.

44. Oliver, *History of the Island of Antigua*, 2:69.

45. Martin, *An Essay Upon Plantership*, 13.

46. Estimate of Martin's Plantation, 1768, British Museum, Additional Manuscripts, 41353, folder 85, quoted in Sheridan, "Samuel Martin, Innovating Sugar Planter of Antigua," 131.

47. Martin, *An Essay Upon Plantership*, 13–14, 27–28.

48. Justin Roberts, *Slavery and the Enlightenment in the British Atlantic, 1750–1807* (Cambridge: Cambridge University Press, 2013), 214.

49. James Alexander, letter addressed to James Stothert, 8 November 1786, box 1, James Stothert Papers, William L. Clements Library, University of Michigan, Ann Arbor.

50. John Fowler, letter addressed to James Stothert at Martha Brae, Jamaica, September 1787, box 1, James Stothert Papers.

51. John Fowler, letters addressed to James Stothert, 6 November 1787, 1 October 1788, 7 October 1788, box 1, James Stothert Papers.

52. Diagrams of the estates are included in box 1, Jarvis Family Papers, William L. Clements Library, University of Michigan, Ann Arbor.

53. Thomas Jarvis, letter to Mary Trant, October 1791, box 2, Jarvis Family Papers.

54. Morgan, *Laboring Women*, 105; Fischer, *Suspect Relations*, 181.

55. *Minutes of the Society for the Improvement of Plantership on the Island of Barbados, instituted 8 December 1804* (Liverpool: Thomas Kaye, 1811). Manuscript copy held at Shilstone Memorial Library, Barbados Museum and Historical Society, Bridgetown, Barbados. Hereafter cited as *MTSIPIB*.

56. 5 January 1805, *MTSIPIB*.

57. Society meeting minutes for 27 March 1805; 9 July and 13 August 1808; 24 March and 29 April 1809, *MTSIPIB*.

58. 27 March 1805, *MTSIPIB*.

59. 3 May 1806, 3 January 1807, *MTSIPIB*.

60. Exposition of Turners Hall Plantation, 1832, Turners Hall Records, microfilm reels 20767–87, Barbados Department of Archives, Black Rock, Barbados; Benjamin M'Mahon, *Jamaica Plantership* (London: Effingham Wilson, 1839), 64.

61. Morgan, *Laboring Women*, 82–83, 89, 91, 107, 128, 138–139, 186.

62. 17 March 1810, *MTSIPIB*.

63. Allan Kulikoff, *Tobacco and Slaves: The Development of Southern Cultures in the Chesapeake, 1680–1800* (Chapel Hill: University of North Carolina Press, 1986), 408–12; Lorena S. Walsh, *Motives of Honor, Pleasure, and Profit: Plantation Management in the Colonial Chesapeake, 1607–1763* (Chapel Hill: University of North Carolina Press, 2010), 105, 144–145, 227, 567.

64. Probate inventories for York County are held at the John D. Rockefeller Jr. Library, Colonial Williamsburg Foundation, Williamsburg, Virginia.

65. Inventory of the Estate of Colonel William Digges, 24 May 1698, York County Estate Inventories, John D. Rockefeller Jr. Library.

66. Kulikoff, *Tobacco and Slaves*, 153; Lorena S. Walsh, "Plantation Management in the Chesapeake, 1620–1820," *Journal of Economic History* 49, no. 2 (1989): 393–406.

67. A true Inventory of the Eastate of William Blaikley Deceased of whats Lying on this side of James river, 20 August 1736, York County Estate Inventories, John D. Rockefeller Jr. Library.

68. Kulikoff, *Tobacco and Slaves*, 326.

69. David Brion Davis, *Slavery in the Colonial Chesapeake* (Williamsburg, VA: Colonial Williamsburg Foundation, 1986), 14.

70. Moore, *Travels into the Inland Parts of Africa*, 69.

71. Thomas Bluett, *Some Memoirs of the Life of Job: The Son of Solomon the High Priest of Boonda in Africa; who was a Slave about Two Years in Maryland* (London: Printed for Richard Ford, 1734), 18–21.

72. Sluyter, *Black Ranching Frontiers*.

73. *Virginia Gazette*, Rind, 22 September 1768, 3, John D. Rockefeller Jr. Library.

74. *Virginia Gazette*, Rind, 29 October 1772, 3, John D. Rockefeller Jr. Library.

75. *Virginia Gazette*, Purdie, 22 March 1776, 3, John D. Rockefeller Jr. Library.

76. *Virginia Gazette*, Purdie and Dixon, 22 April 1773, 3, John D. Rockefeller Jr. Library.

77. *Virginia Gazette*, Purdie, 14 March 14, 1777, 2, John D. Rockefeller Jr. Library.

78. Philip D. Morgan and Michael L. Nicholls, "Slaves in Piedmont Virginia, 1720–1790," *William and Mary Quarterly* 46, no. 2 (1989): 212–51. On the status of drivers in the West Indies and the Chesapeake, see Richard S. Dunn, *A Tale of Two Plantations: Slave Life and Labor in Jamaica and Virginia* (Cambridge, MA: Harvard University Press, 2014), 250, 325, 327, 331. On enslaved drivers in Maryland, see J. Elliott Russo, "'Fifty-Four Days Work of Two Negroes': Enslaved Labor in Colonial Somerset County, Maryland," *Agricultural History* 78, no. 4 (2004): 466–92.

79. Jack P. Greene, ed., *The Diary of Colonel Landon Carter of Sabine Hall, 1752–1778* (Charlottesville: University Press of Virginia, 1965), 1:216, 286; 2:681–82. On horses and plowing in Maryland, see Gloria Lund Main, *Tobacco Colony: Life in Early Maryland, 1650–1720* (Princeton, NJ: Princeton University Press, 1982), 66.

80. Walsh, *Motives of Honor*, 2012.

81. Harold B. Gill, "Wheat Culture in Colonial Virginia," *Agricultural History* 52, no. 3 (1978): 380–93.

82. Luke J. Pecoraro, "'We Have Done Very Little Investigation There; There Is a Great Deal Yet to Do': The Archaeology of George Washington's Mount Vernon," in *Stewards of Memory: The Past, Present, and Future of Historic Preservation at George Washington's Mount Vernon*, ed. Carol Borchert Cadou, Luke J. Pecoraro, and Thomas A. Reinhart (Charlottesville: University of Virginia Press, 2018), 70–91.

83. Greene, *Diary of Colonel Landon Carter*, 1:132.

84. Greene, *Diary of Colonel Landon Carter*, 2:683.

85. Greene, *Diary of Colonel Landon Carter*, 2:687.

86. Greene, *Diary of Colonel Landon Carter*, 1:333.

87. Greene, *Diary of Colonel Landon Carter*, 1:270.

88. Greene, *Diary of Colonel Landon Carter*, 1:561.

89. Greene, *Diary of Colonel Landon Carter*, 1:267, 270.

90. Greene, *Diary of Colonel Landon Carter*, 1:488; 2:672–73.

91. Of course, such labor was not limited to Virginia. Philip D. Morgan notes that Phibbah, an enslaved woman on Vineyard Pen, performed similar kinds of work while enslaved by Thomas Thistlewood. See Morgan, "Slaves and Livestock," 59.

92. Greene, *Diary of Colonel Landon Carter*, 2:577, 583; 2:628–29.

93. Rhys Isaac, *Landon Carter's Uneasy Kingdom: Revolution and Rebellion on a Virginia Plantation* (Oxford: Oxford University Press, 2004), 94.

94. Thomas Jefferson, *Notes on the State of Virginia* [Paris, 1782], 130–34, 253. See also Jordan, *White Over Black*, 29–32, 230, 238.

95. Jefferson, *Notes on the State of Virginia*, 253.

96. Roberts, *Slavery and the Enlightenment*, 91–92, 97; Kiple, *Caribbean Slave*, 64, 84, 87; Kenneth F. Kiple and Virginia H. Kiple, "Deficiency Diseases in the Caribbean," *Journal of Interdisciplinary History* 11, no. 2 (1980): 197–215.

97. Thomas Andrews, "Beasts of the Southern Wild: Slaveholders, Slaves and Other Animals in Charles Ball's *Slavery in the United States*," in *Rendering Nature: Animals, Bodies, Places, Politics*, ed. Marguerite Shaffer and Phoebe Young (Philadelphia: University of Pennsylvania Press, 2015),

21–47, at 26. On discussions of hunger and near-starvation in slave narratives see Vincent Woodard, *The Delectable Negro: Human Consumption and Homoeroticism within U.S. Slave Culture* (New York: New York University Press, 2014), 46–47, 95–97.

98. Nicholas Crawford, "'The reasonable sustentation of human life': Food Rations and the Problem of Provision in British Caribbean Slavery," *Early American Studies* 19, no. 2 (2021): 360–92; Crawford, "'In the Wreck of a Master's Fortune': Slave Provisioning and Planter Debt in the British Caribbean," *Slavery & Abolition* 37, no. 2 (2016): 353–74.

99. Anya Zilberstein, "Bastard Breadfruit and Other Cheap Provisions: Early Food Science for the Welfare of the Lower Orders," *Early Science and Medicine* 21, no. 5 (2016): 492–508.

100. Jennifer L. Anderson and Anya Zilberstein, "Empowering Appetites: The Political Economy and Culture of Food in the Early Atlantic World," *Early American Studies* 19, no. 2 (2021): 195–214. On the issue of minimal nutrition and slavery in the French imperial context, see Bertie Mandelblatt, "'On the excellence of the vegetable diet': Scurvy, Antoine Poissonnier-Desperrières's New Naval Diet and French Colonial Science in the Atlantic World," *Early American Studies* 19, no. 2 (2021): 322–59.

101. Peter Thompson, "Henry Drax's Instructions on the Management of a Seventeenth-Century Barbadian Sugar Plantation," *William and Mary Quarterly* 66, no. 3 (2009): 565–604, at 585–86.

102. Carney, *Black Rice.*

103. Thompson, "Henry Drax's Instructions," 103.

104. Lawson, *New Voyage to Carolina,* 75.

105. Hugh Jones, *The Present State of Virginia* (London: Printed for J. Clarke, 1724), 36, 39–41.

106. Jones, *Present State of Virginia,* 4, 37–38. For similar ideas about African bodies and the "naturalness" of slavery, see William Byrd II, "A Progress to the Mines," 1732, in *The Writings of Colonel William Byrd,* ed. John Spencer Bassett (New York: Doubleday, 1901), 346–60. Byrd believed Africans to be "all Face" and claimed their bodies were naturally suited to labor in intemperately cold or hot climates.

107. Mark Catesby, *Natural History of Carolina, Florida, and the Bahama Islands,* 1:27–28.

108. Frederick C. Knight, *Working the Diaspora: The Impact of African Labor on the Anglo-American World, 1650–1850* (New York: New York University Press, 2010), 60.

109. Writing on rice, for instance, Bernard Romans noted that the plant was a commodity and valued by planters in East and West Florida for its "usefulness in feeding Negroes, cattle and poultry." Romans, *A Concise Natural History of East and West Florida* (New York: Sold by R. Aitken, 1776), 126, 198. Moreover, scholars of slavery in New Spain have demonstrated that corn, specifically maize, was at the center of the "core diets" of enslaved people in Cartagena, Lima, and Portobelo. See Linda A. Newson and Susie Minchin, "Diets, Food Supplies and the African Slave Trade in Early Seventeenth-Century Spanish America," *The Americas* 63, no. 4 (2007): 517–50.

110. Zilberstein, "Bastard Breadfruit," 492–508.

111. Judith Carney and Richard Nicholas Rosomoff, *In the Shadow of Slavery: Africa's Botanical Legacy in the Atlantic World* (Berkeley: University of California Press, 2009).

112. Hughes, *Natural History of Barbados,* 254.

113. Martin, *An Essay Upon Plantership,* 4, 47.

114. Edward Long, *The History of Jamaica; Or, General Survey of the Antient and Modern State of that Island* (London: Printed for Thomas Lowndes, 1774), 2:71–72.

115. Edward Long, *History of Jamaica,* 3:761–62.

116. Martin, *An Essay Upon Plantership,* 8–9. On plantations in North America that provided corn and other provisions for the West Indies, see Heather B. Trigg and David B. Landon, "Labor and Agricultural Production at Sylvester Manor Plantation, Shelter Island, New York," *Historical Archaeology* 44, no. 3 (2010): 36–53; Katherine Howlett Hayes, *Slavery Before Race: Europeans, Africans, and Indians at Long Island's Sylvester Manor Plantation, 1651–1884* (New York: New York University Press, 2014).

117. James Knight, *The Natural, Moral, and Political History of Jamaica, and the Territories thereon Depending: From the First Discovery of the Island by Christopher Columbus to the Year 1746,* ed. Jack P. Greene (Charlottesville: University of Virginia Press, 2021).

118. John Dovaston, *Agricultura Americana, or Improvements in West India Husbandry Considered Wherein the Present System of Husbandry Used in England is Applied to the Cultivation or Growing of Sugar Canes to Advantage, 1774,* Codex Eng. 60, John Carter Brown Library, Brown University, Providence, Rhode Island.

119. Journal of a Jamaican slave overseer, Somerset Vale, 1776–1780, Codex Eng. 180, John Carter Brown Library.

120. Zilberstein, "Bastard Breadfruit," 492–508.

121. Benjamin Thompson, *Essays, Political, Economical and Philosophical* (London: Printed for T. Cadell and W. Davies, 1796), 1:249–50.

122. Philip Gibbes, *Instructions for the Treatment of Negroes* (London: Printed for Shepperson and Reynolds, 1797); T. C. Thomas and J. B. Legg, "Archaeological Evidence of Afro-Barbadian Life at Springhead Plantation, St. James Parish, Barbados," *Journal of the Barbados Museum and Historical Society* 43 (1996/1997): 32–49.

123. Gibbes, *Instructions for the Treatment of Negroes,* 10, 19, 55.

124. Edwin Lascelles et al., *Instructions for the Management of a Plantation in Barbadoes and for the Treatment of Negroes* (London, 1786), 14.

125. [Collins, David], Practical Rules for the Management and Medical Treatment of Negro Slaves in the Sugar Colonies (London: J. Barfield, 1803), 93–94; Roberts, *Slavery and the Enlightenment,* 161.

126. [Collins], *Practical Rules,* 97.

127. Matthew Mulcahy, *Hurricanes and Society in the British Greater Caribbean, 1624–1783* (Baltimore: Johns Hopkins University Press, 2010), 112; Stuart B. Schwartz, *Sea of Storms: A History of Hurricanes in the Greater Caribbean from Columbus to Katrina* (Princeton, NJ: Princeton University Press, 2015), 102; Candice Goucher, *Congotay! Congotay! A Global History of Caribbean Food* (London: Routledge, 2013), 70.

128. [Collins], *Practical Rules,* 114–15.

129. Kenneth F. Kiple and Virginia H. King, "Black Tongue and Black Men: Pellagra and Slavery in the Antebellum South," *Journal of Southern History* 43, no. 3 (1977): 411–28; Kiple and King, *Another Dimension to the Black Diaspora: Diet, Disease and Racism* (Cambridge: Cambridge University Press, 2003).

130. James Grainger, *An Essay on the More Common West-India Diseases; and the Remedies which that Country Itself Produces* (London: Printed for T. Becket and P. A. de Hondt, 1764).

131. James E. McWilliams, *A Revolution in Eating: How the Quest for Food Shaped America* (New York: Columbia University Press, 2005), 113.

132. Hughes, *Natural History of Barbados*, 62–63.

133. *An Abstract of the Evidence Delivered Before a Select Committee of the House of Commons in the Years 1790, and 1791, on the Part of the Petitioners for the Abolition of the Slave Trade* (London: James Phillips, 1791), 58, 67. Copy held at the William L. Clements Library, University of Michigan, Ann Arbor. In addition to documentary testimony, archaeological and physical anthropological evidence also points to the reality of malnourishment on Caribbean plantations. See Jerome S. Handler and Robert S. Corruccini, "Plantation Slave Life in Barbados: A Physical Anthropological Analysis," *Journal of Interdisciplinary History* 14, no. 1 (1983): 65–90.

134. John Gay Alleyne, letter to Sarah Fitzherbert, 1795, microfilm, file E20570, Turners Hall Plantation Records, Fitzherbert Collection, Archives Department, Black Rock, Barbados.

135. Patrick Browne, *The Civil and Natural History of Jamaica* (London: Printed for the author, 1756), 422, 458, 461, 485.

136. Catesby, *Natural History of Carolina, Florida, and the Bahama Islands*, 2:19–20, 68, 83.

137. Alexander Barclay, *Practical View of the Present State of Slavery in the West Indies* (London: Smith, Elder, and Co., 1827), 328–30.

138. Morgan, "Slaves and Livestock," 68–69. Morgan notes that Dick taught the slaveholder Thomas Thistlewood how to hunt and shoot birds using "Negro peppers."

139. Martin Jones, *Feast: Why Humans Share Food* (New York: Oxford University Press 2008).

140. This literature is quite vast by now, and for an incomplete sampling of key works in the field, see first the foundational works of Judith Carney, and then Edda L. Fields-Black, *Deep Roots: Rice Farmers in West Africa and the African Diaspora* (Bloomington: Indiana University Press, 2008); Goucher, *Congotay! Congotay!*; Karen B. Bell, "Rice, Resistance, and Forced Transatlantic Communities: (Re)Envisioning the African Diaspora in Low Country Georgia, 1750–1800," *Journal of African American History* 95, no. 2 (2010): 157–82; Herbert C. Covey and Dwight Eisnach, *What the Slaves Ate: Recollections of African American Foods and Foodways from the Slave Narratives* (Santa Barbara, CA: ABC-CLIO, 2009); Barnet Pavão-Zuckerman et al., "African American Culinary History and the Genesis of American Cuisine: Foodways and Slavery at Montpelier," *Journal of African Diaspora Archaeology and Heritage* 9, no. 2 (2020): 114–47; Frederick Douglass Opie, *Hog and Hominy: Soul Food from Africa to America* (New York: Columbia University Press, 2010); Vivian Nun Halloran, "Recipes as Memory Work: Slave Food," *Culture, Theory and Critique* 53, no. 2 (2012): 147–61; Levi Van Sant, "Lowcountry Visions: Foodways and Race in Coastal South Carolina." *Gastronomica* 15, no. 4 (2015): 18–26.

141. Hilary Beckles, "An Economic Life of Their Own: Slaves as Commodity Producers and Distributors in Barbados," in *The Slave's Economy: Independent Production by Slaves in the Americas*, ed. Ira D. Berlin and Philip Morgan (London: Frank Cass and Co., 1991), 31–47; Jillian E. Galle, "Assessing the Impacts of Time, Agricultural Cycles, and Demography on the Consumer Activities of Enslaved Men and Women in Eighteenth-Century Jamaica and Virginia," in *Out of Many, One People: The Historical Archaeology of Colonial Jamaica*, ed. James A. Delle, Mark W.

Hauser, and Douglas V. Armstrong (Tuscaloosa: University of Alabama Press, 2011), 211–42; Jerome Handler and Diane Wallman, "Production Activities in the Household Economies of Plantation Slaves: Barbados and Martinique, Mid-1600s to Mid-1800s," *International Journal of Historical Archaeology* 18, no. 3 (2014): 441–66. In Vineyard Pen, Jamaica, Phibbah, an enslaved woman, bought and sold pigs and poultry at similar informal markets. See Morgan, "Slaves and Livestock," 59, 68.

142. 3 May 1805, 10 August 1805, 6 December 1805, *MTSIPIB.*

143. 13 February 1808, *MTSIPIB.* On Anderson, see Julie Chun Kim, "Natural Histories of Indigenous Resistance: Alexander Anderson and the Caribs of St. Vincent," *The Eighteenth Century* 55, no. 2–3 (2014): 217–33.

144. 8 October 1808, *MTSIPIB.*

145. M'Mahon, *Jamaica Plantership,* 23, 28, 56–57, 79.

146. Roberts, *Slavery and the Enlightenment,* 107–8, 111, 116, 129; Simon Newman, *A New World of Labor: The Development of Plantation Slavery in the British Atlantic* (Philadelphia: University of Pennsylvania Press, 2013), 198, 208–9; Kulikoff, *Tobacco and Slaves,* 47, 114.

147. Lois Green Carr and Russell R. Menard, "Land, Labor, and Economies of Scale in Early Maryland: Some Limits to Growth in the Chesapeake System of Husbandry," *Journal of Economic History* 49, no. 2 (1989): 407–18.

148. Walsh, "Plantation Management," 393–406.

149. Roberts, *Slavery and the Enlightenment,* 116. See also Gavin Wright, "Slavery and American Agricultural History," *Agricultural History* 77, no. 4 (2003): 543; Glenn A. Crothers, "Agricultural Improvement and Technological Innovation in a Slave Society: The Case of Early National Northern Virginia," *Agricultural History* 75, no. 2 (2001): 135–67.

150. Roberts, *Slavery and the Enlightenment,* 47, 177, 180, 191, 200–201.

151. Edward Littleton, *The Groans of the Plantations* (London: M. Clark, 1698), 18.

152. Martin, *An Essay Upon Plantership,* 3, 5–6.

153. Anna M. Foy, "The Convention of Georgic Circumlocution and the Proper Use of Human Dung in Samuel Martin's *Essay Upon Plantership,*" *Eighteenth-Century Studies* 49, no. 4 (2016): 475–506; Samuel Johnson, *A Dictionary of the English Language: In which the Words are Deduced from Their Originals, and Illustrated in Their Different Significations by Examples from the Best Writers* (London: W. Strahan, 1755), 34, 36.

154. Foy, "Convention of Georgic Circumlocution," 475–76.

155. Martin, *An Essay Upon Plantership,* 15.

156. Martin, *An Essay Upon Plantership,* 16–17.

157. Martin, *An Essay Upon Plantership,* 24–25.

158. Martin, *An Essay Upon Plantership,* 18. On the connections of chemistry and agriculture in the Enlightenment, upon which planters like Martin drew, see Peter M. Jones, "Making Chemistry the 'Science' of Agriculture, c. 1760–1840," *History of Science* 54, no. 2 (June 2016): 169–94.

159. Benjamin R. Cohen, *Notes from the Ground: Science, Soil, and Society in the American Countryside* (New Haven, CT: Yale University Press, 2014), 158; Steven Stoll, *Larding the Lean Earth: Soil and Society in Nineteenth-Century America* (New York: Hill and Wang, 2003), 156–70; Terry G. Sharrer, *A Kind of Fate: Agricultural Change in Virginia, 1861–1920* (West Lafayette: Pur-

due University Press, 2002), 37; Avery Craven, *Soil Exhaustion as a Factor in the Agricultural History of Virginia and Maryland, 1606–1860* (Columbia: University of South Carolina Press, 1925), 136.

160. William Belgrove, *A Treatise Upon Husbandry or Planting* (Boston: D. Fowle, 1755), 2–7.

161. Belgrove, *Treatise Upon Husbandry or Planting,* 9–10.

162. Lascelles et al., *Instructions for the Management of a Plantation,* 8–11.

163. Frank Wesley Pitman, "The Organization of Slave Labor," *Journal of Negro History* 11, no. 4 (1926): 595–609, at 601. John David Smith likewise shows how children labored at manuring on Piedmont North Carolina plantations. See John David Smith, "'I Was Raised Poor and Hard as Any Slave': African American Slavery in Piedmont North Carolina," *North Carolina Historical Review* 90, no. 1 (2013): 12.

164. Roberts, *Slavery and the Enlightenment,* 57.

165. Walsh, "Slave Life," 170–202.

166. Walsh, *Motives of Honor, Pleasure, and Profit,* 472–73, 482, 530.

167. Isaac, *Landon Carter's Uneasy Kingdom,* 73–74.

168. Greene, *Diary of Colonel Landon Carter,* 1:149–50, 155–56, 274, 371, 414.

169. Greene, *Diary of Colonel Landon Carter,* 1:202–3, 347, 415, 566.

170. Lois Green Carr and Lorena S. Walsh, "Economic Diversification and Labor Organization in the Chesapeake, 1650–1820," in *Work and Labor in Early America,* ed. Stephen Innes (Chapel Hill: University of North Carolina Press, 1988), 144–88.

171. Greene, *Diary of Colonel Landon Carter,* 2:1137.

172. Isaac, *Landon Carter's Uneasy Kingdom,* 1:83–84.

173. Herbert C. Covey, *African American Slave Medicine: Herbal and Non-herbal Treatments* (New York: Lexington Books, 2007), 139; [Collins], *Practical Rules,* 363.

174. Andrew Kettler, *The Smell of Slavery: Olfactory Racism and the Atlantic World* (Cambridge: Cambridge University Press, 2020), 33–36.

175. Burnard, "Collecting and Accounting."

176. Ben Kafka, "Paperwork: The State of the Discipline," *Book History* 12 (2009): 340–53. On paperwork and the British Empire, see Bhavani Raman, *Document Raj: Writing and Scribes in Early Colonial South India* (Chicago: University of Chicago Press, 2012).

177. An Inventory of Mr. Thomas Whitby's, 19 March 1711/1712, York County Estate Inventories, John D. Rockefeller Jr. Library.

178. Weilburg Plantation, Accounts Ledger, Rio Demerary, circa August 1767–June 1770, Codex Eng. 52, John Carter Brown Library. On Douglas, see Douglas Hamilton, *Scotland, the Caribbean and the Atlantic World, 1750–1820* (Oxford: Oxford University Press, 2010), 36, 70.

179. Hamilton, *Scotland, the Caribbean and the Atlantic World,* 71–72, 92, 98.

180. Will of Colin Campbell, New Hope, 1761, Will Books, Registrar General's Department, Twickenham Park, St. Catherine Parish, Jamaica.

181. Oliver, *History of the Island of Antigua,* 2:96. On Jarvis's family and plantation, and their connection to the provisioning trade in livestock to Long Island, New York, see Thomas Jarvis Jr., letter to William Whitehead, August 1791, in box 2, Jarvis Family Papers.

182. "Notes and Queries," *Pennsylvania Magazine of History and Biography* 58, no. 4 (1934):

378–84. On Gardner's plantation, see Gardner Family Papers, William L. Clements Library, University of Michigan, Ann Arbor.

183. Drax Hall Plantation Records, call number z/9/11/4/–z/9/11/27, Archives Department, Black Rock, Barbados.

184. Smallwood, "Politics of the Archive."

Chapter 4

BY ONE BARBARITY OR ANOTHER

Sabotage, Slave Resistance, and Animals

1. Lathan A. Windley, ed., *Runaway Slave Advertisements: A Documentary History from the 1730s to 1790*, vol. 2, Maryland (Westport: Greenwood Press, 1983), 26–27.

2. Stephanie M. H. Camp, *Closer to Freedom: Enslaved Women and Everyday Resistance in the Plantation South* (Chapel Hill: University of North Carolina Press, 2005), 7.

3. Greene, *Diary of Colonel Landon Carter*; Isaac, *Landon Carter's Uneasy Kingdom*.

4. On sabotage as a form of industrial resistance, see Timothy Mitchell, *Carbon Democracy: Political Power in the Age of Oil* (London: Verso Books, 2011).

5. The literature on runaway slave advertisements is vast. In particular, however, see David Waldstreicher, "Reading the Runaways: Self-Fashioning, Print Culture, and Confidence in Slavery in the Eighteenth-Century Mid-Atlantic," *William and Mary Quarterly* 56, no. 2 (1999): 243–72; Graham Russell Gao Hodges and Alan Edward Brown, eds., *"Pretends to be Free": Runaway Slave Advertisements from Colonial and Revolutionary New York and New Jersey*, 2nd ed. (New York: Fordham University Press, 2019); Antonio T. Bly, "'Pretends he can read': Runaways and Literacy in Colonial America, 1730–1776," *Early American Studies* (2008): 261–94; Daniel E. Meaders, "South Carolina Fugitives as Viewed through Local Colonial Newspapers with Emphasis on Runaway Notices 1732–1801," *Journal of Negro History* 60, no. 2 (1975): 288–319; John Hope Franklin and Loren Schweninger, *Runaway Slaves: Rebels on the Plantation* (Oxford: Oxford University Press, 2000).

6. "To Thomas Jefferson from Pseudonym: 'A Slave,' 30 November 1808," National Archives, Founders Online, https://founders.archives.gov/documents/Jefferson/99-01-02-9200. For a recent important analysis of slavery and animality, see Bennett, *Being Property Once Myself*.

7. Greene, *Diary of Colonel Landon Carter*, 296.

8. Clay McShane and Joel Tarr, *The Horse in the City: Living Machines in the Nineteenth Century* (Baltimore: Johns Hopkins University Press, 2007).

9. Greene, *Diary of Colonel Landon Carter*, 1:366.

10. Greene, *Diary of Colonel Landon Carter*, 1:367–68.

11. Greene, *Diary of Colonel Landon Carter*, 1:397.

12. Greene, *Diary of Colonel Landon Carter*, 1:442.

13. Greene, *Diary of Colonel Landon Carter*, 1:495.

14. Greene, *Diary of Colonel Landon Carter*, 1:495, 541. The suggestion for the missing word is Greene's.

15. In 1773, while protecting his daughter Sarah from Carter's violence, Manuel assisted in

hiding her from their enslaver for more than a week. Three years later, in 1776, at the outset of the American Revolutionary War, Manuel and eight other men fled Carter permanently to join Lord Dunmore's forces. See Greene, *Diary of Landon Carter*, 2:777, 1051.

16. Greene, *Diary of Colonel Landon Carter*, 1:370.

17. Greene, *Diary of Colonel Landon Carter*, 1:299.

18. Greene, *Diary of Colonel Landon Carter*, 1:376.

19. Rhys Isaac, *Landon Carter's Uneasy Kingdom*, 23.

20. Greene, *Diary of Colonel Landon Carter*, 1:561.

21. Greene, *Diary of Colonel Landon Carter*, 1:385, 544–47.

22. Greene, *Diary of Colonel Landon Carter*, 1:380, 2:762.

23. Greene, *Diary of Colonel Landon Carter*, 2:588.

24. Andrews, "Beasts of the Southern Wild."

25. *The Act of Assembly of the Island of Jamaica, to repeal several acts, and clauses of acts, respecting slaves, and for the better Order and Government of Slaves, and for other Purposes; commonly called the Consolidated Act, as Exhibiting at One View Most of the Essential Regulations of the Jamaica Code Noir; which was passed by the Assembly on the 19th day of December 1787, and by the Lieutenant Governor and the Council on the 22d of the said Month. Respectfully communicated to the public by Stephen Fuller, Esq. Agent for Jamaica* (London: Printed for B. White and Son, 1788), 2.

26. David Barry Gaspar, "Working the System: Antigua Slaves and Their Struggle to Live," *Slavery and Abolition* 13, no. 3 (1992): 131–55, at 142.

27. Diana Paton, "Punishment, Crime, and the Bodies of Slaves in Eighteenth-Century Jamaica," *Journal of Social History* 34, no. 4 (2001): 923–54.

28. Richard B. Sheridan, "From Chattel to Wage Slavery in Jamaica, 1740–1860," in *The Wages of Slavery: From Chattel Slavery to Wage Labour in Africa, the Caribbean, and England,* ed. Michael Twaddle (New York: Frank Cass and Co., 1993), 13–40, at 18.

29. John Fowler to James Stothert, 12 November 1786, James Stothert Papers.

30. Thomas Jarvis to William Gunthorpe, April 1791, box 1, Jarvis Family Papers.

31. Greene, *Diary of Colonel Landon Carter*, 2:588.

32. Greene, *Diary of Colonel Landon Carter*, 1:579.

33. Greene, *Diary of Colonel Landon Carter*, 2:927.

34. Greene, *Diary of Colonel Landon Carter*, 2:1063.

Chapter 5

SHE HAS BRAGG'D

Fugitives, Animals, and the Limits of Slavery

1. Jones, *Present State of Virginia*, 3–7, 38. On white ideas about European rationality versus African irrationality, see Ibram X. Kendi, *Stamped from the Beginning: The Definitive History of Racist Ideas in America* (New York: Random House, 2017), 79–92.

2. Donna Landry, *Noble Brutes: How Eastern Horses Transformed English Culture* (Baltimore: Johns Hopkins University Press, 2008), 1–14, 164–74; Landry, "English Brutes, Eastern Enlightenment," *The Eighteenth Century* 52, no. 1 (2011): 11–30.

3. Monica Mattfeld, *Becoming Centaur: Eighteenth-Century Masculinity and English Horseman-ship* (University Park: Pennsylvania State University Press, 2017); Mattfeld, "'Undaunted all he views': The Gibraltar Charger, Astley's Amphitheatre and Masculine Performance," *Journal for Eighteenth-Century Studies* 37, no. 1 (2014): 19–36; T. H. Breen, "Horses and Gentlemen: The Cultural Significance of Gambling among the Gentry of Virginia," *William and Mary Quarterly* 34, no. 2 (1977): 239–57; Katherine C. Mooney, *Race Horse Men: How Slavery and Freedom Were Made at the Racetrack* (Cambridge, MA: Harvard University Press, 2014), 6–7. Mooney notes that in many West African societies horsemanship denoted a particular mastery over nonhuman nature: "The kings of the Yoruba and the Hausa boasted massive stable complexes, over which slaves presided. Such slaves were valued members of the royal household, supervisors of large staffs, intimates of princes.

4. Lambert, "Master–Horse–Slave, 618–41; Charlotte Carrington-Farmer, "The Rise and Fall of the Narragansett Pacer," *Rhode Island History* 76, no. 1 (2018): 1–38; Mooney, *Race Horse Men*.

5. Jerome S. Handler, "Escaping Slavery in a Caribbean Plantation Society: Marronage in Barbados, 1650s–1830s," *New West Indian Guide* 71, no. 3/4 (1997): 183–225.

6. Gwenda Morgan and Peter Rushton, "Visible Bodies: Power, Subordination and Identity in the Eighteenth-Century Atlantic World," *Journal of Social History* 39, no. 1 (2005): 39–64; Simone Browne, "Branding Blackness," in *Dark Matters: On the Surveillance of Blackness* (Durham, NC: Duke University Press, 2015), chapter 3.

7. Sally E. Hadden, *Slave Patrols: Law and Violence in Virginia and the Carolinas* (Cambridge, MA: Harvard University Press, 2001), 109; Johnson, *River of Dark Dreams,* 222–28.

8. Windley, *Runaway Slave Advertisements,* vol. 3, *South Carolina,* 2.

9. Windley, *Runaway Slave Advertisements,* 2:10.

10. Windley, *Runaway Slave Advertisements,* 3:94.

11. On slavery and disability studies, see Stefanie Hunt-Kennedy, *Between Fitness and Death: Disability and Slavery in the Caribbean* (Champaign: University of Illinois Press, 2020).

12. Windley, Runaway Slave Advertisements, 3:94.

13. Peter H. Wood, *Black Majority: Negroes in Colonial South Carolina from 1670 through the Stono Rebellion* (New York: W. W. Norton & Co., 1996), 304–5; Jane Landers, "Gracia Real de Santa Teresa de Mose: A Free Black Town in Spanish Colonial Florida," *American Historical Review* 95, no. 1 (1990): 9–30.

14. Timothy J. Lockley, ed., *Maroon Communities in South Carolina: A Documentary Record* (Columbia: University of South Carolina Press, 2009).

15. Windley, *Runaway Slave Advertisements,* vol. 1, *Virginia and North Carolina,* 32.

16. Windley, *Runaway Slave Advertisements,* 3:33–34.

17. "24 June 1730, *Weekly Jamaica Courant,*" in Douglas B. Chambers, ed., *Runaway Slaves in Jamaica,* vol. 1, *The Eighteenth Century* (Hattiesburg: University of Southern Mississippi, 2013), 8.

18. Windley, *Runaway Slave Advertisements,* 3:11.

19. Windley, *Runaway Slave Advertisements,* 3:118; Jeanne A. Calhoun, Martha A. Zierden, and Elizabeth A. Paysinger, "The Geographic Spread of Charleston's Mercantile Community, 1732–1767," *South Carolina Historical Magazine* 86, no. 3 (1985): 182–220.

20. Windley, *Runaway Slave Advertisements,* 3:109.

21. Windley, *Runaway Slave Advertisements,* 3:38.

22. Tim Lockley and David Doddington, "Maroon and Slave Communities in South Carolina before 1865," *South Carolina Historical Magazine* 113, no. 2 (2012): 125–45.

23. *South-Carolina Gazette,* Charleston, 23 January 1755.

24. Windley, *Runaway Slave Advertisements,* 3:151.

25. On slavery, frigid environments, and disfigurement in Maryland, see Tony C. Perry, "In Bondage When Cold Was King: The Frigid Terrain of Slavery in Antebellum Maryland," *Slavery & Abolition* 38, no. 1 (2017): 23–36.

26. *North Carolina Journal,* Halifax, 2 October 1797.

27. Windley, *Runaway Slave Advertisements,* 2:38.

28. Windley, *Runaway Slave Advertisements,* 3:223.

29. *South-Carolina Gazette,* Charlestown, 23 January 1755.

30. *South-Carolina Gazette,* Charlestown, 13 July 1747.

31. Windley, *Runaway Slave Advertisements,* 2:72–73.

32. Windley, *Runaway Slave Advertisements,* vol. 4, *Georgia,* 52.

33. Windley, *Runaway Slave Advertisements,* 3:50.

34. Windley, *Runaway Slave Advertisements,* 3:140.

35. *State Gazette of North Carolina,* Edenton, 11 May 1793.

36. *South-Carolina Gazette,* Charlestown, 3 May 1740.

37. Robert E. May, *Yuletide in Dixie: Slavery, Christmas, and Southern Memory* (Charlottesville: University of Virginia Press, 2019).

38. Windley, *Runaway Slave Advertisements,* 2:46.

39. Windley, *Runaway Slave Advertisements,* 2:53. While the archive is silent on Ben's life after this moment, I believe it is probable he offered the other two horses to family members or friends also pursuing their liberation.

40. Cassandra Pybus, *Epic Journeys of Freedom: Runaway Slaves of the American Revolution and Their Global Quest for Liberty* (Boston: Beacon, 2006), 47–48.

41. Windley, *Runaway Slave Advertisements,* 1:449.

42. "12 July 1783, *Cornwall Chronicle,*" in Chambers, *Runaway Slaves in Jamaica,* 79.

43. Windley, *Runaway Slave Advertisements,* 1:18, 32–33.

44. *North Carolina Gazette,* New Bern, 13 March 1752.

45. Windley, *Runaway Slave Advertisements,* 2:48. On Webster's role in the furnace, see James M. Swank, *History of the Manufacture of Iron in All Ages* (Philadelphia: American Iron and Steel Association, 1892), 253.

46. Windley, *Runaway Slave Advertisements,* 2:198–99.

47. *South-Carolina Gazette,* Charleston, 15 February 1748.

48. *North Carolina Journal,* Halifax, 16 January 1793.

49. Anderson, *Creatures of Empire.*

50. Jill H. Casid, *Sowing Empire: Landscape and Colonization* (Minneapolis: University of Minnesota Press, 2005); Judith A. Carney, "Between Land and Sea: Mangroves and Mollusks along Brazil's Mangal Coast," *Fronteiras: Journal of Social, Technological and Environmental Science* 5, no. 3 (2016): 17–38.

51. Thomas M. Wickman, *Snowshoe Country: An Environmental and Cultural History of Winter in the Early American Northeast* (Cambridge: Cambridge University Press, 2018).

52. The classic study in this field remains Carney, *Black Rice*.

Epilogue

1. Sandra L. Dahlberg, "'Doe Not Forget Me': Richard Frethorne, Indentured Servitude, and the English Poor Law of 1601," *Early American Literature* 47, no. 1 (2012): 1–30.

2. Elizabeth Sprigs, "Letter to Mr. John Sprigs in White Cross Street near Cripple Gate, London, 22 September 1756," in *Colonial Captivities, Marches, and Journeys*, ed. Isabel Calder (New York: Macmillan, 1935), 151–52.

3. Petition for freedom to the Massachusetts Council and the House of Representatives, [13] January 1777, manuscript copy, Jeremy Belknap Papers, Massachusetts Historical Society, Boston.

4. Petition of Prince Hall to the Massachusetts General Court, 27 February 1788, Jeremy Belknap Papers.

5. Ottobah Cugoano, *Thoughts and Sentiments on the Evil and Wicked Traffic of the Slavery and Commerce of the Human Species, Humbly Submitted to the Inhabitants of Great-Britain* (London, 1787), 9, 11.

6. Victor C. D. Mtubani, "The Black Voice in Eighteenth-Century Britain: African Writers against Slavery and the Slave Trade," *Phylon* 45, no. 2 (1984): 85–97; George E. Boulukos, "Olaudah Equiano and the Eighteenth-Century Debate on Africa," *Eighteenth-Century Studies* 40, no. 2 (2007): 241–55; Ryan Henley, *Beyond Slavery and Abolition: Black British Writing, c. 1770–1830* (Cambridge: Cambridge University Press, 2018), 180.

7. Cugoano, *Thoughts and Sentiments*, 5.

8. David Hume, *Essays and Treatises on Several Subjects* (Edinburgh: A. Millar; and A. Kincaid and A. Donaldson, 1758), 125; Pauline Kleingeld, "Kant's Second Thoughts on Colonialism," in *Kant and Colonialism: Historical and Critical Perspectives*, ed. Katrin Flikschuh and Lea Ypi (Oxford: Oxford University Press, 2014), 43–67; George Boulukos, *The Grateful Slave: The Emergence of Race in Eighteenth-Century British and American Culture* (Cambridge: Cambridge University Press, 2008), 108–9; Dayan, *The Law Is a White Dog*, 113–37; Suman Seth, "Materialism, Slavery, and *The History of Jamaica*," *Isis* 105, no. 4 (2014): 764–72.

9. Kleingeld, "Kant's Second Thoughts on Race."

10. Cugoano, *Thoughts and Sentiments*, 16–17.

11. Cugoano, *Thoughts and Sentiments*, 112.

12. Cugoano, *Thoughts and Sentiments*, 21.

13. Cugoano, *Thoughts and Sentiments*, 54, 108, 123.

14. Thomas Clarkson, *An Essay on the Slavery and Commerce of the Human Species*, 3rd ed. (Philadelphia: Joseph Crukshank, 1787), 101.

15. Jane Spencer, *Writing about Animals in the Age of Revolution* (Oxford: Oxford University Press, 2020), 170.

16. Dayan, *The Law Is a White Dog*, 151.

17. Bénédicte Boisseron, *Afro-Dog: Blackness and the Animal Question* (New York: Columbia University Press, 2018).

18. Wilderson, *Afropessimism*.

19. Mbembe, *Critique of Black Reason*, 153.

20. Cugoano, *Thoughts and Sentiments,* 22.

21. Thomas N. Baker, "'A Slave' Writes Thomas Jefferson," *William and Mary Quarterly* 68, no. 1 (2011): 127–54.

22. Eran Shalev, "Ancient Masks, American Fathers: Classical Pseudonyms during the American Revolution and Early Republic," *Journal of the Early Republic* 23, no. 2 (2003): 151–72.

23. "Letter of Cato and Petition by 'the negroes who obtained freedom by the late act,'" *Postscript to the Freeman's Journal,* September 21, 1781, at "Black Founders: The Free Black Community in the Early Republic," Library Company of Philadelphia, https://www.librarycompany.org/blackfounders/section7.htm.

24. James A. Steintrager, *Cruel Delight: Enlightenment Culture and the Inhuman* (Bloomington: Indiana University Press, 2004); Lynn Festa, "Humanity without Feathers," *Humanity: An International Journal of Human Rights, Humanitarianism, and Development* 1, no. 1 (Fall 2010): 3–27.

25. Roy E. Finkenbine, "Belinda's Petition: Reparations for Slavery in Revolutionary Massachusetts," *William and Mary Quarterly,* 3rd series, 64, no. 1 (2007): 95–104; Sesay, "Revolutionary Black Roots of Slavery's Abolition in Massachusetts."

26. John Saillant, *Black Puritan, Black Republican: The Life and Thought of Lemuel Haynes, 1753–1833* (Oxford: Oxford University Press, 2002), 17, 21, 102.

27. Mary Prince, *The History of Mary Prince, a West Indian Slave. Related by Herself. With a Supplement by the Editor (T. Pringle). To which is Added, the Narrative of Asa-Asa, a Captured African* (London: F. Westley and A. H. Davis, 1831), 3. On Prince's narrative, see Margot Maddison-MacFadyen, "Mary Prince, Grand Turk, and Antigua," *Slavery & Abolition* 34, no. 4 (2013): 653–62; Barbara Baumgartner, "The Body as Evidence: Resistance, Collaboration, and Appropriation in *The History of Mary Prince,*" *Callaloo* 24, no. 1 (2001): 253–75; Mary Jeanne Larrabee, "'I Know What a Slave Knows': Mary Prince's Epistemology of Resistance," *Women's Studies* 35, no. 5 (2006): 453–73.

28. Prince, *History of Mary Prince,* 4.

29. Prince, *History of Mary Prince,* 5–6.

30. Prince, *History of Mary Prince,* 6.

31. Prince, *History of Mary Prince,* 9.

32. Prince, *History of Mary Prince,* 10–11.

33. Prince, *History of Mary Prince,* 13, 20.

34. Prince, *History of Mary Prince,* 20.

35. Prince, *History of Mary Prince,* 22

36. Prince, *History of Mary Prince,* 23.

37. Bly, "Reed through the Bybell," 1–33.

BIBLIOGRAPHY

Archives and Manuscript Collections

American Philosophical Society, Philadelphia, Pennsylvania
　　Sir Hans Sloane Correspondence, 1647–1743, microfilm
Archives Department, Black Rock, Barbados
　　Drax Hall Plantation Records
　　Turners Hall Plantation Records, Fitzherbert Collection, microfilm
　　Turners Hall Records, microfilm
Beinecke Rare Book and Manuscript Library, Yale University, New Haven, Connecticut
　　Thomas Thistlewood Papers
The British Library, London
　　*Reports of the Lords of the Committee of Council appointed for the consideration of all
　　　matters relating to Trade and Foreign Plantations; submitting . . . the evidence and
　　　information they have collected in consequence of His Majesty's Order in Council,
　　　dated the 11th of February, 1788, concerning the present state of the Trade to Africa,
　　　and particularly the Trade in Slaves, etc,* six volumes.
　　Sloane Manuscripts
Department of Archives and History, Columbia, South Carolina
　　Estate Inventories and Bills of Sale, 1732–1872
Historical Society of Pennsylvania, Philadelphia, Pennsylvania
　　Powel Papers, Series XII, Alexander Johnston Daybook, 1762–1839
The Huntington Library, Art Collections, and Botanical Gardens, San Marino, California
　　William Davenport and Company, Account Book, 1777–1784
Jamaica Archives and Records Department, Spanish Town, Jamaica
　　Estate Inventories and Appraisals
The John Carter Brown Library, Brown University, Providence, Rhode Island
　　John Dovaston, *Agricultura Americana*, manuscript
　　Journal of a Jamaican Slave Overseer, Somerset Vale, 1776–1780, manuscript
　　Weilburg Plantation, Accounts Ledger, 1767–1770
　　William Clark, *Ten Views of Antigua,* 1823
The John D. Rockefeller Jr. Library, Colonial Williamsburg Foundation, Williamsburg,
　　Virginia
　　York County Estate Inventories

The Kislak Center for Special Collections, University of Pennsylvania, Philadelphia
Miscellaneous Manuscripts, Account Book, Box 2, Folder 23
Rebecca Buckley Ferguson Letters, 1747–1819
The Library Company of Philadelphia, Pennsylvania
Patrick Kein, *An Essay on Pen-Keeping and Plantership*, His Majesty's Printing-Office, 1796, Kingston, Jamaica.
Massachusetts Historical Society, Boston, Massachusetts
Jeremy Belknap Papers
The National Archives, Kew, London
Royal African Company, Records, Series T70
The Natural History Museum, London
Sir Hans Sloane Collection, Manuscript Catalogs
Registrar General's Department, Twickenham Park, St. Catherine Parish, Jamaica
Will Books, Will of Colin Campbell, New Hope, 1761
Shilstone Memorial Library, Barbados Museum and Historical Society, Bridgetown, Barbados
Minutes of The Society for the Improvement of Plantership on the Island of Barbados, Instituted 8 December 1804, Thomas Kaye, 1811, Liverpool.
Special Collections, Earl Gregg Swem Library, Williamsburg, The College of William and Mary
Richard Corbin, Account Book, 1786–1797
Skipwith Family Papers
William Selden Papers
Special Collections, Sidney Martin Library, University of the West Indies, Cave Hill, Barbados
Minutes of the Society for the Improvement of Plantership on the Island of Barbados, 1811–1816, manuscript
University Library, Uppsala University, Sweden
Henry Smeathman Collection
The William L. Clements Library, University of Michigan, Ann Arbor
An Abstract of the Evidence Delivered Before a Select Committee of the House of Commons in the Years 1790, and 1791, on the Part of the Petitioners for the Abolition of the Slave Trade, James Phillips, 1791, London.
Charles Winstone Letter Book
Gardner Family Papers
James Stothert Papers
Jarvis Family Papers

Journals

Philosophical Transactions, Royal Society of London
Transactions of the American Philosophical Society

Newspapers

Cornwall Chronicle
Maryland Gazette
South-Carolina Gazette
Virginia Gazette, Purdie
Virginia Gazette, Purdie and Dixon
Virginia Gazette, Rind
Weekly Jamaica Courant

Digital Database

Gale. "Eighteenth Century Collections Online." https://www.gale.com/primary-sources/ eighteenth-century-collections-online.

Primary Printed Works

The Act of Assembly of the Island of Jamaica, to repeal several acts, and clauses of acts, respecting slaves, and for the better Order and Government of Slaves, and for other Purposes; commonly called the Consolidated Act, as Exhibiting at One View Most of the Essential Regulations of the Jamaica Code Noir; which was passed by the Assembly on the 19th day of December 1787, and by the Lieutenant Governor and the Council on the 22d of the said Month. Respectfully communicated to the public by Stephen Fuller, Esq. Agent for Jamaica. London: Printed for B. White and Son, 1788.

Acts of Assembly, passed in the island of Jamaica; from . . . 1681, to . . . 1754, . . . In two volumes. . . . Saint Jago de la Vega, Jamaica, 1769–1771.

Atkins, John. *A Voyage to Guinea, Brasil, and the West-Indies; in His Majesty's Ships, the Swallow and Weymouth.* London: Printed for Caesar Ward and Richard Chandler, 1735.

Atwood, Thomas. *The History of the Island of Dominica.* London: Printed for J. Johnson, 1791.

Banister, John. "The Extracts of Four Letters from Mr. John Banister to Dr. Lister, Communicated by Him to the Publisher." *Philosophical Transactions (1683–1775)* 17 (1693): 667–92.

Barclay, Alexander. *Practical View of the Present State of Slavery in the West Indies.* London: Smith, Elder, and Co., 1827.

Barham, Henry. *Hortus Americanus: The Trees, Shrubs, and other Vegetable Productions, of South-America and the West-India Islands, and Particularly of Jamaica.* Kingston: Printed and published by Alexander Aikman, 1794.

Bate, James, and Alexander Russel. "An Account of the Remarkable Alteration of Colour in a Negro Woman: In a Letter to the Reverend Mr. Alexander Williamson of Maryland, from Mr. James Bate, Surgeon in That Province. Communicated by Alexander Russel, M. D. F. R. S." *Philosophical Transactions (1683–1775)* 51 (1759): 175–78.

Beckford, William. *A Descriptive Account of the Island of Jamaica.* Vol. 1. London: T. and J. Egerton, 1790.

Belgrove, William. *A Treatise Upon Husbandry or Planting.* Boston: D. Fowle, 1755.

Bell, Hesketh. *Obeah: Witchcraft in the West Indies.* 2nd ed. London: Sampson, Low, Marston, and Co., 1893.

Beverly, Robert. *The History and Present State of Virginia.* London: Printed for R. Parker, 1705.

Bluett, Thomas. *Some Memoirs of the Life of Job: The Son of Solomon the High Priest of Boonda in Africa; who was a Slave about Two Years in Maryland.* London: Printed for Richard Ford, 1734.

Bosman, Willem. *A New and Accurate Description of the Coast of Guinea: Divided Into the Gold, the Slave, and the Ivory Coasts.* London: Printed for J. Knapton, 1705.

Bowdich, Thomas Edward. *Mission from Cape Coast Castle to Ashantee, with a Statistical Account of that Kingdom.* London: John Murray, 1819.

Brickell, John. *The Natural History of North-Carolina.* Dublin: James Carson, 1737.

Brodie, James, and Dr. Preston. "An Account of a Faetus, Voided by the Ulcered Navil of a Negro in Nevis, by Mr. James Brodie; Communicated by Dr. Preston." *Philosophical Transactions (1683–1775)* 19 (1695): 580–81.

Browne, Patrick. *The Civil and Natural History of Jamaica.* London: T. Osborne and J. Shipton, 1756.

Byrd, William. "An Account of a Negro-Boy That Is Dappel'd in Several Places of His Body with White Spots. By William Byrd, Esq, F. R. S." *Philosophical Transactions (1683–1775)* 19 (1695): 781–82.

———. "A Progress to the Mines," 1732. In *The Writings of Colonel William Byrd,* edited by John Spencer Bassett, 346–60. New York: Doubleday, 1901.

Carter, Landon, and Colonel Lee. "Observations concerning the Fly-Weevil, That Destroys the Wheat, with Some Useful Discoveries and Conclusions, concerning the Propagation and Progress of That Pernicious Insect, and the Methods to Be Used for Preventing the Destruction of the Grain by It. By Colonel Landon Carter, of Sabine Hall, Virginia; Communicated by Colonel Lee of Virginia." *Transactions of the American Philosophical Society* 1 (1769): 205–17.

Castles, John. "Observations on the Sugar Ants. In a Letter from John Castles, Esq. to Lieut. Gen. Melvill, FRS." *Philosophical Transactions of the Royal Society of London* 80 (1790): 346–58.

Catesby, Mark. *The Natural History of Carolina, Florida, and the Bahama Islands.* Vol. 1. London, 1731.

———. *The Natural History of Carolina, Florida, and the Bahama Islands.* Vol. 2. London, 1743.

Clarkson, Thomas. *An Essay on the Slavery and Commerce of the Human Species.* 3rd ed. Philadelphia: Joseph Crukshank, 1787.

Coke, Thomas. *A History of the West Indies: Containing the Natural, Civil and Ecclesiastical History of Each Island.* Vol. 2. London: Printed for the author, 1810.

[Collins, David]. *Practical Rules for the Management and Medical Treatment of Negro Slaves in the Sugar Colonies.* London: J. Barfield, 1803.

Cugoano, Quobna Ottobah. *Thoughts and Sentiments on the Evil and Wicked Traffic of the Slavery and Commerce of the Human Species, Humbly Submitted to the Inhabitants of Great-Britain, by Ottobah Cugoano, A Native of Africa.* London, 1787.

Dickson, William, and Joshua Steele. *Mitigation of Slavery, in two Parts.* London: Longman, Hurst, Rees, Orme, and Brown, 1814.

Drury, Dru. *Illustrations of Natural History.* 3 vols. London: Printed for the author, 1782.

East India Company, Court of Managers. *London: The Court of Managers for the United-Trade to the East Indies will put up to sale at the East-India-House in Leaden-Hall Street, on the 19th of March, 1705/06, the following goods.* Broadsheet. London, 1706.

Edwards, Bryan. *The History Civil and Commercial of the British Colonies in the West Indies.* 3 vols. London: B. Crosby, 1793, 1805.

Ellis, John. "An Account of an Amphibious Bipes; By John Ellis, Esq; F. R. S. To the Royal Society." *Philosophical Transactions (1683–1775)* 56 (1766): 189–92.

———. "An Account of the Sea Pen, or *Pennatula Phosphorea* of Linnaeus; Likewise a Description of a New Species of Sea Pen, Found on the Coast of South-Carolina, with Observations on Sea-Pens in General. In a Letter to the Honourable Coote Molesworth, Esq; MD and FRS from John Ellis, Esq; FRS and Member of the Royal Academy at Upsal." *Philosophical Transactions (1683–1775)* 53 (1763): 419–35.

———. *The Natural History of Many Curious and Uncommon Zoophytes.* London: Printed for Benjamin White and Son, 1786.

Falconbridge, Alexander. *An Account of the Slave Trade on the Coast of Africa.* London: James Phillips, 1788.

Federal Writers' Project. *Slave Narratives: A Folk History of Slavery in the United States From*

Interviews With Former Slaves. Vol. 4, *Georgia Narratives.* Prepared by the Federal Writers' Project of the Works Project Administration for the State of Georgia. Washington, DC: Library of Congress, 1941.

Federal Writers' Project. *South Carolina Slave Narratives: A Folk History of Slavery in the United States from Interviews with Former Slaves.* Vol. 14. United States Works Progress Administration, 1938.

Flickinger, Daniel Kumler. *Ethiopia, Or, Twenty Years of Missionary Life in Western Africa.* Dayton, OH: United Brethren Printing House, 1873.

"Four Letters from Mr. T. S. Kuckhan, to the President and Members of the Royal Society, on the Preservation of Dead Birds." *Philosophical Transactions (1683–1775)* 60 (1770): 302–20.

A Genuine Narrative of the Intended Conspiracy of the Negroes at Antigua. Extracted from an Authentic Copy of a Report, made to the Chief Governor of the Carabee Islands, by the Commissioners, or Judges appointed to try the Conspirators. Dublin: R. Reilly, 1737.

Gibbes, Philip. *Instructions for the Treatment of Negroes.* London: Printed for Shepperson and Reynolds, 1797.

Godwyn, Morgan. *The Negro's and Indians Advocate.* London, 1680.

Grainger, James. *An Essay on the More Common West-India Diseases; and the Remedies which that Country Itself Produces.* London: Printed for T. Becket and P. A. de Hondt, 1764.

———. *The Sugar-Cane: A Poem in Ten Books.* London: R. and J. Dodsley, 1764.

Herbert, Thomas. *Some Years Travels Into Divers Parts of Africa, and Asia the Great: Describing More Particularly the Empires of Persia and Industan: Interwoven with Such Remarkable Occurrences as Hapned in Those Parts During These Later Times. As Also, Many Other Rich and Famous Kingdoms in the Oriental India, with the Isles Adjacent.* London: R. Everingham,1677.

Houstoun, James. *Some New and Accurate Observations Geographical, Natural and Historical. Containing a True and Impartial Account of the Situation, Product, and Natural History of the Coast of Guinea, so far As Relates to the Improvement of that Trade, for the Advantage of Great Britain in General, and the Royal African Company in Particular.* London: Printed for J. Peele, 1725.

Hughes, Griffith. "A Letter from the Reverend Mr. Griffith Hughes, Minister of St. Lucy's Parish in Barbadoes, to Martin Folkes, Esq; President of the Royal Society, concerning a Zoophyton, Somewhat Resembling the Flower of the Marigold." *Philosophical Transactions (1683–1775)* 42 (1742): 590–93.

———. *The Natural History of Barbados.* London: Printed for the author, 1750.

Hume, David. *Essays and Treatises on Several Subjects.* Edinburgh: A. Millar; and A. Kincaid and A. Donaldson, 1758.

Hutton, William. *A Voyage to Africa: Including a Narrative of an Embassy to One of the Interior Kingdoms in the Year 1820.* London: Longman, 1821.

Jefferson, Thomas. *Notes on the State of Virginia.* [Paris, 1782].

Johnson, Samuel. *A Dictionary of the English Language: In which the Words are Deduced from Their Originals, and Illustrated in Their Different Significations by Examples from the Best Writers.* London: W. Strahan, 1755.

Jones, Hugh. *The Present State of Virginia.* London: Printed for J. Clarke, 1724.

Kalm, Pehr. *Travels into North America: Containing Its Natural History.* Vol. 1. Warrington: William Eyres, 1772.

Knight, James. *The Natural, Moral, and Political History of Jamaica, and the Territories thereon Depending: From the First Discovery of the Island by Christopher Columbus to the Year 1746.* Edited by Jack P. Greene. Charlottesville: University of Virginia Press, 2021.

Lanaghan, Mrs. *Antigua and the Antiguans.* 2 vols. London: Saunders and Otley, 1844.

Lascelles, Edwin, et al. *Instructions for the Management of a Plantation in Barbadoes and for the Treatment of Negroes.* London, 1786.

The Laws of Jamaica: 1792–1799. Kingston: Alexander Aikman and Son, 1811.

Lawson, John. *A New Voyage to Carolina.* London, 1709.

Lettsom, John Coakley. *The Works of John Fothergill.* 3 vols. London: Printed for Charles Dilly, 1784.

Lewis, Matthew Gregory. *Journal of a West-India Proprietor: Kept During a Residence in the Island of Jamaica.* London: John Murray, 1834.

Ligon, Richard. *A True & Exact History of the Island of Barbados Illustrated with a Mapp of the Island, as also the Principall Trees and Plants there, set forth in their due proportions and shapes, drawne out by their severall and respective scales.* London: Printed for Humphrey Moseley, 1657.

Littleton, Edward. *The Groans of the Plantations.* London: M. Clark, 1698.

Long, Edward. *The History of Jamaica; Or, General Survey of the Antient and Modern State of that Island.* 3 vols. London: Printed for Thomas Lowndes, 1774.

Madden, Richard Robert. *A Twelvemonth's Residence in the West Indies: During the Transition from Slavery to Apprenticeship.* Philadelphia: Carey, Lea, and Blanchard, 1835.

Marly, Or, A Planter's Life in Jamaica. Glasgow: Richard Griffin & Co., 1828.

Martin, Samuel. *An Essay Upon Plantership, humbly inscrib'd to all the planters of the British sugar-colonies in America. The Second Edition, Corrected and Enlarged.* Antigua: T. Smith, 1750.

Mather, Cotton. *Small Offers towards the Tabernacle in the Wilderness.* Boston: 1689.

Matthews, John. *A Voyage to the River Sierra-Leone: On the Coast of Africa; Containing an Account of the Trade and Productions of the Country, and of the Civil and Religious Customs and Manners of the People.* London: Printed for B. White and Son, 1788.

Meredith, Henry. *An Account of the Gold Coast of Africa.* Vol. 1. London: Longman, 1812.

M'Mahon, Benjamin. *Jamaica Plantership.* London: Effingham Wilson, 1839.

Moore, Frances. *Travels into the Inland Parts of Africa*. London: D. Henry and R. Cave, 1738.

Moseley, Benjamin. *A Treatise on Sugar*. London: John Nichols, 1800.

Nichols, John. *Illustrations of the Literary History of the Eighteenth Century*. Vol. 1. [London:] Nichols, Son, and Bentley, 1817.

Oliver, Vere Langford. *The History of the Island of Antigua: One of the Leeward Caribbees in the West Indies, from the First Settlement in 1635 to the Present Time*. 2 vols. London: Mitchell and Hughes, 1896.

Parsons, James. "An Account of the White Negro Shewn before the Royal Society: In a Letter to the Right Honourable the Earl of Morton, President of the Royal Society, from James Parsons, M. D. F. R. S." *Philosophical Transactions (1683–1775)* 55 (1765): 45–53.

Peterkin, Joshua. *A Treatise on Planting, From the Origin of the Semen to Ebullition*. 2nd ed. Basseterre: Edward Low, 1790.

Petiver, James. "An Account of Animals and Shells Sent from Carolina to Mr. James Petiver, FRS." *Philosophical Transactions (1683–1775)* 24 (1704–1705): 1952–60, 1953–54.

———. "Botanicum Hortense IV. Continued from No. 345 by James Petiver, F. R. S." *Philosophical Transactions (1683–1775)* 29 (1714): 353–64.

———. *Catalogus Classicus & topicus, omnium rerum figuratarum in V. decadibus, seu primo volumine Gazophylacii naturæ & artis; singulis ad proprias tabulas & numeros relatis. A Jacobo Petiver, . . .* [London, 1709].

———. *Gazophylacii naturae & artis decas septima & octava. In qud Animalia, Quadrupeda, Aves, Pisces, Reptilia, Infecta, Vegetabilia, Fossilia & Lapides Figura insignes, Corpora Marina, Stirpes Minerales e Terra eruta, &c. Item Antiquaria, Numismata, Gemmae excisae, Lucernae, Urnae, Instrumenta varia, Machinae, Busta, Effigies clarorum Virorum, omniaque Arte producta. Descriptionibus brevibus & iconibus illustrantur. Patronis suis & moecenatibus d.d.d. Jacobus Petiver. S.R.S.* [London, 1711?].

———. *Musei Petiveriani centuria prima, rariora naturae continens: viz. animalia, fossilia, plantas, ex variis mundi plagis advecta, ordine digesta, et nominibus propriis signata*. [London], 1695–1703.

Phillips, Thomas. *A Journal of a Voyage Made in the* Hannibal *of London, Ann. 1693, 1694*. London: Walthoe, 1732.

Prince, Mary. *The History of Mary Prince, a West Indian Slave. Related by Herself. With a Supplement by the Editor (T. Pringle). To which is Added, the Narrative of Asa-Asa, a Captured African*. London: F. Westley and A. H. Davis, 1831.

Rask, Johannes. *Two Views from Christiansborg Castle*. Vol. 1, *A Brief and Truthful Description of a Journey to and from Guinea, 1754*, translated and edited by Selena Axelrod Winsnes. Accra: Sub-Saharan Publishers, 2009.

Riddell, Maria. *Voyage to the Madeira and Leeward and Caribbean Isles, with Sketches of the Natural History of these Islands.* Salem, MA: N. Coverly, 1802.

Robertson, Robert. *A Detection of the State and Situation of the Present Sugar Planters of Barbados and the Leeward Islands.* London: Printed and sold by J. Wilford, 1732.

Rogers, George C., Jr., David R. Chesnutt, and Peggy J. Clark, eds. *The Papers of Henry Laurens.* Vol. 6, *August 1, 1768–July 31, 1769.* Columbia: University of South Carolina Press, 1978.

Romans, Bernard. *A Concise Natural History of East and West Florida.* New York: Sold by R. Aitken, 1776.

Rømer, Ludvig Ferdinand. *A Reliable Account of the Coast of Guinea, 1760.* Translated and edited by Selena Axelrod Winsnes. London: British Academy, 2000.

Schaw, Jane. *Journal of a Lady of Quality: Being the Narrative of a Journey from Scotland to the West Indies, North Carolina, and Portugal, in the Years 1774 to 1776.* New Haven, CT: Yale University Press, 1921.

Schomburgk, Robert Hermann. *The History of Barbados.* Longman: London, 1848.

Sloane, Hans. *A Voyage to the Islands Madera, Barbados, Nieves, St Christophers and Jamaica.* 2 vols. London: Printed for the author, 1707, 1725.

Smeathman, Henry. "Some Account of the Termites, Which Are Found in Africa and Other Hot Climates. In a Letter from Mr. Henry Smeathman, of Clement's Inn, to Sir Joseph Banks, Bart. P. R. S." *Philosophical Transactions of the Royal Society of London* (1781), 139–92.

Smith, James Edward, ed. *A Selection of the Correspondence of Linnaeus, and Other Naturalists: From the Original Manuscripts.* 2 vols. London: Printed for Longman, Hurst, Rees, Orme, and Brown, 1821.

Smith, William. *A Natural History of Nevis, and the Rest of the English Leeward Charibee Islands in America.* London: J. Bentham, 1745.

———. *A New Voyage to Guinea.* London: Printed for John Nourse, 1744.

Snelgrave, William. *A New Account of Some Parts of Guinea, and the Slave-Trade.* London: Printed for James, John, and Paul Knapton, 1734.

Spilsbury, Francis. *Account of a Voyage to the Western Coast of Africa: Performed by His Majesty's Sloop* Favourite, *In the Year 1805.* London: Printed for Richard Phillips, 1807.

Sprat, Thomas. *The History of the Royal Society of London, for the Improving of Natural Knowledge.* London: T. R. and J. Allestry, 1667.

Sprigs, Elizabeth. "Letter to Mr. John Sprigs in White Cross Street near Cripple Gate, London, 22 September 1756." In *Colonial Captivities, Marches, and Journeys,* edited by Isabel Calder, 151–52. New York: Macmillan.

Tatham, William. *An Historical and Practical Essay on the Culture and Commerce of Tobacco.* London: T. Bensley, 1808.

"Thomas Walduck's Letters from Barbados, 1710–1712." *Journal of the Barbados Museum and Historical Society* 15, no. 1 (1947–1948): 27–51, 84–88, 137–149.

Thompson, Benjamin. *Essays, Political, Economical, and Philosophical.* Vol. 1. London: Printed for T. Cadell and W. Davies, 1796.

Thompson, Thomas. *An Account of Two Missionary Voyages.* London: Printed for Benj. Dod., 1758.

Toller, William. "Reproducción facsimilar de la 'Historia de un Viaje al Río de la Plata y Buenos Aires desde inglaterra.' Ano MDCCXV por William Toller." *Revista Histórica: Publicación del Museo Histórico Nacional* 23, no. 67-6 (May 1955): 1–33.

Turnbull, Gordon. *Letters to a Young Planter; or, Observations on the Management of a Sugar-Plantation: to which is added, the Planter's Kalendar, Written on the Island of Grenada by an Old Planter.* London: Stuart and Stevenson, 1785.

Secondary Printed Works

Adair, Douglass, and Devereux Jarratt. "The Autobiography of the Reverend Devereux Jarratt, 1732–1763." *William and Mary Quarterly* (1952): 346–93.

Adams, Percy G. "John Lawson's Alter-Ego—Dr. John Brickell." *North Carolina Historical Review* 34, no. 3 (1957): 313–26.

Adey, Peter. *Mobility.* 2nd ed. New York: Routledge, 2017.

Agamben, Giorgio. *Homo Sacer: Sovereign Power and Bare Life.* Stanford, CA: Stanford University Press, 1998.

Aiton, Arthur S. "The Asiento Treaty as Reflected in the Papers of Lord Shelburne." *Hispanic American Historical Review* 8, no. 2 (1928): 167–77.

Alderman, Derek H., and G. Rebecca Dobbs. "Geographies of Slavery: Of Theory, Method, and Intervention." *Historical Geography* 39 (2011): 29–40.

Allewaert, Monique. *Ariel's Ecology: Plantations, Personhood, and Colonialism in the American Tropics.* Minneapolis: University of Minnesota Press, 2014.

Anderson, Virginia DeJohn. *Creatures of Empire: How Domestic Animals Transformed Early America.* Oxford: Oxford University Press, 2004.

Andrews, Thomas. "Beasts of the Southern Wild: Slaveholders, Slaves and Other Animals in Charles Ball's *Slavery in the United States.*" In *Rendering Nature: Animals, Bodies, Places, Politics,* edited by Marguerite Shaffer and Phoebe Young, 21–47. Philadelphia: University of Pennsylvania Press, 2015.

Appleby, John H. "Human Curiosities and the Royal Society, 1699–1751." *Notes and Records of the Royal Society of London* 50, no. 1 (1996): 13–27.

Bankoff, Greg. "Aeolian Empires: The Influence of Winds and Currents on European Maritime Expansion in the Days of Sail." *Environment and History* 23, no. 2 (2017): 163–96.

Barber, Sarah. "'Not worth one Groat': The Status, Gentility and Credit of Lawrence and Sarah Crabb of Antigua." *Journal of Early American History* 1, no. 1 (2011): 26–61.

Bardoe, Samantha Rebovich. "Resistance and Reform: Landscapes at Green Castle, Antigua." In *The Limits of Tyranny,* edited by James A. Delle, 65–92. Knoxville: University of Tennessee Press, 2015.

Bauer, Ralph, and Marcy Norton. "Introduction: Entangled Trajectories: Indigenous and European Histories." *Colonial Latin American Review* 26, no. 1 (2017): 1–17.

Baumgartner, Barbara. "The Body as Evidence: Resistance, Collaboration, and Appropriation in *The History of Mary Prince*." *Callaloo* 24, no. 1 (2001): 253–75.

Bay, Mia. *The White Image in the Black Mind: African-American Ideas about White People, 1830–1925.* Oxford: Oxford University Press, 2000.

Bayly, Christopher A. *Empire and Information: Intelligence Gathering and Social Communication in India, 1780–1870.* Cambridge: Cambridge University Press, 1999.

———. "Knowing the Country: Empire and Information in India." *Modern Asian Studies* 27, no. 1 (1993): 3–43.

Beattie, James, Edward Melillo, and Emily O'Gorman, eds. *Eco-Cultural Networks and the British Empire: New Views on Environmental History.* London: Bloomsbury Publishing, 2014.

———. "Rethinking the British Empire through Eco-Cultural Networks: Materialist-Cultural Environmental History, Relational Connections and Agency." *Environment and History* 20, no. 4 (2014): 561–75.

Beckles, Hilary. "An Economic Life of Their Own: Slaves as Commodity Producers and Distributors in Barbados." In *The Slave's Economy: Independent Production by Slaves in the Americas,* edited by Ira D. Berlin and Philip Morgan, 31–47. London: Frank Cass and Co., 1991.

Beckles, Hilary McDonald. *Natural Rebels: A Social History of Enslaved Black Women in Barbados.* New Brunswick, NJ: Rutgers University Press, 1989.

Beinart, William, and Lotte Hughes. *Environment and Empire.* Oxford: Oxford University Press, 2007.

Bell, Karen B. "Rice, Resistance, and Forced Transatlantic Communities: (Re)Envisioning the African Diaspora in Low Country Georgia, 1750–1800." *Journal of African American History* 95, no. 2 (2010): 157–82.

Bennett, Herman L. *Africans in Colonial Mexico: Absolutism, Christianity, and Afro-Creole Consciousness, 1570–1640.* Bloomington: Indiana University Press, 2005.

Bennett, Jane. *Vibrant Matter: A Political Ecology of Things.* Durham, NC: Duke University Press, 2010.

Berkeley, Edmund, and Dorothy S. Berkeley. "Another 'Account of Virginia': By the Reverend John Clayton." *Virginia Magazine of History and Biography* (1968): 415–36.

———. *Dr. Alexander Garden of Charles Town.* Chapel Hill: University of North Carolina Press, 1969.

———. "The Most Common Rush or Vilest Weed: Some Unpublished Letters of James Petiver to William Byrd II." *Virginia Magazine of History and Biography* 95, no. 4 (1987): 481–95.

Bernasconi, Robert. "Ottobah Cugoano's Place in the History of Political Philosophy." In *Debating African Philosophy: Perspectives on Identity, Decolonial Ethics and Comparative Philosophy,* edited by George Hull. London: Routledge, 2019.

Besson, Jean. *Martha Brae's Two Histories: European Expansion and Caribbean Culture-Building in Jamaica.* Chapel Hill: University of North Carolina Press, 2002.

Bialuschewski, Arne. "A True Account of the Design, and Advantages of the South-Sea Trade: Profits, Propaganda, and the Peace Preliminaries of 1711." *Huntington Library Quarterly* 73, no. 2 (2010): 273–85.

Bijker, Wiebe E., Thomas Parke Hughes, and Trevor J. Pinch, eds. *The Social Construction of Technological Systems: New Directions in the Sociology and History of Technology.* Cambridge, MA: MIT Press, 1989.

Bindman, David. *Ape to Apollo: Aesthetics and the Idea of Race in the Eighteenth Century.* Ithaca, NY: Cornell University Press, 2002.

Blake, John William. *Europeans in West Africa, 1540–1560.* Vol. 2. Farnham: Hakluyt Society, 2010.

Bly, Antonio T. "'Pretends he can read': Runaways and Literacy in Colonial America, 1730–1776." *Early American Studies* (2008): 261–94.

———. "'Reed through the Bybell'": Slave Education in Early Virginia." *Book History* 16, no. 1 (2013): 1–33.

Boaz, Danielle. "'Instruments of Obeah': The Significance of Ritual Objects in the Jamaican Legal System, 1760–Present." In *Materialities of Ritual in the Black Atlantic,* edited by Akinwumi Ogundiran and Paula Saunders, 143–58. Bloomington: Indiana University Press, 2014.

Boehrer, Bruce Thomas. *Animal Characters: Nonhuman Beings in Early Modern Literature.* Philadelphia: University of Pennsylvania Press, 2011.

Bohls, Elizabeth A. "The Aesthetics of Colonialism: Janet Schaw in the West Indies, 1774–1775." *Eighteenth-Century Studies* 27, no. 3 (1994): 363–90.

Boisseron, Bénédicte. *Afro-Dog: Blackness and the Animal Question.* New York: Columbia University Press, 2018.

Borucki, Alex. *From Shipmates to Soldiers: Emerging Black Identities in the Río de la Plata.* Albuquerque: University of New Mexico Press, 2015.

Botkin, Frances R. *Thieving Three-Fingered Jack: Transatlantic Tales of a Jamaican Outlaw, 1780–2015.* New Brunswick, NJ: Rutgers University Press, 2017.

Boulukos, George E. *The Grateful Slave: The Emergence of Race in Eighteenth-Century British and American Culture.* Cambridge: Cambridge University Press, 2008.

Bradley, Keith. *Slavery and Society at Rome.* Cambridge: Cambridge University Press, 1994.

Brandow, James V., ed. "The Diary of Joseph Senhouse." *Journal of the Barbados Museum and Historical Society* 37 (1985): 276–95; 37 (1986): 318–414; 38 (1988): 179–95.

Breen, T. H. "Horses and Gentlemen: The Cultural Significance of Gambling among the Gentry of Virginia." *William and Mary Quarterly* 34, no. 2 (1977): 239–57.

Brewer, Holly. "Slavery, Sovereignty, and "Inheritable Blood": Reconsidering John Locke and the Origins of American Slavery." *American Historical Review* 122, no. 4 (2017): 1038–1078.

Brosnan, Kathleen A. "The Lifting Fog: Race, Work, and the Environment." *Environmental History* 24, no. 1 (2018): 9–24.

Brown, Christopher L. *Moral Capital: Foundations of British Abolitionism.* Chapel Hill: University of North Carolina Press, 2012.

Brown, Ras Michael. *African-Atlantic Cultures and the South Carolina Lowcountry.* Cambridge: Cambridge University Press, 2012.

Brown, Vincent. *The Reaper's Garden: Death and Power in the World of Atlantic Slavery.* Cambridge, MA: Harvard University Press, 2008.

Browne, Randy M. "The "Bad Business" of Obeah: Power, Authority, and the Politics of Slave Culture in the British Caribbean." *William and Mary Quarterly* 68, no. 3 (2011): 451–80.

Browne, Simone. *Dark Matters: On the Surveillance of Blackness.* Durham, NC: Duke University Press, 2015.

Brunton, T. Lauder, and Walter Pye. "On the Physiological Action of the Bark of Erythrophleum Guinense, Generally Called Casca, Cassa, or Sassy Bark." *Philosophical Transactions of the Royal Society of London* 167 (1877): 627–58.

Burnard, Trevor. "Collecting and Accounting: Representing Slaves as Commodities in Jamaica, 1674–1784." In *Collecting Across Cultures: Material Exchanges in the Early Modern Atlantic World,* edited by Daniela Bleichmar and Peter Mancall, 177–91. Philadelphia: University of Pennsylvania Press, 2011.

———. *Planters, Merchants, and Slaves: Plantation Societies in British America, 1650–1820.* Chicago: University of Chicago Press, 2015.

Burnard, Trevor, and John Garrigus. *The Plantation Machine: Atlantic Capitalism in French Saint-Domingue and British Jamaica.* Philadelphia: University of Pennsylvania Press, 2016.

Calhoun, Jeanne A., Martha A. Zierden, and Elizabeth A. Paysinger. "The Geographic Spread of Charleston's Mercantile Community, 1732–1767." *South Carolina Historical Magazine* 86, no. 3 (1985): 182–220

Camp, Stephanie M. H. *Closer to Freedom: Enslaved Women and Everyday Resistance in the Plantation South.* Chapel Hill: University of North Carolina Press, 2004.

———. "The Pleasures of Resistance: Enslaved Women and Body Politics in the Plantation South, 1830–1861." *Journal of Southern History* 68, no. 3 (2002): 533–72.

Carney, Judith. "Between Land and Sea: Mangroves and Mollusks along Brazil's Mangal Coast." *Fronteiras: Journal of Social, Technological and Environmental Science* 5, no. 3 (2016): 17–38.

———. *Black Rice: The African Origins of Rice Cultivation in the Americas*. Cambridge, MA: Harvard University Press, 2001.

———. "Landscapes and Places of Memory: African Diaspora Research and Geography." In *The African Diaspora and the Disciplines*, edited by Tejumola Olaniyan and James Sweet, 101–18. Bloomington: Indiana University Press, 2010.

———. "Landscapes of Technology Transfer: Rice Cultivation and African Continuities." *Technology and Culture* 37, no. 1 (1996): 5–35.

———. "'The Mangrove Preserves Life': Habitat of African Survival in the Atlantic World." *Geographical Review* 107, no. 3 (2017): 433–51.

———. "Seeds of Memory: Botanical Legacies of the African Diaspora." In *African Ethnobotany in the Americas*, edited by Robert Voeks and John Rashford, 13–34. New York: Springer Science and Business Media, 2013.

Carney, Judith, and Richard Porcher. "Geographies of the Past: Rice, Slaves and Technological Transfer in South Carolina." *Southeastern Geographer* 33, no. 2 (1993): 127–47.

Carretta, Vincent, and Ty M. Reese, eds. *The Life and Letters of Philip Quaque, the First African Anglican Missionary*. Athens: University of Georgia Press, 2012.

Casid, Jill H. *Sowing Empire: Landscape and Colonization*. Minneapolis: University of Minnesota Press, 2005.

Catron, John. "Slavery, Ethnic Identity, and Christianity in Eighteenth-Century Moravian Antigua." *Journal of Moravian History* 14, no. 2 (2014): 153–78.

Chambers, Douglas B. *Murder at Montpelier: Igbo Africans in Virginia*. Jackson: University Press of Mississippi, 2005.

Childs, St Julien R. "A Letter Written in 1711 by Mary Stafford to Her Kinswoman in England." *The South Carolina Historical Magazine* 81, no. 1 (1980): 1–7.

Chukwukere, I. "Akan Theory of Conception. Are the Fante Really Aberrant?" *Africa: Journal of the International African Institute* 48, no. 2 (1978): 135–48.

Cockerell, T. D. A. "Dru Drury, an Eighteenth Century Entomologist." *Scientific Monthly* 14, no. 1 (1922): 67–82.

Cohen, Benjamin R. *Notes from the Ground: Science, Soil, and Society in the American Countryside*. New Haven, CT: Yale University Press, 2014.

Cole, Lucinda. *Imperfect Creatures: Vermin, Literature, and the Sciences of Life, 1600–1740*. Ann Arbor: University of Michigan Press, 2016.

Coleman, Deirdre. "'Aetherial Journies, Submarine Exploits': The Debatable Worlds of Natural History in the Eighteenth Century." In *Romanticism's Debatable Lands*, edited by Claire Lamont and Michael Rossington, 223–36. New York: Palgrave Macmillan, 2007.

———. *Henry Smeathman, the Flycatcher: Natural History, Slavery, and Empire in the Late Eighteenth Century.* Liverpool: Liverpool University Press, 2018.

———. *Romantic Colonization and British Anti-Slavery.* Cambridge: Cambridge University Press, 2005.

Coleman, Jon T. *Vicious: Wolves and Men in America.* New Haven, CT: Yale University Press, 2008.

Colpitts, George. "'Animated like Us by Commercial Interests': Commercial Ethnology and Fur Trade Descriptions in New France, 1660–1760." *Canadian Historical Review* 83, no. 3 (2002): 305–37.

———. "Knowing Nature in the Business Records of the Hudson's Bay Company, 1670–1840." *Business History* 59, no. 7 (2017): 1054–80.

———. *Pemmican Empire: Food, Trade, and the Last Bison Hunts in the North American Plains, 1780–1882.* Cambridge: Cambridge University Press, 2014.

Covey, Herbert C. *African American Slave Medicine: Herbal and Non-herbal Treatments.* New York: Lexington Books, 2007.

Covey, Herbert C., and Dwight Eisnach. *What the Slaves Ate: Recollections of African American Foods and Foodways from the Slave Narratives.* Santa Barbara, CA: ABC-CLIO, 2009.

Craven, Avery. *Soil Exhaustion as a Factor in the Agricultural History of Virginia and Maryland, 1606–1860.* Columbia: University of South Carolina Press, 1925.

Crawford, Nicholas. "'In the Wreck of a Master's Fortune': Slave Provisioning and Planter Debt in the British Caribbean." *Slavery & Abolition* 37, no. 2 (2016): 353–74.

———. "The reasonable sustentation of human life": Food Rations and the Problem of Provision in British Caribbean Slavery." *Early American Studies* 19, no. 2 (2021): 360–92.

Crosby, Alfred. *Ecological Imperialism: The Biological Expansion of Europe, 900–1900.* Cambridge: Cambridge University Press, 1986.

Curtin, Philip D. *The Atlantic Slave Trade: A Census.* Madison: University of Wisconsin Press, 1972.

Cwik, Christian. "The End of the British Atlantic Slave Trade or the Beginning of the Big Slave Robbery, 1808–1850." In *The Second Slavery: Mass Slaveries and Modernity in the Americas and in the Atlantic Basin,* edited by Javier Lavina and Michael Zeuske, 19–38. Berlin: LIT Verlag, 2014.

Daaku, Kwame Yeboah. *Trade and Politics on the Gold Coast, 1600–1720: A Study of the African Reaction to European Trade.* Oxford: Clarendon Press, 1970.

Dallett, Francis J., Jr. "Griffith Hughes Dissected." *Journal of the Barbados Museum and Historical Society* 23, no. 1 (1955): 3–29.

Dator, James F. "'Choicest of the Cargoe': Antigua, the Codringtons, and the Slave Trade, ca. 1672–1808." In *An Archaeology and History of a Caribbean Sugar Plantation on*

Antigua, edited by Georgia L. Fox, 145–57. Gainesville: University Press of Florida, 2020.

Datta, Ansu K., and R. Porter. "The Asafo System in Historical Perspective." *Journal of African History* 12, no. 2 (1971): 279–97.

Davidson, James M. "'A Cluster of Sacred Symbols': Interpreting an Act of Animal Sacrifice at Kingsley Plantation, Fort George Island, Florida (1814–39)." *International Journal of Historical Archaeology* 19, no. 1 (2015): 76–121.

Davies, Kenneth. *The Royal African Company*. London: Longmans, Green and Co., 1957.

Davis, Adrienne. "'Don't Let Nobody Bother Your Principle': The Sexual Economy of Slavery." In *Sister Circle: Black Women and Work*, edited by Sharon Harley and the Black Women and Work Collective, 103–27. New Brunswick, NJ: Rutgers University Press, 2002.

Davis, David Brion. *In the Image of God: Religion, Moral Values, and Our Heritage of Slavery*. New Haven, CT: Yale University Press, 2001.

———. *Inhuman Bondage: The Rise and Fall of Slavery in the New World*. Oxford: Oxford University Press, 2006.

———. *The Problem of Slavery in the Age of Emancipation*. New York: Vintage, 2014.

———. *The Problem of Slavery in Western Culture*. Ithaca, NY: Cornell University Press, 1966.

———. *Slavery in the Colonial Chesapeake*. Williamsburg, VA: Colonial Williamsburg Foundation, 1986.

Dayan, Colin. *The Law Is a White Dog: How Legal Rituals Make and Unmake Persons*. Princeton, NJ: Princeton University Press, 2011.

de Asúa, Miguel. *Science in the Vanished Arcadia: Knowledge of Nature in the Jesuit Missions of Paraguay and Río de la Plata*. Leiden: Brill, 2014.

Deb Roy, Rohan. "Introduction: Nonhuman Empires." *Comparative Studies of South Asia, Africa, and the Middle East* 35 no. 1 (2015): 66–75.

DeCorse, Christopher. "Tools of Empire: Trade, Slaves, and the British Forts of West Africa." In *Building the British Atlantic World: Spaces, Places, and Material Culture, 1600–1850*, edited by Daniel Maudlin and Bernard L. Herman, 165–87. Chapel Hill: University of North Carolina Press, 2016.

Delbourgo, James. *Collecting the World: Hans Sloane and the Origins of the British Museum*. Cambridge, MA: Harvard University Press, 2017.

———. "Divers Things: Collecting the World under Water." *History of Science* 49, no. 2 (2011): 149–85.

———. "Listing People." *Isis* 103, no. 4 (2012): 735–42.

———. "The Newtonian Slave Body: Racial Enlightenment in the Atlantic World." *Atlantic Studies* 9, no. 2 (2012): 185–207.

Denny, Margaret. "Linnaeus and His Disciple in Carolina: Alexander Garden." *Isis* 38, no. 3/4 (1948): 161–74.

Dewhurst, Kenneth, and Rex Doublet. "Thomas Dover and the South Sea Company." *Medical History* 18, no. 2 (1974): 107–21.

Dickson, Kwamina B. *An Historical Geography of Ghana.* Cambridge: Cambridge University Press, 1969.

Dierksheide, Christa. *Amelioration and Empire: Progress and Slavery in the Plantation Americas.* Charlottesville: University of Virginia Press, 2014.

Donnan, Elizabeth, ed. *Documents Illustrative of the History of the Slave Trade to America.* 4 vols. New York: Octagon Books, 1965.

Donoso Anes, Rafael. "Accounting and Slavery: The Accounts of the English South Sea Company, 1713–22." *European Accounting Review* 11, no. 2 (2002): 441–52.

Douglas, Starr. "The Making of Scientific Knowledge in an Age of Slavery: Henry Smeathman, Sierra Leone and Natural History." *Journal of Colonialism and Colonial History* 9, no. 3 (2008).

Douglas, A. Starr, and E. Geoffrey Hancock. "Insect Collecting in Africa During the Eighteenth Century and William Hunter's Collection." *Archives of Natural History* 34, no. 2 (2007): 293–306.

Drayton, Richard. *Nature's Government: Science, Imperial Britain, and the "Improvement" of the World.* New Haven, CT: Yale University Press, 2000.

Dunn, Richard S. *Sugar and Slaves: The Rise of the Planter Class in the English West Indies, 1624–1713.* Chapel Hill: University of North Carolina Press, 1972.

———. *A Tale of Two Plantations: Slave Life and Labor in Jamaica and Virginia.* Cambridge, MA: Harvard University Press, 2014.

Dusenberry, William H. "Discriminatory Aspects of Legislation in Colonial Mexico." *Journal of Negro History* 33, no. 3 (1948): 284–302.

Earle, Rebecca. "The Political Economy of Nutrition in the Eighteenth Century." *Past & Present* 242, no. 1 (2019): 79–117

"Early Letters from South Carolina upon Natural History." *South Carolina Historical and Genealogical Magazine* 21, no. 1 (1920): 3–9.

Edelson, S. Max. "Beyond "Black Rice": Reconstructing Material and Cultural Contexts for Early Plantation Agriculture." *American Historical Review* 115, no. 1 (2010): 125–35.

———. *Plantation Enterprise in Colonial South Carolina.* Cambridge, MA: Harvard University Press, 2006.

Edwards, Gary T. "'Negroes . . . and All Other Animals': Slaves and Masters in Antebellum Madison County." *Tennessee Historical Quarterly* 57, no. 1 (1998): 24–35.

Ekirch, A. Roger. "'A New Government of Liberty': Hermon Husband's Vision of Backcountry North Carolina, 1755." *William and Mary Quarterly* (1977): 632–646.

Eltis, David, Philip Morgan, and David Richardson. "Agency and Diaspora in Atlantic History: Reassessing the African Contribution to Rice Cultivation in the Americas." *American Historical Review* 112, no. 5 (2007): 1329–58.

Ephirim-Donkor, Anthony. *African Religion Defined: A Systematic Study of Ancestor Worship among the Akan*. London: Rowman & Littlefield, 2016.

Ewan, Joseph. "The Natural History of John Abbot: Influences and Some Questions." *Bartonia* no. 51 (1985): 37–45.

Ewan, Joseph, and Nesta Ewan. *John Banister and His Natural History of Virginia, 1678–1692*. Urbana: University of Illinois Press, 1970.

Fage, J. D. "African Societies and the Atlantic Slave Trade." *Past & Present* no. 125 (1989): 97–115.

Fajardo, Luis Eduardo. "Dos Comerciantes Británicos en Cartagena a Principios del siglo XVIII." *Boletín Cultural y Bibliográfico* 43, no. 71–72 (2006): 2–19.

Fanon, Frantz. *The Wretched of the Earth*. New York: Grove, 1963.

Fayer, Joan M. "African Interpreters in the Atlantic Slave Trade." *Anthropological Linguistics* 45, no. 3 (2003): 281–95.

Feinberg, Harvey M. "Africans and Europeans in West Africa: Elminans and Dutchmen on the Gold Coast during the Eighteenth Century." *Transactions of the American Philosophical Society* 79, no. 7 (1989): 1–186.

Fernández Bravo, Álvaro. "Catálogo, Colección y Colonialismo Interno: Una lectura de la 'Descripción de la Patagonia' de Thomas Falkner (1774)." *Revista de Crítica Literaria Latinoamericana* (2004): 229–49.

Fields-Black, Edda L. *Deep Roots: Rice Farmers in West Africa and the African Diaspora*. Bloomington: Indiana University Press, 2008.

Finucane, Adrian. *The Temptations of Trade: Britain, Spain, and the Struggle for Empire*. Philadelphia: University of Pennsylvania Press, 2016.

Fischer, Kirsten. *Suspect Relations: Sex, Race, and Resistance in Colonial North Carolina*. Ithaca, NY: Cornell University Press, 2002.

Fissell, Mary. "Imagining Vermin in Early Modern England." *History Workshop Journal* no. 47 (1999): 1–29.

Foucault, Michel. *Discipline and Punish: The Birth of the Prison*. New York: Pantheon, 1977.

Foy, Anna M. "The Convention of Georgic Circumlocution and the Proper Use of Human Dung in Samuel Martin's *Essay Upon Plantership*." *Eighteenth-Century Studies* 49, no. 4 (2016): 475–506.

Franklin, John Hope, and Loren Schweninger. *Runaway Slaves: Rebels on the Plantation*. Oxford: Oxford University Press, 2000.

Frey, Sylvia R., and Betty Wood. *Come Shouting to Zion: African American Protestantism in the American South and British Caribbean to 1830*. Chapel Hill: University of North Carolina Press, 2000.

Fry, Gladys-Marie. *Night Riders in Black Folk History*. Knoxville: University of Tennessee Press, 1975.

Fudge, Erica. *Perceiving Animals: Humans and Beasts in Early Modern English Culture*. Urbana: University of Illinois Press, 2002.

Fuentes, Marisa J. *Dispossessed Lives: Enslaved Women, Violence, and the Archive*. Philadelphia: University of Pennsylvania Press, 2016.

Fulford, Tim, Debbie Lee, and Peter J. Kitson. *Literature, Science and Exploration in the Romantic Era: Bodies of Knowledge*. Cambridge: Cambridge University Press, 2004.

Galle, Jillian E. "Assessing the Impacts of Time, Agricultural Cycles, and Demography on the Consumer Activities of Enslaved Men and Women in Eighteenth-Century Jamaica and Virginia." In *Out of Many, One People: The Historical Archaeology of Colonial Jamaica*, edited by James A. Delle, Mark W. Hauser, and Douglas V. Armstrong, 211–42. Tuscaloosa: University of Alabama Press, 2011.

Gaspar, David Barry. *Bondmen and Rebels: A Study of Master–Slave Relations in Antigua*. Durham, NC: Duke University Press, 1993.

———. "Working the System: Antigua Slaves and Their Struggle to Live." *Slavery and Abolition* 13, no. 3 (1992): 131–55.

Geggus, David. "Marronage, Voodoo, and the Saint Domingue Slave Revolt of 1791." *Proceedings of the Meeting of the French Colonial Historical Society* 15 (1992): 22–35.

Gibbs, Jenna. "Toussaint, Gabriel, and Three Finger'd Jack: 'Courageous Chiefs' and the 'Sacred Standard of Liberty' on the Atlantic Stage." *Early American Studies* 13, no. 3 (2015): 626–60.

Gibson, Susannah. "On Being an Animal, or, the Eighteenth-Century Zoophyte Controversy in Britain." *History of Science* 50, no. 4 (2012): 453–76.

Gijanto, Liza. "Personal Adornment and Expressions of Status: Beads and the Gambia River's Atlantic Trade." *International Journal of Historical Archaeology* 15, no. 4 (2011): 637–68.

Gijanto, Liza, and Sarah Walshaw. "Ceramic Production and Dietary Changes at Juffure, Gambia." *African Archaeological Review* 31, no. 2 (2014): 265–97.

Gilmore, John. *The Poetics of Empire: A Study of James Grainger's* The Sugar-Cane *(1764)*. London: Athlone Press, 2000.

Githens, Thomas S. *Drug Plants of Africa*. Philadelphia: University of Pennsylvania Press, 1949.

Glasson, Travis. *Mastering Christianity: Missionary Anglicanism and Slavery in the Atlantic World*. Oxford: Oxford University Press, 2011.

———. "Missionaries, Methodists, and a Ghost: Philip Quaque in London and Cape Coast, 1756–1816." *Journal of British Studies* 48, no. 1 (2009): 29–50.

Gómez, Pablo F. "Caribbean Stones and the Creation of Early-Modern Worlds." *History and Technology* 34, no. 1 (2018): 11–20.

Gordon-Reed, Annette. *The Hemingses of Monticello: An American Family*. New York: W. W. Norton & Co., 2008.

Goucher, Candice. *Congotay! Congotay! A Global History of Caribbean Food*. London: Routledge, 2013.

Govier, Mark. "The Royal Society, Slavery and the Island of Jamaica: 1660–1700." *Notes and Records of the Royal Society* 53, no. 2 (1999): 203–17.

Graham, Russell, and Alan Edward Brown, eds. *"Pretends to be Free": Runaway Slave Advertisements from Colonial and Revolutionary New York and New Jersey.* 2nd ed. New York: Fordham University Press, 2019.

Grandjean, Katherine A. "New World Tempests: Environment, Scarcity, and the Coming of the Pequot War." *William and Mary Quarterly* 68, no. 1 (2011): 75–100.

Greene, Jack P., ed. *The Diary of Colonel Landon Carter of Sabine Hall, 1752–1778.* 2 vols. Charlottesville: University Press of Virginia, 1965.

———. *Landon Carter: An Inquiry into the Personal Values and Social Imperatives of the Eighteenth-Century Virginia Gentry.* Charlottesville: University Press of Virginia, 1965.

Grigson, Caroline. *Menagerie: The History of Exotic Animals in England.* Oxford: Oxford University Press, 2016.

Grove, Richard H. *Green Imperialism: Colonial Expansion, Tropical Island Edens and the Origins of Environmentalism, 1600–1860.* Cambridge: Cambridge University Press, 1996.

Gunn, Jeffrey. "Creating a Paradox: Quobna Ottobah Cugoano and the Slave Trade's Violation of the Principles of Christianity, Reason, and Property Ownership." *Journal of World History* 21, no. 4 (2010): 629–56.

Hadden, Sally E. *Slave Patrols: Law and Violence in Virginia and the Carolinas.* Cambridge, MA: Harvard University Press, 2001.

Halloran, Vivian Nun. "Recipes as Memory Work: Slave Food." *Culture, Theory and Critique* 53, no. 2 (2012): 147–61.

Hamilton, Douglas. *Scotland, the Caribbean and the Atlantic World, 1750–1820.* Oxford: Oxford University Press, 2010.

Hancock, E. Geoffrey, and A. Starr Douglas. "William Hunter's Goliath Beetle, *Goliathus goliatus* (Linnaeus, 1771), re-visited." *Archives of Natural History* 36, no. 2 (2009): 218–30.

Handler, Jerome S. "An African-type Healer/Diviner and His Grave Goods: A Burial from a Plantation Slave Cemetery in Barbados, West Indies." *International Journal of Historical Archaeology* 1, no. 2 (1997): 91–130.

———. "Escaping Slavery in a Caribbean Plantation Society: Marronage in Barbados, 1650s–1830s." *New West Indian Guide* 71, no. 3/4 (1997): 183–225.

Handler, Jerome S., and Kenneth M. Bilby. *Enacting Power: The Criminalization of Obeah in the Anglophone Caribbean, 1760–2011.* Mona: University of West Indies Press, 2012.

Handler, Jerome S., and Diane Wallman. "Production Activities in the Household Economies of Plantation Slaves: Barbados and Martinique, Mid-1600s to Mid-1800s." *International Journal of Historical Archaeology* 18, no. 3 (2014): 441–66.

Harris, Barbara Jean. *English Aristocratic Women, 1450–1550: Marriage and Family, Property and Careers.* Oxford: Oxford University Press, 2002.

Harrison, Peter. "Curiosity, Forbidden Knowledge, and the Reformation of Natural Philosophy in Early Modern England." *Isis* 92, no. 2 (2001): 265–90.

Hartman, Saidiya V. *Lose Your Mother: A Journey along the Atlantic Slave Route.* New York: Farrar, Straus and Giroux, 2007.

———. *Scenes of Subjection: Terror, Slavery, and Self-Making in Nineteenth Century America.* Oxford: Oxford University Press, 1997.

Hawthorne, Walter. "From "Black Rice" to "Brown": Rethinking the History of Riziculture in the Seventeenth- and Eighteenth-Century Atlantic." *American Historical Review* 115, no. 1 (2010): 151–63.

Hayes, Katherine Howlett. *Slavery Before Race: Europeans, Africans, and Indians at Long Island's Sylvester Manor Plantation, 1651–1884.* New York: New York University Press, 2014.

Henige, David. "John Kabes of Komenda: An Early African Entrepreneur and State Builder." *Journal of African History* 18, no. 01 (1977): 1–19.

Henley, Ryan. *Beyond Slavery and Abolition: Black British Writing, c. 1770–1830.* Cambridge: Cambridge University Press, 2018.

Henry, Paget. "Between Hume and Cugoano: Race, Ethnicity and Philosophical Entrapment." *Journal of Speculative Philosophy* 18, no. 2 (2004): 129–48.

Herbert, Eugenia W. "Portuguese Adaptation to Trade Patterns Guinea to Angola (1443–1640)." *African Studies Review* 17, no. 2 (1974): 411–23.

Hicks, Dan. "Material Improvements: The Archaeology of Estate Landscapes in the British Leeward Islands, 1713–1838." In *Estate Landscapes: Design, Improvement and Power in the Post-Medieval Landscape,* edited by Jonathan Finch and Kate Giles, 205–8. Suffolk: Boydell Press, 2007.

Hill, Matthew H. "Towards a Chronology of the Publications of Francis Moore's *Travels into the Inland Parts of Africa*." *History in Africa* 19 (1992): 353–68.

Hiskett, M. "Materials Relating to the Cowry Currency of the Western Sudan—II: Reflections on the Provenance and Diffusion of the Cowry in the Sahara and the Sudan." *Bulletin of the School of Oriental and African Studies, University of London* 29, no. 2 (1966): 339–66.

Hogarth, Rana A. *Medicalizing Blackness: Making Racial Difference in the Atlantic World, 1780–1840.* Chapel Hill: University of North Carolina Press, 2017.

Hogendorn, Jan S., and H. A. Gemery. "Continuity in West African Monetary History? An Outline of Monetary Development." *African Economic History,* no. 17 (1988): 127–46.

Hogendorn, Jan, and Marion Johnson. *The Shell Money of the Slave Trade.* Cambridge: Cambridge University Press, 1986.

Holsey, Bayo. *Routes of Remembrance: Refashioning the Slave Trade in Ghana*. Chicago: University of Chicago Press, 2008.

Howes, F. N. "Fish-Poison Plants." *Bulletin of Miscellaneous Information (Royal Botanic Gardens, Kew)*, no. 4 (1930): 129–53.

Hutchings, Kevin. *Romantic Ecologies and Colonial Cultures in the British Atlantic World, 1770–1850*. Montreal: McGill-Queen's University Press, 2009.

Ingersoll, Thomas N. "'Releese Us out of This Cruell Bondegg': An Appeal from Virginia in 1723." *William and Mary Quarterly* 51, no. 4 (1994): 777–82.

Irving, Sarah. *Natural Science and the Origins of the British Empire*. New York: Routledge, 2015.

———. "Rethinking Instrumentality: Natural Philosophy and Christian Charity in the Early Modern Atlantic World." *HOPOS: The Journal of the International Society for the History of Philosophy of Science* 2, no. 1 (2012): 55–76.

Isaac, Rhys. *Landon Carter's Uneasy Kingdom: Revolution and Rebellion on a Virginia Plantation*. Oxford: Oxford University Press, 2004.

Isichei, Elizabeth. *Voices of the Poor in Africa: Moral Economy and the Popular Imagination*. Rochester, NY: University of Rochester Press, 2002.

Jackson, L. P. "Elizabethan Seamen and the African Slave Trade." *Journal of Negro History* 9, no. 1 (1924): 1–17.

Jacoby, Karl. "Slaves by Nature? Domestic Animals and Human Slaves." *Slavery and Abolition* 15, no. 1 (1994): 89–99.

Johnson, Marion. "The Cowrie Currencies of West Africa, Part I." *Journal of African History* 11, no. 1 (1970): 17–49.

Johnson, Sherry. *Climate and Catastrophe in Cuba and the Atlantic World in the Age of Revolution*. Chapel Hill: University of North Carolina Press, 2011.

Johnson, Walter. *River of Dark Dreams: Slavery and Empire in the Cotton Kingdom*. Cambridge, MA: Harvard University Press, 2013.

———. "Time and Revolution in African America: Temporality and the History of Atlantic Slavery." In *Rethinking American History in a Global Age*, edited by Thomas Bender, 148–67. Oakland: University of California Press, 2002.

———. "To Remake the World: Slavery, Racial Capitalism, and Justice." *Boston Review*, February 20, 2018. https://bostonreview.net/forum/walter-johnson-to-remake-the-world.

Johnston, Edith Duncan. "Dr. William Houstoun, Botanist." *Georgia Historical Quarterly* 25, no. 4 (1941): 325–39.

Jones, Peter M. "Making Chemistry the 'Science' of Agriculture, c. 1760–1840." *History of Science* 54, no. 2 (June 2016): 169–94.

Jonsson, Frederik Albritton. *Enlightenment's Frontier: The Scottish Highlands and the Origins of Environmentalism*. New Haven, CT: Yale University Press, 2013.

Jordan, Winthrop D. *White Over Black: American Attitudes toward the Negro, 1550–1812.* Chapel Hill: University of North Carolina Press, 1968.

Kafka, Ben. "Paperwork: The State of the Discipline." *Book History* 12 (2009): 340–53.

Keefer, Katrina. "Poro, Witchcraft and Red Water in Early Colonial Sierra Leone: G. R. Nylander's Ethnography and Systems of Authority on the Bullom Shore." *Canadian Journal of African Studies/Revue canadienne des études africaines* 55, no. 1 (2021): 39–55.

Kendi, Ibram X. *Stamped from the Beginning: The Definitive History of Racist Ideas in America.* New York: Random House, 2017.

Kercsmar, Joshua Abram. "Wolves at Heart: How Dog Evolution Shaped Whites' Perceptions of Indians in North America." *Environmental History* 21, no. 3 (2016): 516–40.

Kim, Julie Chun. "Natural Histories of Indigenous Resistance: Alexander Anderson and the Caribs of St. Vincent." *The Eighteenth Century* 55, no. 2–3 (2014): 217–33.

Kindmark, Kristina, and György Nováky. "Imperiets Budbärare: Henry Smeathman å resa i Sierra Leone, 1771–1774." In *Från Karakorum till Silijan: Resor Under Sju Sekler,* edited by Hanna Hodacs and Åsa Karlsson, 163–96. Lund: Historiska Media, 2000.

King, James Ferguson. "Descriptive Data on Negro Slaves in Spanish Importation Records and Bills of Sale." *Journal of Negro History* 28, no. 2 (1943): 204–19.

Kiple, Kenneth F. *The Caribbean Slave: A Biological History.* Cambridge: Cambridge University Press, 2002.

Kiple, Kenneth F., and Virginia Himmelsteib King. *Another Dimension to the Black Diaspora: Diet, Disease and Racism.* Cambridge: Cambridge University Press, 2003.

———. "Black Tongue and Black Men: Pellagra and Slavery in the Antebellum South." *Journal of Southern History* 43, no. 3 (1977): 411–28.

Kiple, Kenneth F., and Virginia H. Kiple. "Deficiency Diseases in the Caribbean." *Journal of Interdisciplinary History* 11, no. 2 (1980): 197–215.

Klein, Herbert. *The Atlantic Slave Trade.* 2nd ed. Cambridge: Cambridge University Press, 2010.

Klein, Martin A. "Servitude among the Wolof and Sereer of Senegambia." In *Slavery in Africa: Historical and Anthropological Perspectives,* edited by Suzanne Miers and Igor Kopytoff, 335–63. Madison: University of Wisconsin Press, 1977.

Kleingeld, Pauline. "Kant's Second Thoughts on Colonialism." In *Kant and Colonialism: Historical and Critical Perspectives,* edited by Katrin Flikschuh and Lea Ypi, 43–67. Oxford: Oxford University Press, 2014.

Klooster, Wim. *Revolutions in the Atlantic World: A Comparative History.* New York: New York University Press, 2009.

Knight, Frederick C. *Working the Diaspora: The Impact of African Labor on the Anglo-American World, 1650–1850.* New York: New York University Press, 2010.

Koerner, Lisbet. *Linnaeus: Nature and Nation.* Cambridge, MA: Harvard University Press, 2000.

Konadu, Kwasi. *The Akan Diaspora in the Americas*. Oxford: Oxford University Press, 2010.

Kulikoff, Allan. *From British Peasants to Colonial American Farmers*. Chapel Hill: University of North Carolina Press, 2000.

———. *Tobacco and Slaves: The Development of Southern Cultures in the Chesapeake, 1680–1800*. Chapel Hill: University of North Carolina Press, 1986.

Kupperman, Karen Ordahl. "Errand to the Indies: Puritan Colonization from Providence Island through the Western Design." *William and Mary Quarterly* 45, no. 1 (1988): 70–99.

Lambert, David. "Master–Horse–Slave: Mobility, Race and Power in the British West Indies, c. 1780–1838." *Slavery & Abolition* 36, no. 4 (2015): 618–41.

———. "'Taken Captive by the Mystery of the Great River': Towards an Historical Geography of British Geography and Atlantic Slavery." *Journal of Historical Geography* 35, no. 1 (2009): 44–65.

Lancaster, James A. T. "Natural Knowledge as a Propaedeutic to Self-Betterment: Francis Bacon and the Transformation of Natural History." *Early Science and Medicine* 17, no. 1/2 (2012): 181–96.

Landers, Jane. "Gracia Real de Santa Teresa de Mose: A Free Black Town in Spanish Colonial Florida." *American Historical Review* 95, no. 1 (1990): 9–30.

Landry, Donna. "English Brutes, Eastern Enlightenment." *The Eighteenth Century* 52, no. 1 (2011): 11–30.

———. *Noble Brutes: How Eastern Horses Transformed English Culture*. Baltimore: Johns Hopkins University Press, 2008.

Larrabee, Mary Jeanne. "'I Know What a Slave Knows': Mary Prince's Epistemology of Resistance." *Women's Studies* 35, no. 5 (2006): 453–73.

Latour, Bruno. *Reassembling the Social: An Introduction to Actor-Network-Theory*. Oxford: Oxford University Press, 2005.

Law, John. "Notes on the Theory of the Actor-Network: Ordering, Strategy, and Heterogeneity." *Systems Practice* 5, no. 4 (1992): 379–93.

Law, Robin. "'The Common People Were Divided': Monarchy, Aristocracy and Political Factionalism in the Kingdom of Whydah, 1671–1727." *International Journal of African Historical Studies* 23, no. 2 (1990): 201–29.

———, ed. *The English in West Africa, 1681–1683*. Oxford: Published for the British Academy by Oxford University Press, 1997.

———, ed. *The English in West Africa, 1685–1688*. Oxford: Published for the British Academy by Oxford University Press, 2001.

———, ed. *The English in West Africa, 1691–1699*. Oxford: Published for the British Academy by Oxford University Press, 2006.

———. "Further Light on Bulfinch Lambe and the 'Emperor of Pawpaw': King Agaja of Dahomey's Letter to King George I of England, 1726." *History in Africa* 17 (1990): 211–26.

———. "Human Sacrifice in Pre-Colonial West Africa." *African Affairs* 84, no. 334 (1985): 53–87.

———. "The Komenda Wars, 1694–1700: A Revised Narrative." *History in Africa* 34, no. 1 (2007): 133–68.

———. *Ouidah: The Social History of a West African Slaving "Port," 1727–1892.* Athens: Ohio University Press, 2004.

———. "West Africa's Discovery of the Atlantic." *International Journal of African Historical Studies* 44, no. 1 (2011): 1–25.

Lindemann, Mary. *Medicine and Society in Early Modern Europe.* Cambridge: Cambridge University Press, 1999.

Livingston, Julie, and Jasbir K. Puar. "Interspecies." *Social Text* 29, no. 1(106) (2011): 3–14.

Lockley, Tim, and David Doddington. "Maroon and Slave Communities in South Carolina before 1865." *South Carolina Historical Magazine* (2012): 125–45.

Lovejoy, Paul E. *Transformations in Slavery: A History of Slavery in Africa.* Cambridge, MA: Cambridge University Press, 2011.

Lucas, Michael T. "Empowered Objects: Material Expressions of Spiritual Beliefs in the Colonial Chesapeake Region." *Historical Archaeology* 48, no. 3 (2014): 106–24.

Lydon, Ghislaine. *On Trans-Saharan Trails: Islamic Law, Trade Networks, and Cross-Cultural Exchange in Nineteenth-Century Western Africa.* Cambridge: Cambridge University Press, 2009.

MacGregor, Arthur, and Alistair McAlpine. *Sir Hans Sloane: Collector, Scientist, Antiquary, Founding Father of the British Museum.* London: British Museum Press, 1994.

MacMaster, Richard K. "From Ulster to the Carolinas: John Torrans, John Greg, John Poaug, and Bounty Immigration, 1761–1768." In *The Irish in the Atlantic World,* edited by David T. Gleeson. Columbia: University of South Carolina Press, 2010.

Maddison-MacFadyen, Margot. "Mary Prince, Grand Turk, and Antigua." *Slavery & Abolition* 34, no. 4 (2013): 653–62.

Main, Gloria Lund. *Tobacco Colony: Life in Early Maryland, 1650–1720.* Princeton, NJ: Princeton University Press, 1982.

Marzano, Annalisa. *Harvesting the Sea: The Exploitation of Marine Resources in the Roman Mediterranean.* Oxford: Oxford University Press, 2013.

Mattfeld, Monica. *Becoming Centaur: Eighteenth-Century Masculinity and English Horsemanship.* University Park: Pennsylvania State University Press, 2017.

———. "'Undaunted all he views': The Gibraltar Charger, Astley's Amphitheatre and Masculine Performance." *Journal for Eighteenth-Century Studies* 37, no. 1 (2014): 19–36.

Maxwell, Clarence. "Enslaved Merchants, Enslaved Merchant-Mariners, and the Bermuda Conspiracy of 1761." *Early American Studies* 7, no. 1 (2009): 140–78.

May, Robert E. *Yuletide in Dixie: Slavery, Christmas, and Southern Memory.* Charlottesville: University of Virginia Press, 2019.

Mazzio, Carl. "Acting with Tact: Touch and Theater in the Renaissance." In *Sensible Flesh: On Touch in Early Modern Culture,* edited by Elizabeth D. Harvey, 159–186. Philadelphia: University of Pennsylvania Press, 2003.

Mbembe, Achille. *Critique of Black Reason.* Translated by Laurent Dubois. Durham, NC: Duke University Press, 2017.

McCaskie, T. C. "Denkyira in the Making of Asante C. 1660–1720." *Journal of African History* 48, no. 1 (2007): 1–25.

McClellan, James E., III. *Colonialism and Science: Saint Domingue and the Old Regime.* Chicago: University of Chicago Press, 1992.

McShane, Clay, and Joel Tarr. *The Horse in the City: Living Machines in the Nineteenth Century.* Baltimore: Johns Hopkins University Press, 2007.

McWilliams, James E. *A Revolution in Eating: How the Quest for Food Shaped America.* New York: Columbia University Press, 2005.

Meacham, Sarah Hand. "Pets, Status, and Slavery in the Late-Eighteenth-Century Chesapeake." *Journal of Southern History* 77, no. 3 (2011): 521–54.

Meaders, Daniel E. "South Carolina Fugitives as Viewed through Local Colonial Newspapers with Emphasis on Runaway Notices 1732–1801." *Journal of Negro History* 60, no. 2 (1975): 288–319.

Melville, Elinor G. K. *A Plague of Sheep: Environmental Consequences of the Conquest of Mexico.* Cambridge: Cambridge University Press, 1997.

Menard, Russell R. "Plantation Empire: How Sugar and Tobacco Planters Built Their Industries and Raised an Empire." *Agricultural History* 81, no. 3 (2007): 309–32.

Meniketti, Marco. *Sugar Cane Capitalism and Environmental Transformation: An Archaeology of Colonial Nevis, West Indies.* Tuscaloosa: University of Alabama Press, 2015.

Merchant, Carolyn. "Shades of Darkness: Race and Environmental History." *Environmental History* 8, no. 3 (2003): 380–94.

Meyers, Amy R. W., and Margaret Beck Pritchard, eds. *Empire's Nature: Mark Catesby's New World Vision.* Chapel Hill: University of North Carolina Press, 1998.

Miller, Joseph. *Way of Death: Merchant Capitalism and the Angolan Slave Trade, 1730–1830.* Madison: University of Wisconsin Press, 1988.

Mitchell, Matthew David. "'Legitimate Commerce' in the Eighteenth Century: The Royal African Company of England under the Duke of Chandos, 1720–1726." *Enterprise & Society* 14, no. 3 (2013): 544–78.

Monzote, Reinaldo Funes. *From Rainforest to Cane Field in Cuba: An Environmental History since 1492.* Chapel Hill: University of North Carolina Press, 2008.

Mooney, Katherine C. *Race Horse Men: How Slavery and Freedom Were Made at the Racetrack.* Cambridge, MA: Harvard University Press, 2014.

Moreau de Saint-Méry, M. L. E. "The Border Maroons of Saint-Domingue: Le Maniel." In *Maroon Societies: Rebel Slave Communities in the Americas,* edited by Richard Price, 107–34. Baltimore: Johns Hopkins University Press, 1979.

Morgan, Gwenda, and Peter Rushton. "Visible Bodies: Power, Subordination and Identity in the Eighteenth-Century Atlantic World." *Journal of Social History* 39, no. 1 (2005): 39–64.

Morgan, Jennifer L. *Laboring Women: Reproduction and Gender in New World Slavery.* Philadelphia: University of Pennsylvania Press, 2004.

———. "'Some Could Suckle over Their Shoulder': Male Travelers, Female Bodies, and the Gendering of Racial Ideology, 1500–1770." *William and Mary Quarterly* 54, no. 1 (1997): 167–92.

Morgan, Kenneth. "Bristol West India Merchants in the Eighteenth Century." *Transactions of the Royal Historical Society* 3 (1993): 185–208.

———. *Slavery and the British Empire: From Africa to America.* Oxford: Oxford University Press, 2007.

Morgan, Philip D. "Slaves and Livestock in Eighteenth-Century Jamaica: Vineyard Pen, 1750–1751." *William and Mary Quarterly* 52, no. 1 (1995): 47–76.

Morgan, Philip D., and Michael L. Nicholls. "Slaves in Piedmont Virginia, 1720–1790." *William and Mary Quarterly* 46, no. 2 (1989): 212–51.

Mtubani, Victor C. D. "The Black Voice in Eighteenth-Century Britain: African Writers against Slavery and the Slave Trade." *Phylon* 45, no. 2 (1984): 85–97.

Mukharji, Projit Bihari. *Doctoring Traditions: Ayurveda, Small Technologies, and Braided Sciences.* Chicago: University of Chicago Press, 2016.

———. "Occulted Materialities." *History and Technology* 34, no. 1 (2018): 31–40.

Mulcahy, Matthew. *Hurricanes and Society in the British Greater Caribbean, 1624–1783.* Baltimore: Johns Hopkins University Press, 2010.

Müller-Wille, Staffan. "Nature as a Marketplace: The Political Economy of Linnaean Botany." *History of Political Economy* 35, no. 5 (2003): 154–72.

Murphy, Kathleen S. "Collecting Slave Traders: James Petiver, Natural History, and the British Slave Trade." *William and Mary Quarterly* 70, no. 4 (2013): 637–67.

———. "A Slaving Surgeon's Collection: The Pursuit of Natural History through the British Slave Trade to Spanish America." In *Curious Encounters: Voyaging, Collecting, and Making Knowledge in the Long Eighteenth Century,* edited by Adriana Craciun and Mary Terrall, 138–58. Toronto: University of Toronto Press, 2019.

Murphy, Trevor. *Pliny the Elder's Natural History: The Empire in the Encyclopedia.* Oxford: Oxford University Press, 2004.

Myers, Jefferey. "Other Nature: Resistance to Ecological Hegemony in Charles W. Chesnutt's 'The Conjure Woman.'" *African American Review* 37, no. 1 (2003): 5–20.

Nagl, Dominik. "The Governmentality of Slavery in Colonial Boston, 1690–1760." *Amerikastudien/American Studies* 58, no. 1 (2013): 5–26.

Nelson, George H. "Contraband Trade under the Asiento, 1730–1739." *American Historical Review* 51, no. 1 (1945): 55–67.

Nelson, John K. *A Blessed Company: Parishes, Parsons, and Parishioners in Anglican Virginia, 1690–1776.* Chapel Hill: University of North Carolina Press, 2003.

Nelson, Louis P. *Architecture and Empire in Jamaica*. New Haven, CT: Yale University Press, 2016.

———. "Architectures of West African Enslavement." *Buildings & Landscapes: Journal of the Vernacular Architecture Forum* 21, no. 1 (2014): 88–125.

Newman, Simon. *A New World of Labor: The Development of Plantation Slavery in the British Atlantic*. Philadelphia: University of Pennsylvania Press, 2013.

Newson, Linda A., and Susie Minchin. "Diets, Food Supplies and the African Slave Trade in Early Seventeenth-Century Spanish America." *The Americas* 63, no. 4 (2007): 517–50.

Newton, John. *The Journal of a Slave Trader (John Newton), 1750–1754*. Edited by Bernard Martin and Mark Spurrell. London: Epworth Press, 1962.

Norman, Neil L. "Hueda (Whydah) Country and Town: Archaeological Perspectives on the Rise and Collapse of an African Atlantic Kingdom." *International Journal of African Historical Studies* 42, no. 3 (2009): 387–410.

Norton, Marcy. "Going to the Birds: Animals as Things and Beings in Early Modernity." In *Early Modern Things: Objects and Their Histories, 1500–1800*, edited by Paula Findlen, 53–83. London: Routledge, 2013.

"Notes and Queries." *Pennsylvania Magazine of History and Biography* 58, no. 4 (1934): 378–84.

Nussbaum, Felicity, ed. *The Global Eighteenth Century*. Baltimore: Johns Hopkins University Press, 2005.

Offen, Karl. "Puritan Bioprospecting in Central America and the West Indies." *Itinerario* 35, no. 1 (2011): 15–48.

Ogborn, Miles. "The Power of Speech: Orality, Oaths and Evidence in the British Atlantic World, 1650–1800." *Transactions of the Institute of British Geographers* 36, no. 1 (2011): 109–25.

———. "Streynsham Master's Office: Accounting for Collectivity, Order and Authority in 17th-Century India." *Cultural Geographies* 13, no. 1 (2006): 127–55.

Ogundiran, Akinwumi. "Of Small Things Remembered: Beads, Cowries, and Cultural Translations of the Atlantic Experience in Yorubaland." *International Journal of African Historical Studies* 35, no. 2/3 (2002): 427–57.

Opie, Frederick Douglass. *Hog and Hominy: Soul Food from Africa to America*. New York: Columbia University Press, 2010.

Orejas Miranda, Braulio R. "The Snake Genus Lystrophis in Uruguay." *Copeia* 1966, no. 2 (1966): 193–205.

O'Shaughnessy, Andrew Jackson. *An Empire Divided: The American Revolution and the British Caribbean*. Philadelphia: University of Pennsylvania Press, 2000.

Otremba, Eric. "Inventing Ingenios: Experimental Philosophy and the Secret Sugar-Makers of the Seventeenth-Century Atlantic." *History and Technology* 28, no. 2 (2012): 119–47.

Palmer, Colin A. "The Company Trade and the Numerical Distribution of Slaves to Spanish America, 1703–1739." In *Africans in Bondage: Studies in Slavery and the Slave Trade,* edited by Philip D. Curtin and Paul Lovejoy, 27–43. Madison: African Studies Program, University of Wisconsin–Madison, 1986.

Palmié, Stephan. "Other Powers: Tylor's Principle, Father Williams's Temptation, and the Power of Banality." In *Obeah and Other Powers: The Politics of Caribbean Religion and Healing,* edited by Diana Paton and Maarit Forde, 316–40. Durham, NC: Duke University Press, 2012.

Parrish, Susan Scott. *American Curiosity: Cultures of Natural History in the Colonial British Atlantic World.* Chapel Hill: University of North Carolina Press, 2012.

Parsons, Christopher M., and Kathleen S. Murphy. "Ecosystems under Sail: Specimen Transport in the Eighteenth-Century French and British Atlantics." *Early American Studies* 10, no. 3 (2012): 503–29.

Pasierowska, Rachael L. "'Screech Owls Allus Holler 'round the House before Death': Birds and the Souls of Black Folk in the 1930s American South." *Journal of Social History* 51, no. 1 (2016): 27–46.

Paton, Diana. "The Afterlives of Three-Fingered Jack." In *Slavery and the Cultures of Abolition: Essays Marking the Bicentennial of the British Abolition Act of 1807,* edited by Brycchan Carey and Peter J. Kitson, 42–63. Suffolk: Boydell and Brewer, 2007.

———. *The Cultural Politics of Obeah: Religion, Colonialism and Modernity in the Caribbean World.* Cambridge: Cambridge University Press, 2015.

———. "Obeah Acts: Producing and Policing the Boundaries of Religion in the Caribbean." *Small Axe* 13, no. 1 (2009): 1–18.

———. "Punishment, Crime, and the Bodies of Slaves in Eighteenth-Century Jamaica." *Journal of Social History* 34, no. 4 (2001): 923–54.

Patterson, Orlando. *Slavery and Social Death: A Comparative Study.* Cambridge, MA: Harvard University Press, 1982.

Pattullo, Polly. *Your Time Is Done Now: Slavery, Resistance, and Defeat: The Maroon Trials of Dominica (1813–1814).* New York: New York University Press, 2015.

Paugh, Katherine. *The Politics of Reproduction: Race, Medicine, and Fertility in the Age of Abolition.* Oxford: Oxford University Press, 2017.

Paul, Helen J. *The South Sea Bubble: An Economic History of its Origins and Consequences.* London: Routledge, 2010.

Pavão-Zuckerman, Barnet, Scott Oliver, Chance Copperstone, Matthew Reeves, and Marybeth Harte. "African American Culinary History and the Genesis of American Cuisine: Foodways and Slavery at Montpelier." *Journal of African Diaspora Archaeology and Heritage* 9, no. 2 (2020): 114–47.

Perdue, Charles L., Thomas E. Barden, and Robert K. Phillips, eds. *Weevils in the Wheat: Interviews with Virginia Ex-Slaves.* Charlottesville: University of Virginia Press, 1992.

Perry, Tony C. "In Bondage When Cold Was King: The Frigid Terrain of Slavery in Antebellum Maryland." *Slavery & Abolition* 38, no. 1 (2017): 23–36.

Pestana, Carla Gardina. *Protestant Empire: Religion and the Making of the British Atlantic
World.* Philadelphia: University of Pennsylvania Press, 2009.

Peterfreund, Stuart. "From the Forbidden to the Familiar: The Way of Natural Theology
Leading Up to and Beyond the Long Eighteenth Century." *Studies in Eighteenth-
Century Culture* 37, no. 1 (2008): 23–39.

Peters, Tacuma. "The Anti-Imperialism of Ottobah Cugoano: Slavery, Abolition, and
Colonialism in Thoughts and Sentiments on the Evil of Slavery." *CLR James Journal*
23, no. 1/2 (2017): 61–82.

Petley, Christer. *White Fury: A Jamaican Slaveholder and the Age of Revolution.* Oxford
University Press, 2018.

Pettigrew, William A. "Free to Enslave: Politics and the Escalation of Britain's Transatlantic Slave Trade, 1688–1714." *William and Mary Quarterly* (2007): 3–38.

———. *Freedom's Debt: The Royal African Company and the Politics of the Atlantic Slave
Trade, 1672–1752.* Chapel Hill: University of North Carolina Press, 2013.

Phillips, Ulrich B. "Slave Crime in Virginia." *American Historical Review* 20, no. 2 (1915):
336–40.

Pietz, William. "The Problem of the Fetish: Bosman's Guinea and the Enlightenment
Theory of Fetishism." *Res: Anthropology and Aesthetics,* no. 16 (1988): 105–24.

Platt, Virginia Bever. "The East India Company and the Madagascar Slave Trade." *William
and Mary Quarterly* (1969): 548–77.

Pluymers, Keith. "Atlantic Iron: Wood Scarcity and the Political Ecology of Early English
Expansion." *William and Mary Quarterly* 73, no. 3 (2016): 389–426.

Pollitt, Ronald. "John Hawkins's Troublesome Voyages: Merchants, Bureaucrats, and the
Origin of the Slave Trade." *Journal of British Studies* 12, no. 2 (1973): 26–40.

Porter, Charlotte. "Natural History Discourse and Collections: The Roles of Collectors
in the Southeastern Colonies of North America." *Museum History Journal* 1, no. 1
(2008): 129–46.

Pybus, Cassandra. *Epic Journeys of Freedom: Runaway Slaves of the American Revolution and
Their Global Quest for Liberty.* Boston: Beacon, 2006.

Raman, Bhavani. *Document Raj: Writing and Scribes in Early Colonial South India.* Chicago:
University of Chicago Press, 2012.

Rangan, Haripriya, Judith Carney, and Tim Denham. "Environmental History of Botanical Exchanges in the Indian Ocean World." *Environment and History* 18, no. 3
(2012): 311–42.

Ratcliff, Marc J. "Temporality, Sequential Iconography and Linearity in Figures: The
Impact of the Discovery of Division in Infusoria." *History and Philosophy of the Life
Sciences* 21, no. 3 (1999): 255–92.

Rauschenberg, Roy A. "John Ellis, Royal Agent for West Florida." *Florida Historical Quarterly* 62, no. 1 (1983): 1–24.

Rawley, James A. "Richard Harris, Slave Trader Spokesman." *Albion: A Quarterly Journal Concerned with British Studies* 23, no. 3 (1991): 439–58.

Rediker, Marcus. "History from Below the Water Line: Sharks and the Atlantic Slave Trade." *Atlantic Studies* 5, no. 2 (2008): 285–97.

Reese, Ty M. "'Sheep in the Jaws of So Many Ravenous Wolves': The Slave Trade and Anglican Missionary Activity at Cape Coast Castle, 1752–1816." *Journal of Religion in Africa* 34, no. 3 (2004): 348–72.

Richardson, Bonham C. *The Caribbean in the Wider World, 1492–1992: A Regional Geography*. Cambridge: Cambridge University Press, 1992.

———. *Caribbean Migrants: Environment and Human Survival on St. Kitts and Nevis*. Knoxville: University of Tennessee Press, 1983.

Richardson, Patrick. *Empire & Slavery*. New York: Harper and Row, 1968.

Ritvo, Harriet. *The Animal Estate: The English and Other Creatures in the Victorian Age*. Cambridge, MA: Harvard University Press, 1987.

Robbins, Louise E. *Elephant Slaves and Pampered Parrots: Exotic Animals in Eighteenth-Century Paris*. Baltimore: Johns Hopkins University Press, 2002.

Roberts, Jonathan. "Medical Exchange on the Gold Coast during the Seventeenth and Eighteenth Centuries." *Canadian Journal of African Studies/Revue Canadienne Des Études Africaines* 45, no. 3 (2011): 480–523.

Roberts, Justin. *Slavery and the Enlightenment in the British Atlantic, 1750–1807*. Cambridge: Cambridge University Press, 2013.

Roberts, Mark S. *The Mark of the Beast: Animality and Human Oppression*. West Lafayette, IN: Purdue University Press, 2008.

Robles, Whitney Barlow. "Flatness." In *The Philosophy Chamber: Art and Science in Harvard's Teaching Cabinet, 1766–1820*, edited by Ethan W. Lasser. 190–209. New Haven, CT: Yale University Press, 2017.

Rodgers, Nini. *Ireland, Slavery and Anti-Slavery, 1612–1865*. New York: Palgrave Macmillan, 2007.

Røge, Pernile. "A Natural Order of Empire: The Physiocratic Vision of Colonial France after the Seven Years' War." In *The Political Economy of Empire in the Early Modern World*, edited by Sophus Reinert and Pernille Røge. London: Palgrave Macmillan, 2013.

Romeiras, Maria M., Maria Cristina Duarte, Arnoldo Santos-Guerra, Mark Carine, and Javier Francisco-Ortega. "Botanical Exploration of the Cape Verde Islands: From the Pre-Linnaean Records and Collections to Late 18th Century Floristic Accounts and Expeditions." *Taxon* 63, no. 3 (2014): 625–40.

Rose, Deborah Bird, Thom van Dooren, Matthew Chrulew, Stuart Cooke, Matthew

Kearnes, and Emily O'Gorman. "Thinking through the Environment, Unsettling the Humanities." *Environmental Humanities* 1, no. 1 (2012): 1–5.

Ross, Doran H. "'Come and Try': Towards a History of Fante Military Shrines." *African Arts* 40, no. 3 (2007): 12–35.

Rountree, Helen C. *The Powhatan Indians of Virginia: Their Traditional Culture*. Norman: University of Oklahoma Press, 1989.

Rucker, Walter C. "Earth from a Dead Man's Grave: Ritual Technologies and Mortuary Realms in the Eighteenth-Century Gold Coast Diaspora." In *Slavery and its Legacy in Ghana and the Diaspora*, edited by Rebecca Shumway and Trevor R. Getz, 62–84. London: Bloomsbury Publishing, 2017.

———. *Gold Coast Diasporas: Identity, Culture, Power*. Bloomington: Indiana University Press, 2015.

———. *The River Flows On: Black Resistance, Culture, and Identity Formation in Early America*. Baton Rouge: Louisiana State University Press, 2006.

Rushforth, Brett. *Bonds of Alliance: Indigenous and Atlantic Slaveries in New France*. Chapel Hill: University of North Carolina Press, 2012.

Russo, J. Elliott. "'Fifty-Four Days Work of Two Negroes': Enslaved Labor in Colonial Somerset County, Maryland." *Agricultural History* 78, no. 4 (2004): 466–92.

Salmon, Michael. *The Aurelian Legacy: British Butterflies and Their Collectors*. Berkeley: University of California Press, 2000.

Samford, Patricia. "The Archaeology of African-American Slavery and Material Culture." *William and Mary Quarterly* 53, no. 1 (1996): 87–114.

Saunt, Claudio. "'The English Has Now a Mind to Make Slaves of Them All': Creeks, Seminoles, and the Problem of Slavery." *American Indian Quarterly* 22, no. 1/2 (1998): 157–80.

Savage, John. "'Black Magic' and White Terror: Slave Poisoning and Colonial Society in Early 19th Century Martinique." *Journal of Social History* 40, no. 3 (2007): 635–62.

Schaffer, Simon, Lissa L. Roberts, Kapil Raj, and James Delbourgo, eds. *The Brokered World: Go-Betweens and Global Intelligence*. Sagamore Beach, MA: Science History Publications, 2009.

Schavelzon, Daniel. "On Slaves and Beer: The First Images of the South Sea Company Slave Market in Buenos Aires." *African and Black Diaspora: An International Journal* 7, no. 2 (2014): 119–28.

Schwartz, Stuart B. *Sea of Storms: A History of Hurricanes in the Greater Caribbean from Columbus to Katrina*. Princeton, NJ: Princeton University Press, 2015.

Scott, James C. *Domination and the Arts of Resistance: Hidden Transcripts*. New Haven, CT: Yale University Press, 1990.

Scott, W. R. "The Constitution and Finance of the Royal African Company of England from Its Foundation Till 1720." *American Historical Review* 8, no. 2 (1903): 241–59.

Seed, Patricia. *Ceremonies of Possession in Europe's Conquest of the New World, 1492–1640*. Cambridge: Cambridge University Press, 1995.

Senior, Emily. *The Caribbean and the Medical Imagination, 1764–1834: Slavery, Disease and Colonial Modernity*. Cambridge: Cambridge University Press, 2018.

Sesay, Chernoh M. "The Revolutionary Black Roots of Slavery's Abolition in Massachusetts." *New England Quarterly* 87, no. 1 (2014): 99–131.

Seth, Suman. *Difference and Disease: Medicine, Race, and the Eighteenth-Century British Empire*. Cambridge: Cambridge University Press, 2018.

———. "Materialism, Slavery, and *The History of Jamaica*." *Isis* 105, no. 4 (2014): 764–72.

Shapin, Steven, and Simon Schaffer. *Leviathan and the Air-Pump: Hobbes, Boyle, and the Experimental Life*. Princeton, NJ: Princeton University Press, 1985.

Sharrer, Terry G. *A Kind of Fate: Agricultural Change in Virginia, 1861–1920*. West Lafayette, IN: Purdue University Press, 2002.

Shaw, Rosalind. *Memories of the Slave Trade: Ritual and the Historical Imagination in Sierra Leone*. Chicago: University of Chicago Press, 2002.

Shepherd, Verene. *Livestock, Sugar and Slavery: Contested Terrain in Colonial Jamaica*. Kingston: Ian Randle Publishers, 2009.

Sheridan, Richard B. "From Chattel to Wage Slavery in Jamaica, 1740–1860." In *The Wages of Slavery: From Chattel Slavery to Wage Labour in Africa, the Caribbean, and England*, edited by Michael Twaddle, 13–40. New York: Frank Cass and Co., 1993.

———. "The Guinea Surgeons on the Middle Passage: The Provision of Medical Services in the British Slave Trade." *International Journal of African Historical Studies* 14, no. 4 (1981): 601–25.

———. "Letters from a Sugar Plantation in Antigua, 1739–1758." *Agricultural History* 31, no. 3 (1957): 3–23.

———. "The Rise of a Colonial Gentry: A Case Study of Antigua, 1730–1775." *Economic History Review* 13, no. 3 (1961): 342–57.

———. "Samuel Martin, Innovating Sugar Planter of Antigua." *Agricultural History* 34, no. 3 (1960): 126–39.

Shumway, Rebecca. *The Fante and the Transatlantic Slave Trade*. Rochester, NY: University of Rochester Press, 2011.

Silverman, David J. "'We Chuse to Be Bounded': Native American Animal Husbandry in Colonial New England." *William and Mary Quarterly* 60, no. 3 (2003): 511–48.

Skabelund, Aaron. "Animals and Imperialism: Recent Historiographical Trends." *History Compass* 11, no. 10 (2013): 801–7.

Sluyter, Andrew. *Black Ranching Frontiers: African Cattle Herders of the Atlantic World, 1500–1900*. New Haven, CT: Yale University Press, 2012.

———. "The Ecological Origins and Consequences of Cattle Ranching in Sixteenth-Century New Spain." *Geographical Review* (1996): 161–77.

———. "The Role of Black Barbudans in the Establishment of Open-Range Cattle Herding in the Colonial Caribbean and South Carolina." *Journal of Historical Geography* 35, no. 2 (2009): 330–349.

———. "The Role of Blacks in Establishing Cattle Ranching in Louisiana in the Eighteenth Century." *Agricultural History* 86, no. 2 (2012): 41–67.

Smalley, Andrea. *Wild by Nature: North American Animals Confront Colonization*. Baltimore: Johns Hopkins University Press, 2017.

Smallwood, Stephanie E. "The Politics of the Archive and History's Accountability to the Enslaved." *History of the Present* 6, no. 2 (2016): 117–32.

———. *Saltwater Slavery: A Middle Passage from Africa to American Diaspora*. Cambridge, MA: Harvard University Press, 2009.

Smith, Beatrice Scheer. "Hannah English Williams: America's First Woman Natural History Collector." *South Carolina Historical Magazine* 87, no. 2 (1986): 83–92.

Smith, David Chan. "Useful Knowledge, Improvement, and the Logic of Capital in Richard Ligon's *True and Exact History of Barbados.*" *Journal of the History of Ideas* 78, no. 4 (2017): 549–70.

Smith, David Livingstone. *On Inhumanity: Dehumanization and How to Resist It*. Oxford: Oxford University Press, 2020.

———. "Paradoxes of Dehumanization." *Social Theory and Practice* 42, no. 2 (2016): 416–43.

Smith, Justin E. H. *Nature, Human Nature, and Human Difference: Race in Early Modern Philosophy*. Princeton, NJ: Princeton University Press, 2015.

Smith, Kimberly K. *African American Environmental Thought: Foundations*. Lawrence: University of Kansas Press, 2007.

Smith, Robert. "Peace and Palaver: International Relations in Pre-Colonial West Africa." *Journal of African History* 14, no. 4 (1973): 599–621.

Smith, Theophus H. *Conjuring Culture: Biblical Formations of Black America*. Oxford: Oxford University Press, 1994.

Smithers, Gregory D. *Slave Breeding: Sex, Violence, and Memory in African American History*. Gainesville: University Press of Florida, 2012.

Snyder, Christina. *Slavery in Indian Country: The Changing Face of Captivity in Early America*. Cambridge, MA: Harvard University Press, 2010.

Spencer, Jane. *Writing about Animals in the Age of Revolution*. Oxford: Oxford University Press, 2020.

Sperling, John G. *The South Sea Company: An Historical Essay and Bibliographical Finding List*. Cambridge, MA: Harvard University Press, 1962.

Spicksley, Judith. "Pawns on the Gold Coast: The Rise of Asante and Shifts in Security for Debt, 1680–1750." *Journal of African History* 54, no. 2 (2013): 147–75.

Stearns, Raymond P. "James Petiver, Seventeenth-Century Promoter of Natural Science." *Proceedings of the American Antiquarian Society* 62, no. 2 (1952): 243–365.

———. *Science in the British Colonies of America*. Urbana: University of Illinois Press, 1970.

Stewart, Mart A. *What Nature Suffers to Groe: Life, Labor, and Landscape on the Georgia Coast, 1680–1920*. Athens: University of Georgia Press, 1996.

Stoll, Steven. *Larding the Lean Earth: Soil and Society in Nineteenth-Century America*. New York: Hill and Wang, 2003.

Swank, James M. *History of the Manufacture of Iron in All Ages*. Philadelphia: American Iron and Steel Association, 1892.

Sweet, David G. "Black Robes and 'Black Destiny': Jesuit Views of African Slavery in 17th-Century Latin America." *Revista de historia de America* 86 (1978): 87–133.

Swingen, Abigail Leslie. *Competing Visions of Empire: Labor, Slavery, and the Origins of the British Atlantic Empire*. New Haven, CT: Yale University Press, 2015.

"Tales of Old Barbados." *Journal of the Barbados Museum and Historical Society* 12, no. 4 (1945): 171–78.

Thomas, Hugh. *The Slave Trade: The Story of the Atlantic Slave Trade, 1440–1870*. New York: Simon & Schuster, 1997.

Thomas, T. C., and J. B. Legg. "Archaeological Evidence of Afro-Barbadian Life at Springhead Plantation, St. James Parish, Barbados." *Journal of the Barbados Museum and Historical Society* 43 (1996/1997): 32–49.

Thompson, Peter. "Henry Drax's Instructions on the Management of a Seventeenth-Century Barbadian Sugar Plantation." *William and Mary Quarterly* 66, no. 3 (2009): 565–604.

Thornton, A. P. "The Organization of the Slave Trade in the English West Indies, 1660–1685." *William and Mary Quarterly* 12, no. 3 (1955): 399–409.

Thornton, John. *Africa and Africans in the Making of the Atlantic World, 1400–1800*. Cambridge: Cambridge University Press, 1998.

———. *Warfare in Atlantic Africa, 1500–1800*. London: University College London Press, 1999.

Tillson, Albert H., Jr. *Accommodating Revolutions: Virginia's Northern Neck in an Era of Transformations, 1760–1810*. Charlottesville: University of Virginia Press, 2010.

Tonkin, Elizabeth. "Autonomous Judges: African Ordeals as Dramas of Power." *Ethnos* 65, no. 3 (2000): 366–86.

Trigg, Heather B., and David B. Landon. "Labor and Agricultural Production at Sylvester Manor Plantation, Shelter Island, New York." *Historical Archaeology* 44, no. 3 (2010): 36–53.

Trouillot, Michel-Rolph. *Silencing the Past: Power and the Production of History*. Boston: Beacon Press, 1995.

Tyler, Lyon G. "Pedigree of a Representative Virginia Planter, Edward Digges, Esq." *William and Mary Quarterly* 1, no. 4 (1893): 208–13.

Van Sant, Levi. "Lowcountry Visions: Foodways and Race in Coastal South Carolina." *Gastronomica* 15, no. 4 (2015): 18–26.

Verdesio, Gustavo. *Forgotten Conquests: Rereading New World History from the Margins.* Philadelphia: Temple University Press, 2001.

Waldstreicher, David. "Reading the Runaways: Self-Fashioning, Print Culture, and Confidence in Slavery in the Eighteenth-Century Mid-Atlantic." *William and Mary Quarterly* 56, no. 2 (1999): 243–72.

Walsh, Lorena S. *Motives of Honor, Pleasure, and Profit: Plantation Management in the Colonial Chesapeake, 1607–1763.* Chapel Hill: University of North Carolina Press, 2010.

———. "Plantation Management in the Chesapeake, 1620–1820." *Journal of Economic History* 49, no. 2 (1989): 393–406.

———. "Slave Life, Slave Society, and Tobacco Production in the Tidewater Chesapeake, 1620–1820." In *Cultivation and Culture: Labor and the Shaping of Slave Life in the Americas,* edited by Ira Berlin and Philip D. Morgan. 170–202. Charlottesville: University of Virginia Press, 1993.

Walvin, James. *Slavery in Small Things: Slavery and Modern Cultural Habits.* Malden, MA: John Wiley and Sons, 2017.

Warsh, Molly A. "A Political Ecology in the Early Spanish Caribbean." *William and Mary Quarterly* 71, no. 4 (2014): 517–48.

Watson, Alan D. "North Carolina Slave Courts, 1715–1785." *North Carolina Historical Review* 60, no. 1 (1983): 24–36.

Watts, David. *The West Indies: Patterns of Development, Culture and Environmental Change Since 1492.* Cambridge: Cambridge University Press, 1987.

Wax, Darold D. "'A People of Beastly Living': Europe, Africa and the Atlantic Slave Trade." *Phylon* 41, no. 1 (1980): 12–24.

Wennerlind, Carl. *Casualties of Credit: The English Financial Revolution, 1620–1720.* Cambridge, MA: Harvard University Press, 2011.

West, Emily. *Chains of Love: Slave Couples in Antebellum South Carolina.* Urbana: University of Illinois Press, 2010.

Wertenbaker, Thomas Jefferson. *The Planters of Colonial Virginia.* Princeton, NJ: Princeton University Press, 1922.

White, Deborah Gray. *Ar'n't I a Woman? Female Slaves in the Plantation South.* New York: W. W. Norton and Co., 1985.

Wickman, Thomas M. *Snowshoe Country: An Environmental and Cultural History of Winter in the Early American Northeast.* Cambridge: Cambridge University Press, 2018.

Wilderson, Frank B. III. *Afropessimism.* New York: Liveright, 2020.

Williams, Eric. "The Golden Age of the Slave System in Britain." *Journal of Negro History* 25, no. 1 (1940): 60–106.

Williams, Gomer. *History of the Liverpool Privateers and Letters of Marque: With an Account of the Liverpool Slave Trade.* London: William Heinemann, 1897.

Windley, Lathan A, ed. *Runaway Slave Advertisements: A Documentary History from the 1730s to 1790.* 4 vols. Westport, CT: Greenwood Press, 1983.

Winterbottom, Anna. *Hybrid Knowledge in the Early East India Company World.* London: Palgrave, 2016.

Wisecup, Kelly. *Medical Encounters: Knowledge and Identity in Early American Literatures.* Amherst: University of Massachusetts, 2013.

Wood, Betty, T. R. Clayton, and W. A. Speck. "The Letters of Simon Taylor of Jamaica to Chaloner Arcedekne, 1765–1775." *Royal Historical Society Camden Fifth Series* 19 (2002): 1–164.

Wood, Peter H. *Black Majority: Negroes in Colonial South Carolina from 1670 through the Stono Rebellion.* New York: W. W. Norton & Co., 1996.

Wood, W. Raymond, "An Archaeological Appraisal of Early European Settlements in the Senegambia." *Journal of African History* 8, no. 1 (1967): 39–64.

Wright, Donald R. "Darbo Jula: The Role of a Mandinka Jula Clan in the Long-Distance Trade of the Gambia River and Its Hinterland." *African Economic History*, no. 3 (1977): 33–45.

Wyatt, Edward. "Dr. James Greenway, Eighteenth Century Botanist, of Dinwiddie County, with an Account of Two Generations of His Descendants." In *Genealogies of Virginia Families: From Tyler's Quarterly Historical and Genealogical Magazine*, 1:130–40. Baltimore: Genealogical Publishing Company, 2007.

Wynter, Sylvia. "Unsettling the Coloniality of Being/Power/Truth/Freedom: Towards the Human, After Man, Its Overrepresentation—An Argument." *CR: The New Centennial Review* 3, no. 3 (2003): 257–337.

Yang, Bin. *Cowrie Shells and Cowrie Money: A Global History.* New York: Routledge, 2019.

Young, Jason R. *Rituals of Resistance: African Atlantic Religion in Kongo and the Lowcountry South in the Era of Slavery.* Baton Rouge: Louisiana State University Press, 2007.

Zilberstein, Anya. "Bastard Breadfruit and Other Cheap Provisions: Early Food Science for the Welfare of the Lower Orders." *Early Science and Medicine* 21, no. 5 (2016): 492–508.

Digital Research Projects

Chambers, Douglas B., ed. *Runaway Slaves in Jamaica.* Vol. 1, *The Eighteenth Century.* Hattiesburg: University of Southern Mississippi, 2013. https://ufdcimages.uflib.ufl.edu/AA/00/02/11/44/00001/JamaicaRunawaySlaves-18thCentury.pdf.

Dissertations and Unpublished Papers

Carrington-Farmer, Charlotte. "Slave Horse/War Horse: The Narragansett Pacer in Colonial and Revolutionary Rhode Island." Paper delivered at the War Horses of the World conference at the School of Oriental and African Studies, University of London, 2014.

Paul, Helen Julia. "The South Sea Company and the Royal African Company's Combined Slaving Activities." Paper presented at the Economic History Society Conference, Reading, 2006.

Rebovich, Samantha Anne. "Landscape, Labor, and Practice: Slavery and Freedom at Green Castle Estate, Antigua." PhD dissertation, Syracuse University, 2011.

INDEX

Printed in the USA
CPSIA information can be obtained
at www.ICGtesting.com
CBHW032321220724
12009CB00002B/9

9 780807 178867